ANGKOR

MICHAEL D. COE

ANGKOR
AND THE KHMER
CIVILIZATION

With 130 illustrations, 22 in color

Ancient Peoples and Places
FOUNDING EDITOR: GLYN DANIEL

To the memory of Sophie Dobzhansky Coe

Frontispiece: Each of the many towers of the Bayon, Angkor Thom, has four smiling faces believed to represent Jayavarman VII (1181–*c.* 1215) as Avalokiteshvara, the Bodhisattva of infinite compassion.

First published in hardcover in the United States of America in 2003 by Thames & Hudson Inc., 500 Fifth Avenue, New York, New York 10110

thamesandhudsonusa.com

Library of Congress Catalog Card Number 2003100796
ISBN 0-500-02117-1

Printed and bound in Singapore by CS Graphics

Contents

Preface

I was first led to Angkor by reading about this astonishing civilization in the pages of *Escape with Me!*, Osbert Sitwell's entertaining and informative account of his various travels to the Orient. But it was not until the spring of 1954 that I was able to visit the ancient city, at the young age of twenty-four and armed with Maurice Glaize's comprehensive 1948 guide to the ruins. Cambodia was then in an early stage of the civil war that was much later to devastate the entire country. French army officers in their tropical whites could be seen everywhere in Phnom Penh and Siem Reap; I was told that to quell the rebels, the king had deployed his royal war elephants, vividly recalling the battles against the Cham recorded in the wonderful Bayon reliefs at the centre of Angkor.

Like many another traveller, I had completely fallen under the spell of Angkor and the culture of the Khmer. On my return to graduate work at Harvard, convinced that comparative study could throw light on the nature of that other great monsoon forest civilization – that of the Maya – I began to read such classic works as George Coedès' *Pour mieux comprendre Angkor* and, above all, the monumental *The Ancient Khmer Empire* by Lawrence Palmer Briggs. Louis Malleret's excavations at the site of Oc Eo in the Delta of southern Vietnam had already revealed something of the more distant, pre-Angkorian past; and it was tempting to think that the ultimate origins of this civilization could be discovered in the drainage basin of Cambodia's Great Lake (the Tonle Sap), and that I could take this, rather than early Mesoamerica, as the theme of my research.

This was but a graduate student's pipe dream. But by good fortune, I remained in the Maya field, since several decades of sheer horror subsequently engulfed the Khmer people and their land. The liberation of at least part of Cambodia from Khmer Rouge rule made it possible to visit the country once more, and in 1993 I returned to Angkor with my late wife Sophie. This time one saw in the streets of Phnom Penh and Siem Reap the blue helmets of United Nations troops, rather than the white kepis of the French, but much of the country was still dangerous. With the beginning of mine clearance, archaeologists were once more working in this great complex, and there were research and conservation teams from many countries. Advanced technologies, including airborne radar survey, had opened entirely new areas of investigation. All of these diverse, multinational efforts have come under the coordination of Cambodia's official APSARA authority (Authority for the Protection and Management of Angkor and the Region of Siem Reap), as well as the recently established Center for Khmer Studies.

In the course of several subsequent trips to Cambodia, I became convinced that while there are several excellent guides to Angkor, there is a need for a concise but comprehensive general book on Khmer civilization, extending from earliest times until the establishment of the French Protectorate, told from an anthropological and archaeological perspective – in other words, a well-illustrated culture history of the pre-colonial Khmer people, with emphasis on the Angkorian Empire and its capital city. The present book is the result of three years of reading, research and travel, including an extended visit to all significant Khmer ruins in northeastern Thailand (the Khorat Plateau). Its perspective has been guided not only by the classic works of the great École Française d'Extrême-Orient (EFEO), but by more recent published studies of such scholars as Claude Jacques, Michael Vickery and Roland Fletcher. Readers will note that I have by no means neglected the period from the decline of Angkor until the arrival of the French, which is absolutely critical not only to the understanding of early times, but also to the culture of present-day Cambodia.

I wish first of all to acknowledge the contributions of three outstanding Cambodian guides based in Siem Reap. These are my good friend Nhean Samban, who showed me many aspects of Angkor; Savuth of Phnom Penh Tourism, for his information on contemporary rice cultivation; and Muon Monirom, who took me to Phnom Kulen. In Thailand, my guide for the Khorat Plateau (and for the breathtaking Preah Vihear, across the border inside Cambodia) was Supoth Hongthon, a Khmer-speaking native of Surin and a mine of information on the area.

My gratitude also goes to Mary Dell Lucas of Far Horizons Travel, who made possible two of my journeys to Angkor and one to Champassak (Laos).

During my several sojourns in the Angkor area, I have been enormously helped by various specialists in the Khmer civilization. These include John Sanday, Field Director of the Preah Khan Conservation Project (World Monuments Fund), and Chhan Chamroeun, then also with the project. At the Center for Khmer Studies, I have benefited by the advice of William A. Southworth and Philippe Peycam, both of whom steered me in the right directions. Marc Franiette of the Mission Arquéologique au Cambodge devoted an afternoon showing me the ceramics from EFEO excavations in Angkor's Royal Palace. Ashley Thompson, then of the APSARA Authority and now with the University of California (Berkeley), shared with me her deep knowledge of Angkor, took me to the summit of Phnom Bok, and persuaded me that the civilization by no means perished with the city's decline. Thanks also go to Vann Molyvann, chairman of APSARA, and to Ith Sotha, Director of the Geography Department of the Ministry of Land Management, Urban Planning and Construction, for allowing me access to the recent JICA (Japan International Cooperation Agency) detailed mapping of Angkor.

I owe a special debt to Masako Marui and Hisao Arahi and their colleagues of the Angkor International Mission, Sophia University, who introduced me to the Tani Kiln site, and generously shared with me important information on their archaeological research. Michael Dega, then with the University of

Hawaii's Anthropology Department, kindly provided me with a full account of the latest findings on the so-called 'red soils' circular earthworks of eastern Cambodia. My friend Jeff Chouinard has generously made available several of his photographs of Cambodia and Laos.

My deepest gratitude goes to several specialists in the archaeology of mainland Southeast Asia who have very kindly read all or part of the manuscript. These include Miriam Stark, Co-Director of the University of Hawaii's LOMAP Project in Angkor Borei; Charles Higham of the University of Otago (New Zealand); Roland Fletcher of the School of Archaeology, University of Sydney; and Elizabeth Moore of the School of Oriental and African Studies, University of London. I would also like to acknowledge the comments and support of my friend and neighbour Ben Kiernan, the leading authority on Cambodia's terrible Khmer Rouge genocide. As a kind of 'new boy' to this field, and writing my book in a city located almost on the other side of the world from Angkor, I have learned much from all of these colleagues, but the reader should be warned that any errors of fact or interpretation in this volume are mine alone.

Thames & Hudson have been my publishers for over four decades, with six books, two of which have been through many editions. I have always found their staff, whether editorial, production, or design, uniformly helpful and knowledgeable. It has been an especial pleasure to have collaborated over the course of many years and many book projects with Colin Ridler, in my opinion one of the very best archaeological editors in the business. I also thank Susan Crouch for her editorial work on this volume.

Readers should note that some of the terminology for cultural-historical periods used in the book differs from that used by others, being based largely upon developmental criteria that will be defined in the chapters that follow.

This book	Elsewhere
Early Farmers	Neolithic, Bronze Age
Early Kingdoms	'Funan', 'Zhenla', pre-Angkorian
Classic	Angkorian
Post-Classic	Post-Angkorian

There is probably no other area in the world where our understanding of past history and prehistory is changing so fast as in this part of Southeast Asia. For the very first time we are beginning to comprehend the kind of city that ancient Angkor really was, where it came from, and what happened to it. With so many projects from a variety of nations active, and so many new investigative techniques being applied to old archaeological problems, Khmer studies are going through a period of great intellectual excitement. I hope that the present volume conveys at least some of this to the general reader.

DATES	PERIODS	MAJOR RULERS	SIGNIFICANT DEVELOPMENTS
1900	**Protectorate**	Norodom	1863 Treaty with French
		Ang Duong	Phnom Penh the capital;
1800			Vietnamese control of Cambodia
			Vietnamese annex Delta
1700			
1600	**Post-Classic**	Chai Chettha II	Udong the capital
			Fall of Lovek to the Thai
		Ang Chan I	
1500			
1400			Court moves to Quatre Bras region
			End of Khmer Empire; Thai invasions
1300		Jayavarman VIII	Anti-Buddhist iconoclasm
1200		Jayavarman VII	Angkor Thom; apogee of Khmer Empire
		Suryavarman II	Cham invasion of Angkor
1100		Udayadityavarman II	Angkor Wat
			Phimai
	Classic	Suryavarman I	Baphuon
1000		Rajendravarman II	Banteay Srei
		Jayavarman IV	Yashodharapura the capital; Bakheng
900		Indravarman I	Hariharalaya the capital
		Jayavarman II	Founding of the Khmer Empire
800			
		Jayadevi	
700		Jayavarman I	
		Bhavavarman II	
600		Chitrasena, Bhavavarman I	
			Ishanapura (Sambor Prei Kuk)
500		Rudravarman	
	Early Kingdoms		
400			Angkor Borei
300			
			Oc Eo culture
200			
			Hinduism and Buddhism arrive in
100			Southeast Asia
0	**Iron Age**		Circular earthworks

Introduction

Had the ancient Greeks and Romans known of Angkor, they surely would have counted that great city as the eighth wonder of the world. When the French naturalist and explorer Henri Mouhot – to whom was given the honour of first bringing its ruins to the general attention of Europe – entered Angkor in 1860, he questioned the local people about its origin. Among the explanations that they gave him was the suggestion that it might have been 'the work of the giants', leading Mouhot to exclaim:

> The work of giants! The expression would be very just, if used figuratively, in speaking of these prodigious works, of which no one who has not seen them can form any adequate idea; and in the construction of which patience, strength, and genius appear to have done their utmost in order to leave to future generations proofs of their power and civilization.[1]

Almost every early explorer (and virtually every other subsequent visitor to these prodigious ruins) has been wonder struck by the beauty and multiplicity of the sculptures that can be seen everywhere – on lintels and on walls, and freestanding before and within temples. They have also been overwhelmed by the sheer size of Angkor, one of the few ancient archaeological complexes that can actually be seen from outer space (China's Great Wall is another). The entire urban complex covers about 1,000 square km (386 square miles), and its core area *c*. 200 square km (77 square miles). There is nothing else to equal it in the archaeological world. Scholars and travellers are suitably impressed by the size of the Classic Maya cities of Mexico and Guatemala, yet one could fit ten Tikals or Calakmuls (the largest Classic Maya sites) within the bounds of Angkor and still have room to spare.

pl. 1

Western scholars have been intrigued by the puzzle of Angkor ever since its 'discovery' by Mouhot. Who had built this city and others like it in the tropical forests of Cambodia and Thailand? How old was Angkor? How could a nation of poor farmers such as Cambodia was in the nineteenth century ever have supported such mighty works from a bygone era? And what was the cause of the Angkor civilization's decline and fall into jungle-covered ruins? The first two of these questions were answered by a century of research and restoration conducted by the French archaeologists, art historians and epigraphers of the École Française d'Extrême-Orient (EFEO). Be that as it may, the burning questions of the origin, support base and decline of the brilliant Classic Khmer culture are still being hotly debated on both sides of the Atlantic and in Southeast Asia itself. Sadly, these puzzles have been far from academic, for the horrific 'reforms' carried out by the genocidal Khmer Rouge regime against its own people during the 1970s were based not merely on Maoist principles but also on a mistaken conception of the mechanisms by which the ancient Khmer Empire marshalled its labour forces to build and maintain Angkor and its stupendous system of reservoirs and canals.

The two most renowned monsoon-forest civilizations in the history of the world were the Classic Khmer and the Classic Maya. Both of these arose and flourished in tropical lowlands with strongly marked rainy and dry seasons, and middling to poor soils – in fact, in areas that were not exactly optimum for the staple crops (rice for the Khmer and maize for the Maya) on which they depended. Some grandiose and influential theories have been advanced in each case to support the idea that such spectacular public works as we see at sites like Angkor and Tikal must have been supported by hydraulic agriculture carried out on a grandiose scale; some of these theories are now considered to be untenable (as we shall see in the case of the 'hydraulic city' model for Angkor), but the debate goes on.

The similarity in many aspects of art and architecture between these complex cultures has led some very distinguished scholars to claim that one (the Maya) was in part derived from the other (the Khmer).[2] Unfortunately for such a hypothesis of trans-Pacific diffusion, the dates are all wrong! By the time the Cambodian King Jayavarman II declared himself a universal monarch in AD 802, thereby initiating the Classic Khmer period of the Angkorian state and empire, the Classic Maya civilization was already in steep decline, and within the following century underwent complete collapse, many centuries before the demise of Angkor. It cannot be denied that Khmer temple-pyramids such as Baksei Chamkrong in the centre of Angkor are strikingly similar to their counterparts in southeastern Mexico and northern Guatemala, but stepped temple-pyramids and huge cities were already being built as early as 200 BC in the Maya lowlands, at a time when most of mainland Southeast Asia had nothing more complex than simple circular villages of pile dwellings.

Yet even though long-range diffusion now seems unlikely, the comparative study of these two civilizations[3] can throw much light on the phenomenon of state evolution (and devolution) in the tropics, and help specialists in one region to develop insights and devise new research strategies from looking at what has happened and is happening on the other side of the Pacific Basin. One just has to ask the right questions.

The age of 'discovery'

The Western notion that Angkor and its empire had to be 'discovered' by Europeans such as Mouhot seems foolish to the Khmer, since they (the Cambodians) had never forgotten Angkor. As will become clear in Chapter 8, parts of the city continued to be occupied by the Khmer long after its conquest and sacking by the Siamese in the fifteenth century, and the subsequent transfer of the capital downstream to the Quatre Bras region. The imperial

city's best-known monument, the world-famous Angkor Wat temple com- pl. VIII
plex, has been continuously occupied by an active community of monks ever pl. IX
since the introduction to Angkor of Theravada Buddhism as a state religion
at the beginning of the fourteenth century. It is quite clear from late inscriptions and from the earliest European pictures of this huge, moated structure
that the monks had largely kept it clear of the jungle and in a state of fair to
good repair until the arrival of the French authorities and beyond, for that
matter.

We now know that the first European account of Angkor, dating from 1585
to 1588, is by the official Portuguese chronicler Diogo do Couto (*c.* 1543
–1616), based on an eyewitness report by a Capuchin friar named Antonio da
Magdalena.[4] According to Couto, in 1550 or 1551, a Cambodian king came
across the jungle-shrouded remains of the 'city' (in this case, Angkor Thom)
while hunting wild elephants, and subsequently had the ruins cleared by a
force of 5,000–6,000 men. This story probably had no basis in fact. On the
other hand, Couto's account of the city walls, five imposing gates, moat, and
other features is quite accurate. As for Angkor Wat, situated on a flat, open
plain to the southeast of 'the city', Couto exclaims that it is 'of a construction
so strange that one can hardly describe it with the pen, nor can one compare it
to any other monument in the world'.[5]

The Couto record was never printed until modern times. Nevertheless,
because Cambodia had excited the rival imperial ambitions of Portugal and
Spain during the sixteenth and seventeenth centuries (France at this time
was busy devising a takeover of Siam, which luckily never happened), other
missionaries and military adventurers from these countries began hearing
wild and exaggerated rumours about this 'lost' city, one such even speculat-
ing that it must have been built by Alexander the Great or the Romans.[6] But
the truly knowledgeable observers from foreign lands were most probably
Buddhist pilgrims and merchants from Asian countries like Japan. In recent
decades, there has appeared in a private Japanese collection an extraordinar- 96
ily accurate plan of Angkor Wat, copied in 1715 from a drawing by a Japanese
pilgrim who had been to Angkor in the early part of the previous century.[7] In
addition, a number of ink graffiti painted on interior columns of Angkor Wat
testify to the continuing presence of pious merchants from that country and
from China.

But the admittedly sketchy Portuguese and Spanish notices of a great civilization and city buried in the Cambodian jungles made no impression
whatever on the Western world. It was the zoologist (Alexandre-) Henri
Mouhot (1826–61) who changed all this.[8] A nephew by marriage of Mungo
Park, the famous Scottish explorer of Africa's Niger River, Mouhot was
commissioned by England's Royal Geographical Society and the Zoological
Society of London to explore Siam, Cambodia and Laos, which he did in a
series of journeys beginning in 1858. By January 1860, he had reached
Angkor. Even he admitted that he was not its actual 'discoverer'; that honour
goes to his fellow countryman Charles-Émile Bouillevaux, a missionary who
had spent two days in Angkor in 1850.[9] Yet Mouhot (who died of fever in
Luang Prabang, Laos, the next year) was its *effective* discoverer; it was his

vivid and perceptive account, posthumously published in French in 1863 and more extensively in English in 1868, that first fired the world's imagination about the ruined city.

The engravings in Mouhot's book, based on his own sketches and photographs, were hardly up to the standards set by the great topographical artists of the early nineteenth century, such as David Roberts in Egypt or Frederick Catherwood in the Maya area. The case was very different with John Thomson (1837–1921), an English explorer whose remarkably fine photographs of Angkor were published in 1867, in his *Antiquities of Cambodia*.[10]

The Mekong Exploration Commission[11]

The French established their 'protectorate' over the fragile Cambodian state in 1863. Then, alarmed by the British takeover of southern Burma and the influence that their old enemy had over the Kingdom of Siam, the French colonial government newly installed in Saigon decided to mount an exploration of the mighty Mekong River. They clearly had hopes that this would enable them to circumvent the British in Hong Kong and directly link Vietnam with the Chinese market (unfortunately, they failed to realize that the enormous Khong Falls on what is now the Laos–Cambodian border rendered this ambition nothing but a dream). The commission was accordingly

1 Members of the Delaporte expedition among the Khmer ruins, 1873.

2 Transport of a statue from the ruins of Preah Khan (Kompong Svai) by the Delaporte Expedition of 1873. This eventually ended up in Paris. The party had to cross a large swamp created by the silting up of Preah Khan's reservoir or *baray*.

set up in 1866, under the direction of Ernest Doudart de Lagrée, with the talented and ambitious Francis Garnier as second-in-command.

The results of this major expedition appeared in 1873 and included a detailed study of Angkor – even though this and the whole northwestern part of Cambodia were then under Siamese rule, and remained so until 1907. The *Voyage d'Exploration en Indo-Chine*[12] had numerous illustrations by the expedition artist, a naval officer named Louis Delaporte (1842–1925), and while these transmit something of the grandeur of the site, his vivid reconstructions of monuments like the Bayon at the centre of Angkor Thom owe much to the imagination. Nevertheless, it was Delaporte who, by importing Khmer sculptures and casts to Paris, first brought this great artistic tradition to the attention of the world.

Other French *savants* followed on the heels of the Mekong Commission. Lucien Fournereau, an architect who went to Angkor in 1887–88, produced the first truly accurate plans, cross-sections and elevations of the city's major architectural complexes.[13] By then, it was becoming clear that dozens – perhaps hundreds – of sites of the same ancient civilization were scattered throughout much of Cambodia, including the portion under Siamese control, and beyond the Dangrek Range in what is now northeastern Thailand and the Champassak region of southern Laos. The task of compiling an inventory of

3 Early French archaeologists in Angkor wisely left the monastic complex of Ta Prohm exactly as they had found it, with the ruins in the grip of giant trees and their root systems.

all these ruins fell to Étienne Aymonier (1844–1929). Aymonier, a naval man, could read the Sanskrit and Khmer inscriptions and the dates inscribed on these monuments, and his 1901 reports (republished in English translation in Bangkok in 1999) are still important for Khmer research, since his descriptions, plans, photographs and drawings are all we have for a few ruins.[14]

The age of EFEO

The return of Angkor and the province of Battambang from Siam (Thailand) to Cambodia in 1907 meant that the French colonial government now had exclusive jurisdiction over all of Cambodia's cultural heritage, including the great city itself. The colonial research apparatus was already in place for an intensive programme of study. This was the École Française d'Extrême-Orient (EFEO), founded in Saigon in 1898, and headquartered in Hanoi until 1957 (its Cambodian branch was forced by the Khmer Rouge to close down in 1975). For most of the twentieth century, this magnificent institution, the counterpart and contemporary of the Oriental Institute in the Near East and of the Carnegie Institution of Washington in the Maya area, was responsible for all of the restoration of Angkor, and for 95 per cent of the scholarship that was conducted on the Classic Khmer civilization and its forerunners. One of the first acts of the EFEO was to commission Étienne-Edmond Lunet de Lajonquière to continue Aymonier's work, and his remarkable atlas of early sites in what used to be French Indo-China is still a key resource for Khmer studies.[15]

By the 1920s, Angkor had become a magnet destination for well-travelled and well-heeled tourists, a situation that lasted up until the Second World War. Accordingly, the efforts of most EFEO archaeologists stationed in Siem Reap were directed towards reconstructing Angkor's ruined structures, and putting them in some sort of a chronological scheme. Contributing to this effort were outstanding EFEO figures like Jean Commaille, Louis Finot, George Groslier, Maurice Glaize, Henri Marchal, and Henri Parmentier. In contrast to the beauty and size of their mortarless buildings, the ancient architects had occasionally been poor engineers, and putting the jumbled stones back in order was no easy task. From the Dutchman who had reconstructed Borobudur in Java, the EFEO staff had learned the technique of *anastylosis*: taking a building apart stone by stone, rebuilding the core with modern materials (like concrete), and then putting the numbered stones back where they belonged. The supremely lovely Banteay Srei was the first complex to be so treated, not long after it had been illegally pillaged by the adventurer and novelist André Malraux. 45 46

This was an age not only of massive reconstruction, but also of epigraphy and art history. George Coedès (1886–1969) spent most of his adult life recording and translating the Sanskrit and Khmer-language inscriptions of Cambodia and Thailand, and it is thanks to him and his colleagues that we know the dates and histories of Angkor's rulers, and of their predecessors in 'Funan' and 'Zhenla' (more of these in Chapters 5 and 6).[16] On the basis of these inscriptions, and on the evolution of relief and in-the-round stone carving, a kind of history was built up by the EFEO scholars that was concentrated on specific Angkor kings, their works, and their conquests. All of this was summed up in masterly fashion by the American diplomat Lawrence Palmer Briggs, in his still-unsurpassed magnum opus of 1951.

The ancient Khmer Empire[17]

But even within the ranks of traditionally oriented EFEO archaeologists there were a few scholars who reflected the kind of holistic and anthropologically based archaeology that had begun to be practised in Western Europe and North America. One of these was the Russian-born Victor Goloubew (1873–1945), who pioneered the use of aerial photography in the detection of ancient Khmer hydraulic works. After the disruptions of the Second World War (during much of which Cambodia was under the jurisdiction of the Vichy regime), a new breed of French archaeologists arrived on the scene. The most brilliant of these may have been George Groslier's son Bernard-Philippe (1926–86), who was a professional, modern archaeologist in every respect, interested in larger questions regarding the evolution of Classic Angkor, not just king-lists and sequences of carved lintels. Although a *gaulliste* by political affiliation, B.-P. Groslier's view of Angkor as a 'hydraulic city' was heavily influenced by Marxist theory, and opened a continuing debate over the nature of the city and society that has not yet been fully resolved.[18]

Not the least of the younger Groslier's innovations was his introduction of true field archaeology to Cambodia, including his stratigraphic excavations in the Srah Srang pool area and in the Royal Palace enclosure of Angkor Thom, as well as his work on an early, circular, moated settlement in southeastern Cambodia near the Vietnam border (see Chapter 4). All this boded well for the future, but then came disaster in its worst conceivable form. In 1970 the civil war, and by extension the war in Indo-China, engulfed Angkor. For the following three years Siem Reap and Angkor were the scene of hostilities, and Groslier himself was severely wounded by a Khmer Rouge bullet. Many of Groslier's notes and collections were lost, including the catalogue for the huge Baphuon pyramid, by then dismantled for *anastylosis*. Groslier was forced at last to return to France. Phnom Penh fell to the Maoist fanatics in April 1975, and four years of savage, uninterrupted genocide began.

The rebirth of Khmer archaeology

Following the liberation of most of Cambodia by the Vietnamese army in 1979, and the retreat of the Khmer Rouge to the Thai border region, conservation efforts resumed at Angkor. Miraculously, or perhaps because the Khmer Rouge had wished to preserve it as the ideal to which the nation's enslaved populace was supposed to strive, the ancient city had been only slightly damaged by past military actions. An exception was the temple atop Phnom Bakheng; through its use as a stronghold by various factions, it has been disfigured in places by bullet holes. The major obstacle was the thousands of land mines left behind by the combatants. These had to be cleared before any kind of work could begin. Another serious problem consisted of occasional guerrilla attacks on Cambodian government forces by Khmer Rouge remnants (when my wife and I visited Angkor in 1993, on the eve of the UN-supervised elections, we could hear mortar explosions and machine-gun fire in the distance).

The first post-liberation project at Angkor was an attempt to restore Angkor Wat by a team from the Archaeological Survey of India, an undertaking that has come under heavy criticism for the drastic methods used to clean the walls and carvings at this great complex.[19] Under the official aegis of APSARA (French acronym for the Authority for the Protection and Management of Angkor and the Region of Siem Reap),[20] there are now at least eight research and/or restoration teams working at Angkor, from a wide variety of countries – including Japan, France, the UK, Australia, New Zealand, Germany, Hungary, China, and Cambodia itself. In addition, for some years the New York-based World Monuments Fund has been actively involved in the conservation of Preah Khan, Jayavarman II's vast monastic establishment in the north-central part of Angkor.[21] Outside the Angkor area proper, a research group from the University of Hawaii has a large project underway at Angkor Borei, a very early Cambodian site in the upper region of the Mekong Delta.[22] As the rest of Cambodia returns to normalcy, we may expect to see much more attention devoted to the empire's provincial sites – many of great size – and to the pre-Angkor past.

At long last, Angkor is being mapped and surveyed in its totality, by means of photogrammetric techniques. Most recently, airborne synthetic radar (AIRSAR) developed by NASA's Jet Propulsion Laboratory has been used to generate large-scale images of Angkor and its surroundings, resulting in the discovery of pre-Angkor and Classic-period features that were otherwise undetectable.[23]

Of course, as we shall see, the Khmer Empire extended over much of Thailand, especially the Khorat Plateau of the northeast. Because that country was spared the horrors of the Indo-China War, archaeological research by Thai and foreign archaeologists has continued unabated. Almost from the beginning, Thai archaeology has had a very different and more modern orientation than that of the older EFEO, being less focused on epigraphy and art history, and more upon actual stratigraphic excavation and analysis, assisted by all of the scientific techniques of modern field research, including aerial survey. These investigations have extended from intensive survey and excavation of early villages of the Neolithic, Bronze and Iron Ages (the Early Farming period and Iron Age of this book), to large, Classic Khmer centres such as Phimai and Phnom Rung.[24]

After so many setbacks and with the return of peace to the region, it appears that the study of the Khmer past has a bright future.

Periods

Compared to Europe, the Near East, and, in the New World, Mesoamerica and the Andes, the study of Southeast Asian cultural history is in its infancy. Only Thailand and Vietnam have adequate, long chronologies based upon 'dirt' archaeology and radiocarbon dating. For most of the region, the kind of evolutionary scenario proposed by such pioneers as Gordon Childe for western Eurasia, and Julian Steward and Gordon Willey for the pre-Columbian Americas, has never been considered. The turbulent and tragic history of twentieth-century Southeast Asia and, in the case of Cambodia, an almost exclusive reliance on art history and epigraphy, have all contributed to this intellectual state of affairs.

For the area with which we are most concerned – northeastern Thailand, Cambodia, and the Delta of southern Vietnam – we shall see that the record of its first peopling (the 'hunters and gatherers' period) is very spotty indeed, even though it is likely that this extended over hundreds of thousands of years. It is not until we get to the earliest settled villages and the beginnings of pottery production that we start to have solid archaeological data, especially from Thailand, and the possibility of comparing the archaeological record with cultural-historical schemes worked out elsewhere in the world. In this book I have taken the liberty of applying to some of the different evolutionary stages of Khmer culture history terms that have served well for Mesoamerican studies, and that can be integrated with the one proposed in 1984 for Thailand by the New Zealand prehistorian Donn Bayard,[25] and used in Charles Higham's standard text on mainland Southeast Asian archaeology.[26] Here are the periods into which the chapters will be organized:

Hunters and gatherers (? to *c.* 3600–3000 BC). This little-known period marks the initial peopling of mainland Southeast Asia by modern *Homo sapiens*, and is the equivalent of the Palaeolithic and Mesolithic eras of the western part of the Old World. During it, small bands of hunters with a technology centred on fairly rudimentary tools of chipped stone and possibly bamboo occupied rockshelters and open-air sites.

Early Farming period (3600–3000 BC to *c.* 500 BC). This is the age of villages, and corresponds to Bayard's General Periods A and B; it is marked by the advent of settled, village-farming life, with rice agriculture. At first, social ranking is fairly weak, but in time these societies become increasingly stratified into chiefdoms. Bronze working is introduced around 2000–1500 BC, and at some point circular, fortified village plans.

Iron Age (*c.* 500 BC to *c.* AD 200–500). Iron tools and weapons are introduced, perhaps from China. Some of the circular, 'red soils' village sites of eastern Cambodia may last into this period.

Early Kingdoms period (*c.* AD 100–200 to AD 802). In this era (known elsewhere as the 'pre-Angkorian period' or General Period C) the first truly centralized societies, mostly modest-sized kingdoms, appear along with maritime trading networks extending from the Mediterranean to India to the Mekong Delta. Some of these kingdoms were in touch with China, either through trade or tribute, or both, and they appear grouped in the sketchy Chinese records as 'Funan' and 'Zhenla'. More importantly, the Early Kingdoms period saw the long-term and at times intense Indianization of mainland and insular Southeast Asia, with the adoption of Buddhism and/or Hinduism as state religions. The first written records, in a script derived from Indian prototypes, appear during this era.

Classic (AD 802–1327) (General Period D). Sometimes called the Angkorian period, the Classic is the time of Angkor's greatness, from the founding of the city as a capital in AD 802, through its apogee as the immense centre of a mighty empire, until the inscribing of its last Sanskrit text in AD 1327, after which the great city declined and Cambodia's capital was ultimately transferred downriver. During this time, and even after, the Classic Khmer civilization becomes the model for all subsequent states in the Indianized (that is, non-Vietnamese and non-'sinicized') portion of Southeast Asia.

Post-Classic (AD 1327–1863). The least known and understood period in Khmer culture history, the Post-Classic opens with various poorly documented invasions by Thai armies, and ends with the establishment of the French Protectorate over Cambodia in 1863. During this period, as Cambodia's fortunes fell, those of its neighbours Siam and Vietnam rose, and Cambodia lost many of its lands, including the Delta, which fell into Vietnamese hands. Theravada Buddhism became the established religion, Buddhist monks rather than Hindu Brahmins became the state clergy, and spacious wooden pagodas for congregational worship replaced the stone-built royal temples that had been dedicated to the old Hindu and Mahayana Buddhist gods.

2 · The Setting

The Lower Mekong Basin

The Khmer people of today are largely (but not entirely) confined to the Kingdom of Cambodia, yet the story of their origins and of their empire extends over three geographical areas: the Khorat Plateau of northeastern Thailand, Cambodia proper, and the Delta of southern Vietnam. We shall concentrate on these three, but it should be kept in mind that the far smaller Champassak region of southernmost Laos belongs with them too. Together, these comprise the Lower Mekong Basin.

The Mekong, the world's seventh-longest river, rises in the high plateau of Tibet, cuts down through the mountains of China, forms the border of northeastern Myanmar, separates Thailand and Laos, and flows south through Cambodia before it empties through the Delta. All along its upper stretches, from Tibet to southern Laos, there are treacherous rapids and rocks (especially visible in low water), so that except in its lower part it has constituted more of a barrier than a waterway for the peoples of this part of Asia.

4 The massive Khong Falls on the Mekong mark the boundary between Laos and Cambodia. They effectively block all boat communication between the lower and upper reaches of the river.

5 Physiographic map of mainland Southeast Asia.

4   At the northern Cambodian border the Mekong must pass over the Khong Falls, where it forms a series of stupendous cataracts that together comprise the largest waterfall in the world, twice the size of Niagara in volume. This is what dashed French hopes of ever exploiting the river as a commercial route to China; in fact, the Mekong's gradient only becomes gentle enough for boats of even moderate size when it passes Kompong Cham in Cambodia.

   As it proceeds by Phnom Penh on its way to the Delta, the now deeper Mekong splits into two branches – the Mekong proper and the Bassac. This is the Quatre Bras ('Four Arms') region, the fourth 'arm' formed by the Tonle Sap River that alternately drains and fills the Great Lake, of which more later. Finally, the Mekong and the Bassac reach the South China Sea in a maze of sediment-loaded channels in what is now southern Vietnam.[1]

The Lower Mekong Basin, and in fact all of Southeast Asia, is subject to the annual cycle of the monsoons, that is, to the alternation between a wet, rainy season and a strongly marked dry season.[2] The 'summer monsoon', during which the prevailing winds are from the southwest, begins in late May or early June, and is marked by heavy rains and afternoon thunderstorms. The main course of the Mekong and its tributaries rise rapidly and begin flooding low-lying land; at the same time, melting snows in Tibet and southwestern China contribute to the volume. Eventually, so much water is flowing into the Delta that its channels can no longer discharge it properly, and like an overloaded septic system, one of the Mekong's tributaries – the Tonle Sap River above Phnom Penh – reverses its 'normal' flow and begins swelling the waters of the Great Lake.

Devastating typhoons may strike the Southeast Asian mainland at any time from July to November, but only the Delta region is subject to these great cyclones. By mid-November the 'winter monsoon' has begun, bringing in northeast winds, dry weather, and somewhat cooler temperatures. When the floods subside, the Tonle Sap River changes direction once more, and water flows from the lake down towards Phnom Penh and the Delta. By the last months of the dry season, thousands upon thousands of square kilometres of once-green rice fields have been harvested and lie fallow, sunbaked and brown.

In spite of appearances, the total amount of rainfall in the Lower Mekong Basin is never very high; furthermore, it fluctuates from year to year, with serious consequences for rice agriculture. This, the 'core area' of Khmer culture, receives on the average about 1,500 mm (59 in) annually; at Phnom Penh, Cambodia's capital, the mean is 1,432 mm (56 in), but in any one year it may be as high as 2,310 mm (91 in) and as low as 969 mm (38 in). The highest amount of rainfall is reached in the mainly unpopulated, heavily forested Cardamom and Elephant Mountains and contiguous coast of southwestern Cambodia; and the lowest on the Khorat Plateau.

The regions

The Khorat Plateau

Thailand's northeastern region, known to the Thai as 'Isan', is the poorest part of an otherwise prosperous nation.[3] Because its inhabitants occupy an enormous area of some 180,000 square km (70,000 square miles), the northeast actually contains one third of the country's population. Physically and culturally speaking, this is the Khorat Plateau, a vast tableland bounded on the west by the Petchabun Range, and on the south by the Dangreks. The plateau, which is generally 200 m (650 ft) above sea level, is tilted down towards the east, and is drained by the Chi and Mun Rivers; these flow together as the Mun, to join the Mekong on the Lao border.

6 The Dangrek Range, view east from Preah Vihear. This escarpment marks the southern edge of the Khorat Plateau, and looks south over the Cambodian Plain.

Since these rivers are deeply cut into the underlying Cretaceous sandstone, they have relatively restricted alluvial plains (compared to Cambodia), and water levels are usually 10–20 m (33–66 ft) below the level of the rice paddies, obviating any meaningful ways of irrigating them. In general, the soils of the Khorat Plateau are low in fertility, except in the narrow alluvial valleys, and rainfall is even more capricious than further south in Cambodia. It is estimated that 40 per cent of the land is unsuitable for any kind of agriculture, and another 30 per cent is covered by sparse, deciduous forests that, if removed, would result in rapid soil deterioration. Another inhibiting factor is the uncertainty of the drinking water supply, especially in the southern part of Khorat, where wells often become brackish in the dry season due to underlying salt deposits.[4]

Even with these limitations, the fertile Chi and Mun drainage system – the Khorat Basin, properly speaking – was the locus for some of the earliest farming villages yet known in Southeast Asia. And some of the most spectacular Classic Khmer temple complexes, such as Phimai and Phnom Rung, lie along the broader part of the Mun Valley and its tributaries.

As one reaches the southern edge of the plateau, the land rises to form the 6 Dangrek Range. Sloping gradually to an average height of about 450–600 m (1,480–1,970 ft), these sandstone hills drop off sharply on their southern flank to form a steep west–east escarpment overlooking the lushly forested, humid Cambodian Plain. The Dangrek escarpment then curves north to front the Champassak province of Laos, on the Mekong's right bank.

The Cambodian Plain

As the geographer Jean Delvert has pointed out,[5] Cambodia is actually a great, depressed basin, studded with isolated heights, few rising over 100 m (330 ft) above the surrounding lowlands; such island-like prominences are called *phnom* in Khmer. One of these heights, however, should claim our attention for the outstanding economic, religious, and political role that it played in the formation and maintenance of the city of Angkor. This is Phnom Kulen, a formation of folded and uplifted sandstones about 20 km (12 miles) northeast of Angkor.[6] Visible on clear days from the Dangreks, Phnom Kulen, along with the contiguous Phnom Kbal Spean, forms the source of all the waters that nourish the canals, moats, and giant reservoirs of the ancient city; in addition to this role, Angkor's architects and sculptors obtained all of the sandstone used in their monuments from Kulen's quarries. And, finally, it was on one of Phnom Kulen's heights that the Khmer Empire was founded by the early ruler Jayavarman II.

Most of the habitable part of Cambodia consists of the Mekong drainage, and back swamps created by it. The most striking feature of the Cambodian Plain is the Great Lake, the Tonle Sap ('Freshwater Lake') to the Khmer; the most extensive body of fresh water in Southeast Asia.[7] During the dry season the Great Lake covers an area of about 2,700 square km (1,050 square miles), but at the height of the monsoon rains it expands fourfold to about 10,360 square km (4,000 square miles) and resembles a vast inland sea. This is in large part the result of the annual reversal of the Tonle Sap River's flow, bringing the waters of the Mekong back into the flood plain and drowning the low forest that borders the dry season lake. Varying in depth throughout the year from 1.5 to 9.2 m (5 to 30 ft), the lake contains per cubic metre the greatest concentration of fish in the world, and supports an intensive fishing industry based upon the trapping, netting and fattening of various species of carp and catfish. Henri Mouhot, who was on the Great Lake in January 1860, remarks:

> ...the fish in it are so incredibly abundant that when the water is high they are actually crushed under the boats, and the play of oars is frequently impeded by them.[8]

This is a seasonal activity (from December until May) mainly under the control of many thousands of migratory Vietnamese and Cham fishermen, dwellers in either so-called 'floating villages' or in villages formed of houses supported by pilings that may be up to 15 m (50 ft) in height.

The catch may be towed as fresh fish from the Great Lake to downstream markets in huge, floating pounds, but most of it is dried, salted and smoked, or processed into fish pastes and sauces used to flavour rice.

The entire Cambodian Basin is relatively isolated from the sea, that is, from the Gulf of Siam, by the Cardamom and Elephant Mountain ranges. As any traveller flying from Bangkok to Phnom Penh can appreciate, these mountains, which average over 1,000 m (3,300 ft) in height, are covered by a dense, high, forest, sustained by the area's heaviest rainfall, and have been largely shunned by Cambodian farmers. On their southwest side, these mountains drop precipitously into the Gulf, which is bordered by narrow beaches and few natural harbours. This geographical situation may in part account for the exclusively inland orientation of Classic Khmer civilization.

Towards the east, abutting the Vietnam border, are more mountains, all part of the highlands that comprise much of that country, and which apparently never formed part of the Classic Angkorian realm. Nonetheless, these, and other upland areas around and within the Cambodian Basin, were the traditional homelands of tribal peoples (hunters, gatherers and swidden farmers); in past times, these much-scorned groups were the unfortunate targets of Khmer slaving expeditions.

The Delta

The vast, low, alluvial plain of the Delta actually begins just below Phnom Penh, and extends beyond the Cambodian border to form the southernmost part of Vietnam – what used to be called 'Cochin China' in the days of French colonialism.[9] For most of its history, the Vietnamese portion of the Delta was in Khmer hands, and speakers of Khmer still form a significant minority within the population. It was only in the late seventeenth century and throughout most of the eighteenth century that the Kingdom of Dai Viet annexed most of the Delta, and ethnic Vietnamese moved into the area. The process of vietnamization was accelerated by the French, who transferred large numbers of rice farmers from the overpopulated Tonkin Plain of northern Vietnam to 'Cochin China', as a source of ready labour for the great agricultural tracts owned by them and by a powerful, native landlord class.

Few parts of the Delta are more than 3 m (10 ft) above the monotonous, largely unforested plain, and most of the region is devoted to rice paddies. In contrast to the Khorat Plateau, the major problem here is not too little water, but too much, and the area is crisscrossed with drainage canals, some probably pre-dating the French colonial regime; most of them lie on the Vietnamese side of the border, as the French considered the Vietnamese to be more industrious and reliable than the Cambodians. Simply because the Delta is so low lying, salinity poses a threat to growing rice, as brackish water may penetrate far inland from the coast, especially in the Ca Mau Peninsula.

As the Mekong nears the South China Sea, it splits into a tangle of mangrove-lined waterways. In 1295, the Chinese envoy Zhou Daguan travelled this way *en route* to Angkor, and left this description:

> There are several dozen mouths, but only the fourth one allows free passage; all the others are choked with sandbars, which cannot be crossed by large vessels. Whatever way one looks nothing is to be seen but tall canes, old trees, yellow sands, and pale reeds; at first glance it is impossible to orient oneself, and even the sailors hold it difficult to find one's way into the right channel.[10]

This scene will be familiar to those who have viewed Francis Ford Coppola's film of the Vietnam War, *Apocalypse Now*.

Because of the fertility of the nitrogen-rich alluvium along both banks of the Mekong, the Delta is definitely one of Asia's 'rice baskets', providing about one half of all rice produced in Vietnam. But in early times, long before the great land-reclamation programmes carried out by the French, the Delta was less important for its agriculture than for its strategic location along the trading lanes linking the Indic and Sinitic worlds. It may also have played a critical role in the initial adoption by the Khmer of Indian models of religion and society. This complex topic will be more fully explored in Chapter 5.

Flora and fauna

Given the thousands of years that the resources and agricultural potential of the Khmer area have been exploited by human groups, the entire landscape has been seriously altered from what may have been its condition before the adoption of rice farming. The characteristic members of the forest wherever it is found are various species of dipterocarp, a tree with broad, elongated leaves and distinctive winged fruits. Visitors to Angkor will see them everywhere, the bases of their tall, smooth trunks often marked by blackened cavities where the local people have been extracting resin.

True evergreen rainforest is actually very localized, being mostly confined to the relatively inaccessible Cardamom and Elephant ranges of Cambodia. In contrast, the forests of most of the region are subject to the annual fluctuation of the monsoons, and are thus semideciduous to deciduous. The most extreme conditions are found on the Khorat Plateau, with its low average rainfall and poor soils; there, away from the alluvial valleys, one finds what is termed Dry Dipterocarp Forest, interspersed with savannas. Much of the Cambodian Basin away from the low-lying rice-growing areas is covered by Monsoon Forest; during the winter dry months, the dipterocarps drop most of their leaves to form a brown carpet on the forest floor.[11]

An analysis by Judith Jacob of inscriptions of the pre-Classic and Classic Khmer periods has indicated a number of domesticated and wild trees and plants that were exploited in ancient times.[12] Included among the fruits grown by Khmer farmers were mangoes, jackfruit, bael fruit (Malabar orange), carambola, various citruses, tamarind, Chinese dates and watermelon. Vegetables and grain crops mentioned in the texts are rice, sorghum, millet, sesame, mung beans, cucumbers, eggplants, wax gourds and Chinese cabbage. Even though no recipes have come down to us from those days, dishes were enhanced by spices, including cardamom, ginger, turmeric, nutmeg, cane sugar and black pepper (the ubiquitous, fiery chile pepper of modern Southeast Asia was introduced in post-Angkor times, most likely by the Portuguese).

A feature of the contemporary landscape throughout village Cambodia is the sugar palm (*Borassus flabellifer*), the country's national tree, a tall, slender, and astonishingly useful plant that furnishes leaves for palm-leaf books, thatch, and matting; wood for construction; and (from its inflorescence) 7 wine, vinegar and sugar. Not surprisingly, this tree also appears in the inscriptions. So do the coconut palm and the areca palm – the latter being the source of the alkaloid-rich nut that is mixed with lime and wrapped with *Piper Betle* leaves to produce the famous betel chew, a masticatory found throughout South and Southeast Asia.

Other plants economically useful to the early Khmer were cotton, the mulberry tree, bamboos and the silk-cotton tree (*Ceiba pentandra*), a majestic plant containing kapok in its seedpods.

Wild game animals once abounded in the monsoon forests of Southeast Asia, but twentieth-century wars have taken a heavy toll on their numbers, especially in Cambodia during the Khmer Rouge period.[13] The primates consist of gibbons, langurs and macaques, the last still common among the ruins of Angkor. The ancient Khmer were familiar with the huge and formidable Asiatic tiger, as well as with leopards and smaller members of the cat family, and undoubtedly hunted deer. Besides the tiger, other dangerous large mammals in their environment included the gaur, banteng and wild buffalo (all members of the cattle family), wild boars and the Indian elephant.

Some of the reptiles of mainland Southeast Asia played important roles in the art and culture of the Classic Khmer. There are two saurian species, one or both of which appear in the famous reliefs of Angkor Wat. The largest and most fearsome is the estuarine crocodile (*Crocodilus porosus*), familiar to many as the 'saltie' of northern Australia and a common inhabitant of the Delta; when the thirteenth-century Chinese diplomat Zhou Daguan speaks of crocodiles 'as large as boats',[14] he must be speaking of these. The Siamese crocodile (*C. siamensis*) is considerably smaller, and abounds in the swamps of Cambodia, and in the Tonle Sap. Even more significant in Khmer religion and iconography are two snakes: the common cobra (*Naja naja*), found everywhere but the thickest jungle, and the much rarer king cobra or hamadryad (*Ophiophagus hannah*), the world's largest venomous snake.

Among the wild birds of Khmer country, the most economically significant would have been peafowl and jungle fowl (the wild ancestor of the familiar chicken), hornbills (prized by Southeast Asian carvers for their huge bills), and various kingfishers. It was the brilliant, iridescent blue feathers of the kingfishers that attracted Chinese traders to the city of Angkor, for they were much sought after to embellish court headdresses in the Chinese capital.

Animal domestication is very ancient in mainland Southeast Asia. Excavations in Khorat Plateau sites have shown that cattle, water buffalos, pigs and domesticated chickens were bred and kept there at least three millennia ago, and the same would probably be true for Cambodia were its prehistoric archaeology better known. The principal use of oxen and buffalos was and still is to draw ploughs in rice paddies; as in the rest of the Far East, cows are seldom if ever milked. The Khmer generally prefer to eat pork rather than beef, but meat is rare in their diet compared to fish and fish sauces.

On the testimony of relief sculpture, horses were probably more prevalent in Classic Angkor times than today, being extensively used for cavalry and for drawing chariots. The same is true of elephants, which are barely 'domesticated' in the full sense of the word since they do not breed well in captivity;

new animals must be hunted and then tamed and trained. The Angkorian kings maintained huge numbers of the beasts as war elephants and for royal processions. Until the eve of the Second World War, elephants were extensively used throughout Cambodia in logging and forest clearance, and even to conduct well-heeled tourists to the ruins.

Rice: the Khmer staff of life

Asian civilization would not exist without rice (*Oryza sativa*, an annual semiaquatic grass): over half the world's population subsists on its starchy grains, grown under a wide variety of conditions.[15] So much part of life is it that in many Asian countries the word for 'food' is 'cooked rice' (*bai* in Khmer); in Cambodia, rice with fish is the basis of the economy. The origins of domesticated rice are still obscure. Although a semiaquatic annual grass, it is generally thought to have originated as dry rice sown and harvested in upland fields. As for 'paddy rice' (rice grown in well-watered fields edged by bunds, or low dikes), this appears in the archaeological record about 8,000 years ago

7

7 Rice fields near Siem Reap, at the end of the rainy season. In the distance are tall sugar palms, the Cambodian national tree.

8 Rice harvest in the southern Khorat Plateau of Thailand. These farmers are ethnic Khmer.

in the Yangtze and Huai River drainages of central China, and in all likelihood spread from there to other parts of Asia.

8   In Cambodia, and in most of Southeast Asia, there are four kinds of rice cultivation, all of them practised in both ancient and modern times.[16]

1 *Dry rice farming*, using swidden ('slash-and-burn') techniques, is the norm for the more upland hilly regions, particularly those inhabited by the non-Khmer ethnic minorities such as the Brao and the Pear (see next chapter), but sometimes even Khmer paddy farmers will cultivate dry rice on non-inundated soils. The low vegetation – or higher forest, in the case of newly pioneered lands – is cut and burned during the dry season, following which the rice is planted in holes made with a digging stick. There is no bunding or any other method of water retention, and the crop is totally dependent on sufficient rainfall.

2 *Bunded field farming*. There is little question that farming in rain-fed paddies was, and remains, the principal method of rice production throughout both Cambodia and the Khorat Plateau. The Cambodian lowland landscape is one of small, generally square or rectangular fields of between 0.5 and 2 hectares (1.2–4.9 acres), built upon soils that are said by agronomists to be of medium to poor quality. Yields generally average 1–1.5 tons per hectare, which is not very high compared with other Asian countries like China or Japan, but they exceed 2 tons on the rich, black soils of Battambang Province in western Cambodia. The typical Khmer farmer begins working and sowing his seedbed in mid-May, at the start of the rainy season. About

one month later, on an auspicious day, he commences ploughing his bunded rice field with cattle or water buffalo. In contrast to Chinese practice, animal or human manure, being considered impure, is seldom used in Cambodia as a fertilizer, although it is widely employed in Thailand. Transplanting of the young rice onto the now rain-flooded paddies is mainly women's labour, and takes about 20 days of hard work by cooperative teams.

The timing of the harvest is set by the particular variety of rice being culti-vated. Paddy farmers in this part of Southeast Asia can choose between up to twenty-five different races of rice, each differing in length of growing season, adaptability to particular soils, resistance to pests, and even in flavour (the jasmine rice that matures in five months is considered the best-tasting). 'Sticky' rice comes in two varieties, a highly prized white one used in sweet desserts, and a black one for making wine. It is this arsenal of botanic vari-ability that ensures adequate harvests in the face of uncertain rainfall and less-than-ideal soils, above all in the relatively dry Khorat Plateau alluvial river valleys. After harvest, during the dry season, the parched, stubble-cov-ered paddies are grazed by farm animals.

3. *Flood-retreat farming.* This type of rice cultivation is highly productive, with average yields of 2–3 tons per hectare, and is carried out on the shores of the Great Lake and in the alluvial plain of the Lower Mekong (including the Phnom Penh 'Quatre Bras' region and part of the Delta). Essentially, flood-retreat farmers store floodwaters in bunded areas and man-made reservoirs. During the dry season they release water to supply paddies below these sim-ple, cooperatively built structures. According to the geographers who have studied it in the Lower Mekong, flood-retreat farming may actually have been the key factor in the rise to greatness of the Khmer civilization, a propo-sition that will be examined in Chapter 7.

As described by the geographer W. J. van Liere[17] for the plains adjacent to the Great Lake, especially in the Siem Reap-Angkor region, the flood-retreat system is quite sophisticated. Along the tributaries of the Great Lake there are broad levees, with shallow depressions between. During the summer monsoon, the run-off water from higher lands drains towards the depres-sions, where it is bunded and retained in swampy areas and then spread across the landscape through a multitude of small ditches. In the annually-flooded margins of the Great Lake itself, there are even larger, rectangular, bunded structures called *tnub*, with one side left open towards higher land, in which water is retained as the dry season progresses, and the lake level drops.

Flood-retreat fields are ploughed in June, after the first rains. As the flood-waters recede at the beginning of the next dry season, transplanting begins, proceeding from higher to lower areas as the water level drops – the Khmer say that the 'farmers chase the water'. Five to six days after transplanting, they begin spreading water from the impoundments by small ditches. Finally, harvesting takes place from March onwards.

4. *Floating rice farming.* So-called 'floating' rice is an oxymoron: it doesn't really float. Rather, this is a variety of *Oryza sativa* that is planted in flooded localities; as the water rises, the stalk lengthens so that the seed heads are always above water. Mature plants may be as much as 5 m (16.4 ft) long. This

used to be planted in some areas around the Great Lake and in the Delta, but it is now in bad repute not only because the Khmer Rouge forced the people to plant it as a staple food while exporting most of the white rice harvest, but also because it is said to have an indifferent flavour. Although it is mentioned with some wonder by Zhou Daguan,[18] the Chinese chronicler of thirteenth-century Angkor, 'floating' rice probably never played a significant role in the ancient economy.

Professional agronomists bemoan the fact that the Khmer do not practise large-scale hydraulic rice cultivation, and point to the mediocrity of most Cambodian soils, but throughout its modern history the country has managed not only to adequately feed all of its people, but also to export approximately ten per cent of its rice crop. Until the devastation triggered by the Khmer Rouge leadership in the 1970s, starvation was unknown. Cambodia was and still is a land of relatively poor, but independent and well-fed farmers. A family of five can subsist on one hectare of bunded paddy land, but one hectare of flood retreat land can feed this same family and at least five other souls. Khmer civilization must have depended on this surplus; it was indeed the 'gift of the Mekong'.

3 · Peoples and Languages

Cambodian genesis

For the Khmer peoples no great origin myths comparable to those in the biblical Book of Genesis, or to the *Popol Vuh* among the Maya, have survived in written form. Nonetheless, intriguing fragments of such a story or stories have come to us from early Chinese sources, from stone inscriptions, and from Khmer folklore. Two such legends seem to be set in the Delta, in a country known to the Chinese annalists as 'Funan' (of which more in Chapter 5). One of them concerns a Brahman named Kaundinya, apparently a prince of a 'solar' dynasty or lineage of India or possibly Malaya.[1] Following his arrival in the region, he threw a javelin to mark the location of his future capital, then took as his wife the daughter of the local *naga* (cobra) king. Kaundinya's marriage to this snake-woman (*nagi*), named Soma or 'Moon', thus united the solar and lunar dynasties, a union that would be celebrated by all subsequent Cambodian rulers. The notion of a king wedding a *nagi* bride is echoed in popular tales about a mythical ancient king Prah Thon, and often invoked in song during modern marriage ceremonies.

The ethnologist Éveline Porée-Maspero[2] sees a deeper meaning behind these stories: the *nagi* snake-woman symbolizes an original, local tradition of matrilineal descent associated with the Moon, and the foreign husband an introduced one of patrilineal descent connected with the Sun. Basing her study on dynastic records preserved in Cambodian inscriptions, she has found that the matrilineal principle continued to govern or at least influence dynastic succession from earliest times right through the period of Angkor's ascendancy.

The second and apparently unrelated legend involves a hermit named Kambu, who was given an *apsaras* or celestial nymph named Mera by the great god Shiva (the major patron deity of Khmer rulers).[3] From this marriage sprang the Khmer royal line as well as the people themselves. The Khmer thus came to call their land *Kambudesa* or 'Country of Kambu', later abridged to *Kambuja*; it is from this latter that the modern name 'Cambodia' is derived.

The peopling of Southeast Asia

All of the land of the Khmer, and by extension all of mainland Southeast Asia, has actually been occupied by humans and their near-human ancestors for a very long period of time, far beyond the reach of tribal memory. 'Out of Africa' is the theme most often struck by palaeoanthropologists studying ancient hominid fossils, for it is now certain that our immediate progenitor, *Homo erectus*, began moving out from that continent to the rest of the Old World about 1.5 million years ago. Certainly by a million years ago this low-browed but upright and tool-making creature had occupied what is now continental Southeast Asia and much of the Indonesian island archipelago. I say 'now' because at that distant time the geography of that vast region was very different from what it is at present. During the Pleistocene or Ice Age, at least during the times of glacial maxima in northern latitudes, the sea was between 50 and 90 m (165–200 ft) below today's level, exposing a vast shelf of land (the 'Sunda Shelf') uniting Java, Sumatra and Borneo with the mainland.[4]

The story of the origin of modern humans – *Homo sapiens* – is, according to most specialists, a repetition of the 'out of Africa' theme, with archaic forms of *H. sapiens* having evolved there some 400,000 years ago from *H. erectus*, and then into *H. sapiens sapiens* about 130,000 years before present. So, from East Africa came the ancestral Adams and Eves who would give rise to the various populations that came to occupy all the world save Antarctica. But, a still highly controversial rival scenario would have each of the various races of the world arising separately from geographically dispersed *H. erectus* populations. Be that as it may, we may safely assume that our area was fully occupied by physiologically modern men and women by at least 50,000 years ago, all of whom were following a hunting and gathering way of life.

We shall see in the next chapter that simple, chipped-stone industries assignable to these early people have been found in the Khmer area of Cambodia and Thailand, perhaps mostly predating the end of the Pleistocene in about 8000 BC, after which time sea level became what it is today and the land of the Khmers took on its present appearance. Over the next few millennia, rice cultivation spread from its probable hearth in China into Southeast Asia, and certainly by 2300 BC paddy farming had become the dominant way of life for the inhabitants of these tropical lowlands. The next great transformation, other than the adoption of metal technology after 1500 BC, was the progressive cultural Indianization of these farmers from about AD 100 onwards, beginning in the Delta and spreading from there to the rest of what was to become the Khmer culture area (Chapter 5). With the first Indian-script writings on stone monuments, we can begin to talk about languages and state origins.

Languages: the big picture

9   A language map such as the one for our part of Southeast Asia is static – it does not and cannot reflect the evolution of language, the borrowings of vocabulary and grammar, or, above all, the movements of the peoples who spoke and speak these tongues.[5] A glance at this particular map will highlight the dilemma: while Thai-speakers now dominate the Khorat Plateau, as well as the rest of Thailand, we know that they are relatively recent arrivals from southern China. The same situation holds true for the southern coast of Vietnam and the Delta: these have not always been Vietnamese-speaking, and the Delta so only since the eighteenth century. Such a map drawn up in the tenth century would look very different.

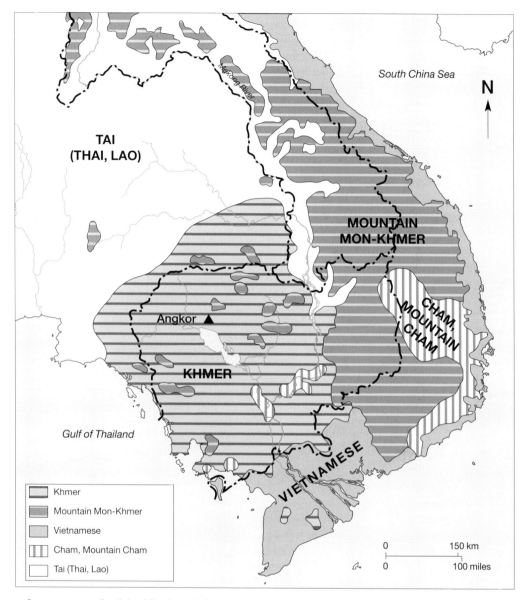

9 Language map of mainland Southeast Asia.

As the linguist H. L. Shorto tells us,[6] the characteristic speech family of mainland Southeast Asia from Thailand's Mae Nam Valley eastward is *Mon–Khmer*; its ancestral form was once the dominant, perhaps the only, language family in this region during the prehistoric era. With upwards of about 150 non-tonal tongues, it is actually distributed from northeastern India to the Vietnamese coast, north to northern Laos and down south into Malaysia. Mon is spoken in southern Burma by a people who once, in the eighteenth century, came close to seizing power in that country.

10 Aboriginal Mon-Khmer, from the mountains of eastern Cambodia.

It is now generally recognized that Vietnamese is a Mon-Khmer language, but it shows the effects of long contact with Chinese in its vocabulary, in its use of tones, and in its tendency to be monosyllabic. Initially it was even written with Chinese characters, as the Vietnamese rulers adopted the Chinese administrative model, but during the French colonial period the Roman alphabet came into general use. There are many ethnic Vietnamese in Cambodia today, particularly in fishing communities along the Mekong and around the Great Lake. Largely because of bitter national conflicts between Vietnam and Cambodia that have occurred over the centuries, relationships between the Khmer and the Vietnamese minority have not been good.

Khmer proper, which we shall examine in greater detail later, is the national language of the wet-rice farmers of the Cambodian lowlands, and of more isolated populations in the southern Khorat Plateau and the Delta. Scattered in more hilly uplands within the Cambodian Basin, in the Dangreks, and quite extensively throughout the highlands of Laos and Vietnam are Mon-Khmer-speaking tribal populations. Called *Montagnards* by the French, and all kinds of pejorative names by their more settled neighbours, they are consummate hunters, as well as cultivators of upland, dry rice using swidden or shifting cultivation techniques. Animists, adept in shamanic practices, they have traditionally been despised by the lowland Khmer, and subject to their slave raids right up to the establishment of the French Protectorate. Not so many decades ago, this state of affairs made it relatively easy for the Khmer Rouge to recruit the 'Mountain Khmer' in a struggle against the Cambodian government. Contrariwise, in the mountains of Vietnam and Laos, others of these tribal peoples became close allies of the US forces during the Indo-China conflict.

The Kui, also known as Souei, are one of the largest of these upland groups, found in the hilly flanks of the Dangreks along the Thai–Cambodian border; they now number about 380,000 souls. Although some Kui remain hoe-farmers and animists (some have a reputation as elephant-hunters), many are now wet-rice cultivators and Buddhists. A far smaller Mon-Khmer group is called the Pear, scattered on the northern slopes of the Cardamoms; in an area between the Great Lake and the Dangreks; and even in the Siem Reap region, where they are called the Samre. According to Étienne Aymonier,[7] the inhabitants of Phnom Kulen, to the north of Angkor, were originally Samre, but, ashamed of admitting their aboriginal origin, changed their language to Khmer. The Stieng occupy the mountain lands of eastern Cambodia and southern Vietnam. Finally, there are the Saoch, on the western side of the Elephant Mountains, towards the coast.

Next must be considered the *Cham*, speakers of a language closely akin to Malay. Cham is Austronesian, that is, it is a member of an extraordinary linguistic family spread over half the globe. At some time before 600 BC the Cham probably settled in south Vietnam from either peninsular Malaysia or Borneo; the language is first attested in inscriptions of the early fifth century AD, when the Cham state had become a powerful presence between the Delta and the northern Vietnamese of the Tonkin coast. Originally the Champa kingdom was Hindu–Buddhist, and had various conflicts with the Khmer Empire (at one point claiming to have captured Angkor), but began to be converted to Islam in the eleventh century. Finally, Champa was decisively defeated by the Vietnamese emperor in 1471, and the Cham began their diaspora. The 220,000 Cham in modern Cambodia are confusingly called 'Khmer Islam', and make a living as fishermen, traders and butchers (in a Buddhist land where killing animals is not a valued occupation). Mainly settled in the Quatre Bras region and along the Mekong above Phnom Penh, they were the special objects of the Khmer Rouge's genocidal programme.[8]

Tribal peoples speaking Austronesian languages are also located in the uplands of northeast Cambodia and adjacent Vietnam.

The *Tai* language family, of which Thai proper and Lao are the principal members, represents an intrusion from a homeland in south China during the twelfth and thirteenth centuries. Archaeologist Donn Bayard has suggested that these tongues were brought in by modest-sized groups, each probably consisting of little more than a royal family and a small standing army, political expediency leading the natives (most probably Mon-Khmer speakers) to adopt the language.[9] All the same, this incursion drove 'a wedge down the centre of South East Asia', as Professor Shorto has told us, splitting areas of Mon-Khmer speech.[10]

Unlike Mon-Khmer, all of the Tai languages are tonal. Thai and Lao are very closely related, to the extent that they might even be considered dialects rather than separate languages. Lao has been dominant in northeastern Khorat, to the north of the area's Khmer speakers, but is now losing ground to Thai proper.

Apart from its language, Thai culture has many distinctive features, but a significant part of it, including statecraft and the Hindu-inspired royal cult, along with much of its art, architecture, music and dance, has been adapted from Khmer prototypes following the defeat of Angkor by Thai armies in the fifteenth century. The Thai script and a portion of its vocabulary have also been borrowed from the Khmer. It thus comes as no surprise to find that in Bangkok there is a massive scale model of Angkor Wat right next to the Temple of the Emerald Buddha – the Thai kingdom's Royal Chapel and one of its holiest sites. But the Khmer–Thai relationship has been complex, for the Thai gave to the Khmer what may be the most important gift of all: Theravada Buddhism.

The Khmer language

Khmer is a remarkably concrete and down-to-earth language, and thus poor in abstract terms, which it has been constrained to borrow from Indian languages. In an example given by the linguist François Martini,[11] there are seventeen different ways to say 'to carry or wear', depending on the mode of carriage ('with the hand', 'suspended from the hand', etc.). In contrast, Khmer has taken so many abstract words from Sanskrit for its administrative, legal and literary vocabulary that it was once thought to be a Sanskritic language. After Theravada Buddhism was introduced at the beginning of the fifteenth century, its sacred Pali texts (Pali is another Indic language) proved to be a rich source of new words; in fact, Pali rather than Sanskrit continues to be a source of neologisms for the modern administration, the media and the technological sector.

Unlike Thai and Vietnamese, Khmer (or Cambodian as it is sometimes termed) is completely non-tonal, with a high percentage of two-syllable words that are usually stressed on the second syllable; words that have more than two syllables are probably of non-Khmer origin. It is rich in vowels and dipthongs, giving a decidedly nasal sound to Khmer speech as heard by Western ears. Khmer grammar has neither gender (i.e. no distinction between 'he', 'she' or 'it') nor number. What it does have is a grammatical system of prefixing, infixing and reduplication. Here are some examples given by Professor Martini:

> *slàp*, to die   *bôl*, to augur
> *samlàp*, to kill   *phnôl*, auspice (-*n*- is infixed)
>   *praphnôl*, to presage (infix *n* + prefix *pra*)

Certain infixes allow one to distinguish nouns from verbs, to form nouns of agents and instruments, and to designate the result of an action, as in:

> *sûn*, to mould, model   *čhok*, to plug up   *bèk*, to break
> *smûn*, potter   *čhnok*, plug, cork   *bamnèk*, debris

As in English, the usual word order is subject – verb – object, but the modifier follows the thing modified.

Cambodian villagers speak colloquial Khmer among themselves, but the educated use far more formal speech. There is an obligatory distinction between the popular and the noble language, and special vocabularies are used to address the king, great personages, and Buddhist monks (or to talk about them). Personal pronouns are also thoroughly hierarchized. For 'I, myself', a person uses entirely different words when addressing an inferior, an equal, a superior, a princely personage, and a monk. This linguistic emphasis on social inequality and respect is as true today as it was during the height of Angkor's greatness.

Writing

According to linguist Franklin Huffman,[12] all mainland Southeast Asian scripts are derived from some form or forms of the ancient Brahmi script of South India. The earliest example of such writing in the region is a Sanskrit inscription of the second or third century AD from Vo-canh, near Nha Trang on the south Vietnamese coast. It is not until AD 611 that we have the first known inscription in the Khmer language, from Angkor Borei, which is located on the lower Mekong at the head of the Delta, and which was clearly a key site for the early development of Khmer civilization.

Although the Khmer writing system is basically phonetic, like all Indic scripts it is far more complex than a mere alphabet would be. 'Quasi-syllabic' would be a more accurate description. There are thirty-three consonants, some aspirated and some not, and each with one of two inherent back vowels – thus, there are two consonant series. As for the vowels themselves, there are 20 signs for these, consisting of 'pure' vowels, dipthongs, and vowels followed by –m. Confusingly to Westerners, one and the same vowel sign is pronounced differently depending on the consonant that it vocalizes. Even further, the vowels are arranged around the consonants: they can appear above it, below it, before it, after it, or divided in two parts that flank the consonant! To add to the complexity, with diacritics one may convert a consonant in one series into a consonant in the other; and when two consonants occur at the beginning of a word (as they often do), the second is written as a sub-script to the first. A consonantal sub-script can also be used beneath another consonant in the middle of a word. Nonetheless, linguists consider this and other Indian-derived writing systems to be phonetically sophisticated and remarkably accurate at reproducing the spoken tongue (which is more than one can say about English script).

Khmer is written from left to right and top to bottom, with no breaks between words. There are now two forms: 1) 'round script', virtually identical with what one finds on Classic Khmer inscriptions, and applied to religious texts, newspaper headlines, and formal texts like those inscribed on public buildings and monuments, and 2) 'oblique script', derived from popular handwriting and used for all other printed works.

There are some 1,200 surviving stone inscriptions from the Cambodian past, many of great calligraphic elegance; these are usually incised on free-standing stelae or on the door-jambs of temples. The majority of them are in Sanskrit (using a very similar script to Khmer), and consist of poetic invocations, dedications and the like involving the Hindu deities and royal

92

personages. The other corpus of texts is in Khmer, and while they also largely concern religious foundations, they usually provide us with more mundane but critical information of great anthropological and economic interest, as we shall see in subsequent chapters.[13]

What we do not have from the past are all the books that must have been in daily use everywhere. As a result of their having been written on perishable materials, the tropical climate, insects and constant wars have seen to their total destruction; with only those records inscribed on stone, we are thus dealing with a very skewed and fragmentary sample of indigenous texts from past eras. It is known that there were two kinds of books (see Chapter 7). One consisted of long, narrow palm leaves incised with a stylus, and loosely strung along one long edge. The other was a screenfold: paper from the inner bark of a tree was folded back and forth like an accordion, and then written on with a pen (some books, though, had smooth, blackened surfaces on which texts were written with something like white chalk). Unfortunately, we do not know whether the palm leaf books had different contents from the screenfolds.

93

Who are the Khmer?

In spite of the devastation of the Indo-China War and the Khmer Rouge terror, the Khmer people – those who speak the Khmer language and follow the Khmer way of life – have experienced a remarkable demographic rebound. There are now about 10.8 million ethnic Khmer in Cambodia (where they comprise 90 per cent of the population); about 700,000 in the Delta of southern Vietnam; and perhaps as many as 1 million in Thailand's Khorat Plateau. Then there is the wartime and post-war Cambodian diaspora, with at least 50,000 Khmer speakers in France, and more than twice that number in the United States of America: the ethnic Khmer community in Long Beach, California, numbers about 55,000, the largest Khmer population outside Cambodia. Quite naturally, the children of these exiles are rapidly losing their native tongue, although they retain a strong sense of identity with their roots in Cambodia's past. There is hardly an ethnic Khmer over the age of six, either in Cambodia or elsewhere, who does not know about the glories of Angkor and its empire, and take pride in them.

So who, exactly, is a 'Khmer'? Basically, a Khmer can be defined as a person of Southeast Asian descent who speaks the Khmer language and practises the Theravada Buddhist religion (or at least has done so since this form of Buddhism was introduced as a state cult to Cambodia in the fifteenth century). In Chapter 8 we shall examine in detail Khmer culture as it was in Cambodia on the eve of the French Protectorate of the nineteenth century, but here it will suffice to give a basic list of traits, other than the common language, that have characterized these people down through the ages.

The Khmer are overwhelmingly lowland cultivators of wet rice in fixed, bunded fields: almost a half of Cambodia's population is still agricultural (as compared with a mere 2 per cent in the United States of America). These fields are generally small, of no more than 1–2 hectares (2.5–4.9 acres), and are traditionally held by individual farmers in usufruct, that is, land belonged

11 Ox-drawn wooden carts. Left: modern Cambodian cart on a road in Siem Reap Province. Right: detail of a relief on the Bayon, Angkor Thom, twelfth to thirteenth centuries.

to the peasant as long as it was not left uncultivated for three years. Cambodia has never had latifundia (huge estates held by absentee landlords), although in Angkorian times there were tenant-farmed lands the produce of which went for the upkeep of temples and religious foundations and to support a hierarchy of civil bureaucrats.[14]

Indispensable to the Khmer farmer for working the rice fields are the metal-tipped wooden plough drawn by yoked oxen or buffaloes, the similarly powered harrow, and the hoe. Rice is harvested with the sickle. Along the dirt roads and in house compounds can be seen the characteristic and elegant ox-drawn cart, one that has hardly changed its form since the days of Angkor's greatness. Lining the roads, dykes and bunds are tall sugar palms, a symbol of Cambodia itself.

A people can be defined by its cuisine, but there are two Khmer cuisines: a courtly tradition consisting of the most refined and varied dishes, and the popular cuisine basically consisting of steamed rice and fish (the latter usually in the form of *prahok* (fish paste) or fish sauce), and vegetables.[15]

The Khmer realm is a land of villages and hamlets with the houses strung out along roads, streams and dykes. All houses are rectangular in shape, and are generally raised on wooden piles driven into the ground; the lower storey serves as shelter for the animals and as storage space, while the upper is the living space for the family, often an extended one. For poorer families, the roof is simply thatched, while more affluent ones have tiled roofs.

Except perhaps in very early, pre-state times, the Khmer seem never to have had lineages or clans; Khmer social organization rather resembles that of the Western world in that there exist loose groupings of relatives or 'kin-folk' from both the father's and mother's side of the family. Anthropologists call such amorphous groups 'kindreds'; as in the United States of America and Europe, an individual's obligations are to these. There is no hereditary Khmer aristocracy, either. It is true that there has been a nobility defined by contiguity to the royal house, but membership in this dies out beyond five degrees of relationship to a king. As shall be seen in Chapter 8, in pre-French Cambodia there were 'mandarin' bureaucrats appointed by the king, but their privileges were not inherited.

There are three components to Khmer religion and religious behaviour, assignable to different epochs in Khmer history and prehistory, but all are still

41

operative today. The first and certainly oldest is an indigenous animism based on a belief in local spirits or genie (*neak ta*), and the propitiation of these with the aid of shaman-specialists. This animistic complex is something that the lowland Khmer share with their brethren, the upland Mon-Khmer. The second element is Hinduism, introduced to Southeast Asia at the beginning of our era, and even in this day closely involved, as it is in Thailand, with royal power and ceremony. The third is Theravada Buddhism, here among the Khmer almost identical in tenets and practice to other countries – Sri Lanka, Thailand, Burma and Laos – where it is the state religion.

Even the Khmer Rouge could not obliterate the Khmer devotion to the Buddha, or abolish the respect and honour that all pay to the Buddhist clergy from novice to abbot. Even though these evil people managed to demolish a vast number of Buddhist pagodas, many of these have been rebuilt, and today there is hardly a Khmer village without one.

Lastly, we must consider the king and the royal family as integral parts of 'Khmerness', of being a khmer. It is no fluke of history that even after devastating wars and genocide, intervals of non-monarchical republican rule, and Marxist-Leninist dictatorship, the name of the country is once again 'The Kingdom of Cambodia', and the titular head is still the king. While the present incumbent, H. R. H. Norodom Sihanouk, no longer wields the temporal power that was held by his predecessors before the arrival of the French, his royal descent, affiliation in the Khmer mind with the ancient kings of Angkor, and role as protector of Buddhism gives him an immense spiritual prestige. Regardless of the vagaries of modern politics (and he has at times been part and parcel of these), at least in theory the king is the very essence of the Khmer state.

12 Typical two-storey house, near Siem Reap, Cambodia. The roof is tiled; the sides consist of palm-leaf mats.

4 · The Khmer Before History

Hunters and gatherers

For over one million years, early humans of the species *Homo erectus* – bipedal, but with smaller brains – roamed over mainland Southeast Asia and the Sunda Shelf, hunting large and small game, gathering wild vegetable foods, and perhaps even fishing, until they were replaced about 60,000 years ago by modern men and women – *Homo sapiens*, like ourselves.[1] These new populations were probably the distant ancestors of the Mon-Khmer peoples and of all their linguistic and cultural relatives. This immense span of time was the last half of the Pleistocene epoch or Ice Age, which was to come to a close between 13,000 and 10,000 years ago, when worldwide temperatures rose dramatically, and the ice caps of the Northern Hemisphere receded. As a consequence of rising sea levels, the Sunda Shelf was largely drowned, and the Southeast Asian mainland and the islands of the Indonesian Archipelago began to look very much as they do today.

These morphologically modern human populations apparently lived a way of life not very different from that pursued by the archaic *Homo erectus* whom they had displaced or replaced. From about 11,000 BC until the adoption of rice agriculture in the third millennium BC, the material remains of these simple societies belong to a very rudimentary lithic tradition called 'Hoabhinian', first defined in the 1920s by the French archaeologist Madeleine Colani, who had excavated rockshelter sites in the Hòa-bình area of northern Vietnam.[2] Hoabhinian tools are generally chipped or flaked from river cobbles of chert and other hard stones, and consist of little more than unifacial choppers and small hide scrapers. Compared with the Late Pleistocene and early Holocene sites of western Eurasia, Hoabhinian stone tools are both crude and remarkably scarce. How may one account for this? A plausible and widely-held explanation is that instead of stone, the ancient peoples of Southeast Asia mainly relied on cutting and scraping implements fashioned from the ubiquitous bamboo and various hard woods, which in many respects would have surpassed stone tools in efficiency, but which would have left no archaeological traces in this rainy environment.

14

There has been very little search for Hoabhinian occupations in Cambodia, with the notable exception of the work carried out in the 1960s by Cécile and Roland Mourer at the site of Laang Spean, a large rockshelter located on a hill between the towns of Battambang and Pailin in northwestern Cambodia.[3] Beneath a top layer containing Early Farming-period ceramics were four deeper strata with the usual Hoabhinian tools of chert and metamorphic stone: side and end scrapers, and unifacial axes or choppers. In one level with

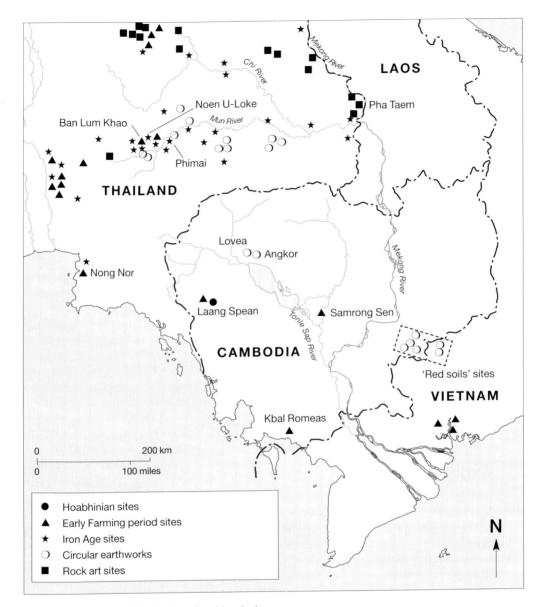

13 Distribution of prehistoric sites.

a radiocarbon date of 4290 BC ± 70 the Mourers excavated numerous faunal remains of hunted and/or scavenged animals, including rhinoceros, deer, small carnivores, monkeys, numerous freshwater turtles, bandicoot rats and fishes. There were even bones from the king cobra, an edible but formidable target for early hunters! A certain degree of mobility of the small band that occupied the cave is suggested by snail shells of marine origin found in the debris; their nearest source, the Gulf of Thailand, is about 100 km (60 miles) from Laang Spean.

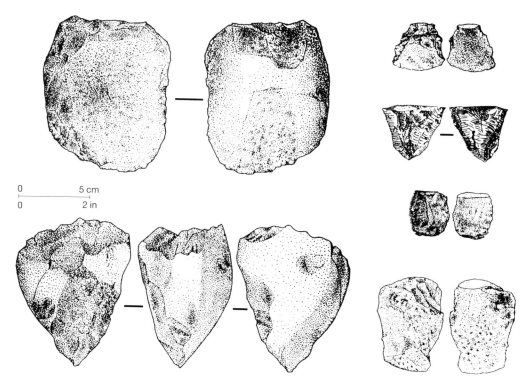

0   5 cm
0   2 in

14 Hoabhinian stone tools from the cave of Laang Spean, northwestern Cambodia.

The Early Farming period

Prior to the arrival of the French and other European powers, there have been three great revolutions in the culture history of mainland Southeast Asia:

- the advent of food production, the so-called 'Neolithic Revolution';
- the rise of kingdoms and the accompanying Indianization of the region; and
- the rise and florescence of Angkor and its empire.

All across Eurasia, from Europe and the Middle East to China, the 'Neolithic Revolution' involving the gradual domestication of plant foods eventually resulted in burgeoning populations, full-blown villages, and the arts associated with a settled way of life, particularly the production of pottery and loom-woven textiles. Here in the land of the Khmer, we shall call this the Early Farming period.

Although claims have been made that the cradle of rice domestication was in Southeast Asia, the evidence seems conclusive that this lay in central China, specifically in the basin of the Yangtze and Huai Rivers and their tributaries. At the Neolithic site of Jiahu in Henan Province, in a level dated to 6800–5800 BC, Chinese archaeologists have recovered carbonized rice grains along with polished stone tools used in rice cultivation.[4] While about 14 per cent of these grains could be identified as wild rice, the rest were domesticated. Jiahu was a permanently settled village, and the excavators speculate that an insufficient food supply stemming from cold winters and limited hunting resources had led the people to develop wild into cultivated rice.

Yet this great transformation may have begun at an even earlier time, for by about 8000 BC, the inhabitants of Yuchan Cave in Hunan Province were both gathering wild rice and cultivating a domesticated variety, while at the same time hunting wild animals and tending domesticated ones.[5] Thus, they had attained a kind of incipient sedentism.

These ancient farmers were almost certainly practising slash-and-burn, shifting cultivation of the same type still found among the upland peoples of mainland Southeast Asia, but in the Pengtoushan culture of 6500 to 5500 BC, the rice had begun to resemble modern paddy varieties in morphology.[6] And a millennium later, in the lower Yangtze Basin, there is good evidence not only for such rice, but also for limited irrigation of rice fields, along with a range of domesticated farm animals, including water buffalo, pigs, sheep, and dogs. The traditional rice-based farmstead thus has an antiquity in China that reaches back over 8,000 years. Thus far, there is nothing in Southeast Asia to challenge the Chinese priority in the adoption of rice as a food crop.

The diffusion of rice and village life

For many millennia, while the moated villages of the Yangtze Basin flourished, the peoples of Thailand and Cambodia, both upland and lowland, persisted in their semi-nomadic life as hunters and gatherers. According to the New Zealand archaeologist Charles Higham, a leading expert on the prehistory of mainland Southeast Asia, domestic rice finally reached that area about 2300 BC, with profound consequences.[7] Higham has suggested that this introduction might have been the result of migrations out of central and southern China by Austroasiatics, the linguistic ancestors of the Mon-Khmer who subsequently came to dominate much of mainland Southeast Asia. If this is true, then those early rice-growing villages of central China described above may not have been 'Chinese' at all, but Austroasiatic. Unhappily, this interesting theory is untestable, since prehistoric remains tell us little or nothing of linguistic affiliations: pottery fragments and stone artifacts don't talk!

Be that as it may, there are very good archaeological data on Early Farming-period settlements throughout the Khorat Plateau, as well as in southern Thailand. In contrast, due to the disruptive events of the last half-century, such information is tantalizingly rare for Cambodia. The marker for this early horizon throughout the region is a range of ceramic decorative techniques that emphasize smoothed versus roughened zones, to produce curvilinear or geometric motifs. This roughening is often carried out by means of cord-marking – impressing the pottery surface with a paddle wrapped in string – but also by 'rocker-stamping': walking the crinkly or smooth edge of a shell across the wet clay surface in a zigzag motion, or simply stamping it repeatedly to produce a dentate pattern.

There is a compelling reason why we know a great deal about burial customs in the Khorat Plateau in the Early Farming period, but very little indeed about settlement patterns and village size: in much of Southeast Asia, historically as well as today, ordinary dwellings are almost totally made from wood, bamboo, palm thatch and other perishable materials. Thus, in a wet, tropical environment, the archaeological traces of such structures are extremely difficult to find. What one *does* find are burials in quantity – whole cemeteries of individuals in extended posture, with accompanying offerings. These burial places were sometimes used over long periods of time, with considerable superposition, so that cultural changes can be detected. Of course, once one enters the historic period, such a treatment of the dead is unknown, since cremation was and is the rule in the Hindu–Buddhist world.

After about 1500 BC, objects of bronze begin to appear in prehistoric Khorat cemeteries.[8] Bronze is an alloy of copper and varying percentages of tin. While the technology of smelting, alloying and casting was in all likelihood imported from China, the objects themselves were locally produced. The copper was probably obtained from ore sources in the lowlands of north-central and northeastern Cambodia; from Champassak in southern Laos; and from northwesternmost Khorat.[9] Tin, however, is another story, since it is extremely rare in much of Southeast Asia; the nearest sources would have been in far western Thailand, at least 560 km (350 miles) from the principal Cambodian copper sources.

Specialists in Southeast Asian prehistory have used the term 'Bronze Age' to describe the period between the advent of bronze and the first use of iron at about 500 BC, but this metal occurs only sporadically and was initially used mainly (but not exclusively) to produce body ornaments such as bracelets rather than weaponry or tools, and so had little economic impact. In contrast, in Europe, the Near East and China, the 'Bronze Age' was marked by the rise of powerful chiefdoms and even of early states, as well as a degree of urbanism, but no such pattern can be detected in our area. With or without metals, there seems to have been little or no economic or social differentiation within or between these simple farming villages for some eighteen centuries.

Non Nok Tha, excavated by E. Green in 1965, and subsequently by Donn Bayard and R. H. Parker, is an early site in the upper reaches of the Chi River system in Khorat, with an Early Farming stratum underlying one with bronze. Probably dating about 2000–1500 BC,[10] these were rice agriculturalists who used rice chaff to temper their pottery; they also hunted local game with dogs, and fished. The villagers of Non Nok Tha variously accompanied their dead with strings of shell disk beads, stone adze heads, grinding stones, bivalve shells and offerings of domesticated cattle or pig bones.

At the site of Ban Lum Khao, located in the Mun River drainage of the Khorat Plateau, not far from the Classic Angkor centre of Phimai, Higham and his associates revealed a cemetery dating to *c.* 1500–500 BC with dozens of graves in rows.[11] Although there were no bronze ornaments with these interments, the excavators found over 500 pottery vessels, some with painted designs, marble 'bangles' (disk bracelets), marine shells, stone adzes, dog bones, and the foot bones from pigs.

With the coming of peace to Cambodia, research on the Early Farming period can be expected to have many successes. But one site is worthy of mention: Samrong Sen, once an enormous midden some 350 m (1000 ft) long, on the right bank of the Stung Chinit (Chinit River), a tributary of the Tonle Sap River. Samrong Sen was investigated by the French authorities as long ago as 1876, but they never scientifically excavated in the modern sense. It was mined for its vast quantities of shells by the villagers who lived on the mound, which they burned to make lime to be wrapped in the betel chew (the lime releases the alkaloids in the areca nut); collections of artifacts were bought from them at various times by visitors such as the French prehistorian Henri Mansuy, over a period of many decades.[12] Finely made, ground stone tools were recovered, including many shouldered adzes of a type widespread in Southeast Asia during the Early Farming period. The abundant pottery included dentate-stamped potsherds, with curvilinear and rectilinear motifs, largely from pedestal (annular-based) bowls, as well as pottery earspools with cruciform designs. There were disk-shaped 'bangles' of shell, bone arrowheads and harpoons, and a few bronze objects that probably came from the upper strata, among them arrowheads, a fishhook and a chisel. Besides molluscs, the faunal remains included bones from python, crocodile, turtle, rhinoceros, pig, deer, elephant, dog, tiger, otter, and probably water buffalo.

Samrong Sen was clearly one of the most important sites of the Early Farming period of mainland Southeast Asia, and probably was occupied from c. 2300 to 500 BC; some of it still exists, and has been recently re-excavated by the Cambodian archaeologist Ly Vanna of Sophia University.[13] Samrong Sen cannot have been unique. According to Roland Mourer, a similar 'kitchen-midden' still exists at Anlong Prao, about 30 km (19 miles) southeast of Samrong Sen; another at Kbal Romeas ('Rhinoceros Head') on the coast facing the Gulf of Thailand has now been destroyed through limestone quarrying.[14] A thorough archaeological survey of the entire Tonle Sap drainage would surely turn up many more middens of comparable age.

Iron Age chiefdoms (c. 500 BC to c. AD 200–500)

Socially undifferentiated and egalitarian as the villages of the Early Farming period may have been, the introduction of iron tools c. 500 BC was accompanied by profound changes of several kinds. As for iron itself, this technology might have been diffused from Asia Minor, perhaps overland but possibly via India; China may have been the proximal source, but the first iron implements there are not significantly older than those in Southeast Asia. In all events, it was a far more significant economic innovation than bronze, since iron ore sources are abundant compared to those for copper and tin. There are fairly rich iron concentrations in Cambodia not far from where copper is extracted, as well as in northwestern Khorat,[15] but iron may also be smelted from the ubiquitous laterite. A high heat must be applied to the ore over several hours to reduce it to metallic form, but all that is needed is a charcoal-burning furnace with foot bellows; simple furnaces of this kind can still be seen in many places in Thailand, Cambodia and Laos, even among the mountain tribes.

Iron was used not only in axes (for land clearance) and digging implements, but also in weaponry, principally knives, spears and arrowheads; in
fact, weapons are often found in burials. Other sophisticated technical innovations of the later Iron Age include glass, used only for body ornament such
as bracelets and beads, and bimetallic (iron and bronze) objects.[16]

Noen U-Loke, investigated by Higham and his Thai colleague Rachanie
Thosarat, is one of the most significant Iron Age sites yet discovered, and lies
to the east of the Khorat Plateau city of Nakhon Ratchasima in the upper
drainage of the Mun River.[17] In fact, it is the largest site ever excavated in
Thailand, with no fewer than 126 extended burials uncovered. Several of the
interments were of great richness, a striking indication of strong social strat-
ification within this settlement: the corpses had been adorned with bronze
bangles, torques and belts. One adult male, who could only have been a powerful chief of this settlement, had silver ear coils covered in gold foil, and 75
bronze bangles on each arm; near his neck were bronze and iron rings, his
finger bones were covered with rings, and his waist was circled with three
bronze belts. The grave also contained pottery vessels, glass beads and an
iron knife. Here and at other Iron Age sites were exotic trade items such as
beads of carnelian and agate; these latter were once thought to have been
imported from India, but geochemical analysis tells us that they were quarried and manufactured locally.

During the 1963–68 restoration of the spectacular Classic Khmer sanctuary of Phimai, also in the upper Mun River basin, in a deep layer beneath the
temple base was found a type of pottery characteristic of the Iron Age in the
southern Khorat Plateau.[18] This is known as Phimai Black, a fine, thin, chaff-
tempered and streak-burnished ware; as one moves east into the middle Mun
Valley this becomes replaced with local painted and cord-marked pottery (a
leftover from the Early Farming period).

What effect did the adoption of iron for agricultural tools have? It is notoriously difficult to estimate population densities from archaeological remains
alone, but Iron Age sites are ubiquitous in Khorat, and many of them are
quite large. Food must have been in plentiful supply, as testified by the lavish
use of rice to pack graves at Noen U-Loke. In many parts of the ancient
world, burgeoning population densities seem to have led to conflict over
resources, and conflicts that were ultimately resolved by the transition from
egalitarian to ranked societies, and ultimately to the state (not to appear in the
Khmer area until after AD 500).

The circular earthworks puzzle

It was as long ago as 1930 that notice was given to a line of circular earthworks
or 'moated mounds' in rubber plantations at Xa Cat, in southern Vietnam
not far from the Cambodian border.[19] They were given the name 'Moi forts',
implying that they had been built by ancestors of the modern 'Mountain
Khmer' hill tribes of the area. Two decades later Peter D. R. Williams-Hunt,
using aerial photographs, located some 200 'moated mounds' in the Chi and
Mun River basins of the Khorat Plateau, some of which were circular in lay-

out and others roughly rectangular. Then, in 1959, the French archaeologist Louis Malleret (of whom more in the next chapter) revisited the original 'Moi forts', describing 17 such earthworks that he assigned, on the basis of surface finds, to the 'Neolithic' (Early Farming) age; he also felt that they were fortifications, and once had a palisade on top.[20]

In 1962, intrigued by Malleret's report, B.-P. Groslier of the École Française d'Extrême-Orient excavated a circular 'Moi fort' near Memot, on the Cambodian side of the border.[21] Sadly, because of the ravages of war and due to his premature death, his research on this topic was never published, but happily his collections have survived and have been studied by a new generation of Cambodian archaeologists (see below).[22]

During the 1980s, Dr Elizabeth Moore, now of London's Institute of Archaeology, analyzed the Williams-Hunt photographic archive.[23] On the aerial photographs of the Mun River area were 91 'irregular', but mostly circular, moated sites, and another 115 that were more-or-less rectangular. The former are located close to watercourses, and are probably Iron Age or earlier, while the latter almost certainly may be ascribed to the period of dominance by Classic Angkor, with its tradition of moat-building around planned enclosures of rectangular or square outline. Of course, in the Cambodian lowlands to the south of the Dangrek chain, small rectangular moated sites can be seen wherever the water table is high enough, but Moore has pointed out that there are circular ones as well.

During the past decade, considerable debate has been aroused within the community of Southeast Asian archaeologists over all these circular earthworks. How old are they? Are they all of the same period? Were the 'Moi forts' really fortifications as Groslier had thought, or did the earthworks serve some other function or functions? What kind of society built all of these? (Groslier was certain that his Memot site belonged to the 'Neolithic', i.e. Early Farming period.) These are questions that only controlled excavation can solve, and it is heartening to know that with the return of peace to the region, this is being done.

The 'red soils' earthworks

An important part of the French colonial enterprise in Indo-China was the establishment of rubber plantations. It was found that the best region for the cultivation of this New World tree (*Hevea brasilensis*) was an expanse of *terres rouges* or 'red soils' that extends from the Delta to the sandstone plateaus of southeastern Cambodia and adjacent south Vietnam. This is exactly where Groslier, Malleret and other investigators have found a number of circular earthworks, and it is for these that we have the most information.

A team of Cambodian archaeologists has reinvestigated Groslier's own site in the Memot district; a joint German–Cambodian–Japanese group under Dr Gerd Albrecht and Dr Miriam Haidle has mapped and excavated Krek 52/62, the westernmost of the 'red soils' earthworks; and a team from the University of Hawaii conducted research on further such sites on the Cambodian side of the border.[24] We now have radiocarbon dates, stratigraphic data, and plans and

15

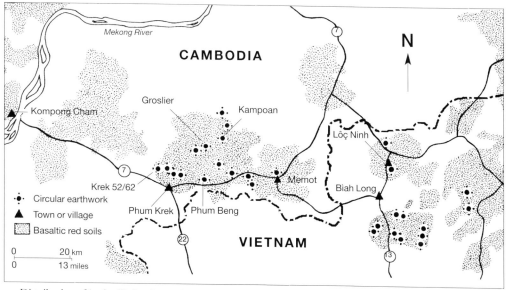

15 Distribution of 'red soil' circular earthworks in Cambodia and Vietnam.

maps for a number of sites. Of these, Krek 52/62 is more-or-less representa- 16
tive. It consists of a circular mound about 255 m (837 ft) in diameter, with an
inner ditch surrounding a level inner plateau. The entrance was on the southwest, and the principal habitation area (or at least the area with highest artifact
density) in the northeast part of the 'plateau'.

16 The Krek 52/62 circular earthwork, eastern Cambodia. The line cutting through the site
is a modern plantation road.

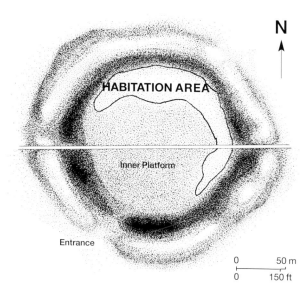

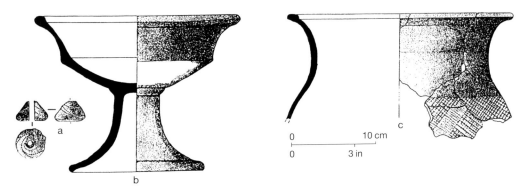

17 Ceramics from the Krek 52/62 circular earthwork. *a*, spindle whorl; *b*, pedestal bowl; *c*, storage jar.

According to Michael Dega, formerly a graduate student at the University of Hawaii, the ceramics and ground stone tools excavated at Krek 52/62, Memot, and other 'red soils' earthworks are strikingly similar to those recovered from Early Farming levels at Samrong Sen, Laang Spean, and Khorat Plateau sites, and more generally to pre-Iron Age occupations elsewhere in Southeast Asia.[25] Although no bronze has been found in the 'red soils' sites, a find of a glass bracelet fragment at Krek 52/62 suggests that this site, at least, was occupied into the Iron Age. With a handful of radiocarbon dates now available, Dega suggests that within a time span of about 2,000 years, from *c.* 2300 to 300 BC, the oldest of these enigmatic earthworks are in or adjacent to Vietnam, and as one moves west towards the Mekong River, they get progressively later.

Prehistoric artifacts may not speak, but some of them 'sing'! In 1996, near the southern Vietnamese village of Loc Ninh in the 'red soils' area, a farmer accidentally struck on two sets of chipped basalt bars of different sizes, each set placed along side of the other.[26] These were carefully excavated, and proved to be associated with cultural material identical with that from Krek 52/62 and the Groslier site near Memot, and with a radiocarbon date of 1240 ± 70 BC. These bar sets are, in fact, tuned lithophones (stone xylophones) with a scale ranging from 400.9 hz to 1,240.66 hz, and are therefore a kind of prehistoric gamelan. A similar lithophone fragment was found in the Krek excavations, and another in Groslier's materials from Memot; but at least ten complete lithophone sets have been found elsewhere in Vietnam since the mid-nineteenth century, and a few are still in use by aboriginal Mon-Khmers in the highlands in ceremonies that include rainmaking or buffalo sacrifice. The traditional Khmer *roneat*, a xylophone of wood or bamboo strung on chords and played in modern Cambodian ensembles, has very old roots, indeed.

Perhaps an answer to the question of the function and nature of the earthworks may lie in an ethnographic analogy pointed out by Japanese archaeologist Yasushi Kojo.[27] The Mon-Khmer-speaking Brao (Brau) people occupy another 'red soils' region to the east of the Mekong in northeastern

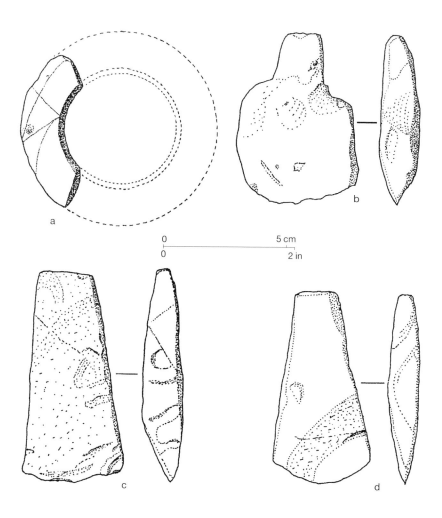

18 Ground stone artifacts from the Groslier circular earthwork. *a*, disk arm ornament; *b*, shouldered adze; *c, d*, celts.

Cambodia, and like some other 'Mountain Khmer' groups live in circular villages; the central axis of each village is determined by the direction of a local river, and houses are arranged in a radial pattern around a central community house. A soil auger survey of artifact densities carried out by Kojo at Krek 52/62 revealed the probable presence of a central structure and of houses laid out in a very similar pattern. It is reasonable to suppose, then, that this and other circular earthworks in Khorat, Cambodia and southern Vietnam represent the villages, in all likelihood fortified with palisades, of Mon-Khmer chiefdoms before the formation of the trading kingdoms that were to characterize the next age (see Chapter 5). The old term 'Moi forts' may not have been so far off the mark, after all.

Elizabeth Moore has emphasized that these structures not only are found in Khorat and the 'red soils' area, but have been detected by aerial photography and remote sensing elsewhere in the Cambodian lowlands, even within the confines of the mighty city of Angkor itself.[28] The present-day village of Lovea, for example, located just west of Angkor in the midst of a sea of rice fields, is clearly built on the central occupational 'plateau' within a circular mound-cum-moat complex of probably great antiquity, and this and many others like it await modern archaeological testing. This is in truth the basic prehistoric culture upon which Khmer civilization and the Angkor Empire were built.

Rock paintings

The eastern edge of the Khorat Plateau is a rocky shelf covered with a somewhat dry and scrubby forest; this shelf suddenly drops down in a series of cliffs or escarpments to the bed of the Mekong River; on the other side of the river are the hills of southern Laos. Hunters and farmers of the Early Farming period found that the smoother faces of these sandstone cliffs made excellent 'canvases' for rock paintings, some of the larger and most spectacular of which can be seen by visitors to Pha Taem National Park. Here those ancient people used red ochre or hematite to draw humans with strange tri-

19

19 Rock paintings in red, Pha Taem National Park, Thailand. Depicted in this view of the cliff face overlooking the Mekong River are giant catfish, stylized human figures, and negative hand silhouettes.

angular heads, parallel wavy lines, positive and negative handprints, turtles, an elephant, and the famous Mekong giant catfish (*Pangasianodon gigas*). The latter creature was probably a prime target for early fishermen, as it still is today, for it can reach a length of 3 m (9.8 ft) and a weight of 200 kg (441 lbs) – one of the largest freshwater fish known.

Similar galleries of prehistoric paintings can be seen at a number of places around the fringes of the Khorat Plateau where there are suitably flat rock surfaces, such as Tham Lai Thaeng in the upper drainage of the Chi River, where the images show kilted humans, a woman resting with a baby and several bulls. More kilted men, or men wearing waist sashes, appear at Khao Chan Ngam in the Petchabun Range (on the western edge of the plateau), along with children, a bow-and-arrow and a dog.

Although rock art is a wonderful window into the past, it is notoriously difficult to date archaeologically. But sophisticated physical and chemical techniques to do just this have been developed for petroglyphs and pictographs in Australia and western North America, and some day these may be applied to the ancient art of Khorat. In the meantime, the best estimate is that of Charles Higham and Rachanie Thosarat,[29] who place these galleries in their 'Bronze Age', that is, in the interval between 1300 and 500 BC. Nonetheless, one should keep in mind that they may be substantially older.

The Khmer before the great transformation

By the first one or two centuries AD, the land occupied by the Khmer during the Iron Age was a prosperous one: dotted everywhere – on the Khorat Plateau, in the Cambodian Basin, and in the Delta – with large settlements, many of them circular, palisaded villages and towns, under the authority of powerful chiefs and their lineages (of whom more in the next chapter). All the domestic animals still familiar in Cambodian villages were there, the most important being the water buffalo and cattle, both perhaps used in tillage of the rice fields. As it is today, the greatest source of protein for all these people must have been fish, and although the archaeological evidence has yet to be gathered, the Great Lake would have been an incredibly rich resource for these ancestral Khmer.

One can only speculate about the way rice was grown. The upland and mountain Khmer, like their modern descendants, would surely have cultivated dry rice in swidden patches during the rainy season. And rainfall-dependant rice would have been the norm for most of mainland Southeast Asia, even in the lowlands. But this could be highly productive if it took the form of flood-retreat farming (see Chapter 2), as it must have in the basin of the Great Lake, along the lower Mekong drainage, and in the Delta.

Technologically, these people were sophisticated metal workers in iron, bronze, and even in gold and silver. Luxury objects of local manufacture, sometimes in lavish amounts, were given as grave offerings for their honoured dead: chiefs, their spouses, and other family members.

Since so much of their way of life was bound up in materials that seldom survive archaeologically – for instance, their pile-supported houses of pole and thatch – it is difficult to speculate about the mental culture of these late prehistoric Khmer on the eve of Indianization, as it has been called. Ethnography may be invoked here, for the mountain-dwelling Mon-Khmer-speaking tribes of Cambodia and the neighbouring highlands of Vietnam, so despised by the Buddhist lowland Khmer and by the Vietnamese, preserve much of what was once the common culture of all.[30] Farmers of dry rice in swidden fields, they are almost all skilled makers of iron tools and weapons. Living in villages of pile dwellings in the midst of the forest, these aboriginal tribesmen find themselves in a natural world that is very much alive and animate: not only animals and plants, but mountains, rocks, and rock outcrops are inhabited by spirits, which may bring misfortune and illness, as well as good. Humans are not mere bodies, but have multiple souls, that may wander or be lost. When people die (and are buried rather than cremated), they become ancestral spirits, to be propitiated. To communicate with, and to control, all of these spiritual forces for good or for evil, every group has its shamans or sorcerers, many of great power and fame.

Ritual may be simple or complex, but almost always requires the blood sacrifice of an animal (and formerly, it is said, of a human), while rice beer or rice wine is sucked from a pot through a bamboo tube. The occasion may be a marriage or a celebration of some point in the agricultural year, and the victim may be a chicken, a pig, or a water buffalo. Among the Mon-Khmer-speaking Mnong and Maa' of southern Vietnam, the spectacular Feast of the Sun, held about every seven years, obliges every household in the village to contribute a buffalo for the sacrifice.

This animistic and shamanistic mental life is not a monopoly of the upland aborigines of mainland Southeast Asia, for it still forms the substratum of village life throughout the Khmer domain, even among the paddy farmers of lowland Cambodia. For example, their Iron Age ancestors would be perfectly at home in the circular village of Lovea, not far from Angkor and modern Siem Reap, where animistic beliefs survive in the form of the ever-present *neak ta* spirits, and in the rituals that these Buddhist villagers still carry out at the world post that stands in the centre of the village.[31]

Onto this Iron Age 'basement culture' was to be grafted a belief system that had its origin over two millennia ago in the plain of India's Ganges River, laying the foundation for what was eventually to become the civilization of Angkor.

5 · Winds of Change: The Early Kingdoms Period

During the colonial era, European authorities – French and British alike – looked upon the countries of mainland Southeast Asia as 'Indo-China'. This was a term with geographical meaning, in that it designated all the land between India and southern China, but it had a cultural sense as well: on the one hand Burma, 'Siam' (Thailand), Cambodia, and Laos were clearly Indianized, while on the other 'Tonkin' (northern Vietnam) had been 'sinicized' at a far later date. That the process of Indianization had taken place some centuries before the founding of Angkor was soon made apparent by the early dates of many Cambodian inscriptions with texts in Sanskrit, the language of the Hindu religion. Although modern scholars debate the degree and scope of these outside influences, and stress the underlying strengths, unity and distinctiveness of native Southeast Asian culture, there can be little doubt that much of what we see in these countries derives from India and, to a far lesser extent, from China.

Surprisingly, Indian historical records from the first millennium AD have very little to say about Southeast Asia, other than that it was a 'Land of Gold' from which bold and enterprising traders might, if they survived the voyage, return as rich men.[1] In contrast, the Chinese annals tell us a great deal about these lands; but, as we shall see, even though these records have been heavily relied upon by generations of scholars,[2] they are difficult to interpret, and sometimes downright misleading. Part of the problem lies in the traditional disdain that the Chinese have had for 'barbarian' peoples, and part with the pitfalls inherent in trying to link personal and place names supposedly transcribed into Chinese, a tonal and largely monosyllabic language, from ones in non-tonal, polysyllabic tongues like Sanskrit and Khmer. In all events, considered in the light of recent scholarship, the ethnographic picture that they give seems to be a great deal more reliable than the historical one.

'Funan' and 'Zhenla'

In about AD 245, during the bloody and turbulent Three Kingdoms period, the Chinese Wei emperor sent a fact-finding, cultural embassy to the countries lying south and southwest of the Middle Kingdom. They reported that there was a barbarous but rich country named 'Funan' in what seems to have been the Delta, ruled by a king whom they called Fan-hsun, to whom foreigners and subjects offered presents of bananas, sugar cane, turtles and birds.

There are walled villages, palaces, and dwellings. The men are all ugly and black, their hair frizzy; they go about naked and barefoot. Their nature is simple and they are not at all inclined toward thievery. They devote themselves to agriculture. They sow one year and harvest for three. Moreover, they like to engrave ornaments and to chisel. Many of their eating utensils are silver. Taxes are paid in gold, silver, pearls, or perfumes. There are books and depositories of archives and other things. Their characters resemble those of Hu [a people of Central Asia using a script of Indian origin].[3]

According to later imperial records, between the date of this embassy and AD 649, there were no fewer than twenty-five tribute missions dispatched by the 'Funanese' to the Chinese court (of course, the emperor and his court have customarily considered as 'tribute' all ambassadorial gifts presented to the ruler of the Middle Kingdom, as King George III's envoy Lord Macartney was to discover in the eighteenth century!). From these, and from their own visits to the Delta, the Chinese had built up a fairly detailed picture of 'Funan' and its supposed history. For instance, the brief ethnographic description of that kingdom given in the annals of the Southern Qi Dynasty (AD 479–501) is probably to be trusted, if one adjusts for its somewhat xenophobic bias:

20

The people of Funan are malicious and cunning. They take by force the inhabitants of the neighbouring cities who do not render them homage, and make them slaves. As merchandise, they have gold, silver, silks. The sons of the well-to-do families wear sarongs of brocade. The poor wear a piece of cloth. The women pull a piece of cloth over the head. The people of Funan make rings and bracelets of gold and vessels of silver. They cut down trees to build their houses. The King lives in a storied pavilion. They make their enclosures of wooden palisades. At the seashore grows a great bamboo, whose leaves are eight or nine feet long. The leaves are tressed to cover the houses. The people also live in houses raised from the ground. They make boats 80 or 90 feet long and 6 or 7 feet wide. The bow and stern are like the head and tail of a fish. When the King goes out, he rides on elephant-back. The women also ride elephants. For amusements, the people have cock-fights and hog-fights…. They have sugar cane, pomegranates, oranges, and much areca nuts [the nut of the betel chew].[4]

Further ethnographic information is contained in the *History of the Liang Dynasty* (AD 502–56):

Where they live, they do not dig wells. By tens of families, they have a basin in common where they get water. The custom is to adore the spirits of the sky. Of these spirits, they make images in bronze; those which have two faces, have four arms; those which have four faces, have eight arms. Each hand holds something – a child, a bird, or quadruped, the sun, the moon. The King, when he travels rides an elephant. So do his concubines, the people of the

20 Modern Cambodian girl with headcloth, selling brocade cloth.

palace. When the King sits down, he squats on one side, raising the right knee, letting the left knee touch the earth. A piece of cotton is spread before him, on which are deposited the gold vases and incense burners.

In the case of mourning, the custom is to shave the beard and the hair. For the dead, there are four kinds of disposal: burial by water, which consists of throwing the body into the water; burial by earth, which consists of interring it in a grave; burial by the birds, which consists of abandoning it in the fields; burial by fire, which consists in reducing it to ashes. The people are of a covetous nature. They have neither rites nor propriety. Boys and girls follow their penchants without restraint.[5]

As Lawrence Briggs has pointed out,[6] many of the customs described above point to the thoroughgoing Indianization that the Delta Khmer had undergone: the basins dug for water, the multi-armed bronze figures of their gods, the seated posture of the king and the elephant as the royal mount, the incense burners, the cremation burials. But others are from an indigenous Southeast Asian tradition: houses on piles, animal fights, long boats, interment burials, and relative freedom of the sexes. Such an amalgam of the native and the foreign has characterized Khmer civilization for the past two millennia.

These same annals give us a dynastic 'history' complete with mythological beginnings, endless battles with neighbours in central Vietnam and elsewhere, and a succession full of usurpations and other events. Names of places and rulers in Chinese are attached to these, and learned French scholars like Étienne Aymonier, Paul Pelliot and George Coedès have done their best to link these to Khmer toponyms and to the Sanskrit names of ancestral rulers appearing in Angkorian inscriptions of the Classic period. In this vein, it has been claimed the 'Fan' appearing in the names of various 'Funanese' kings is a transcription of the typical Sanskrit terminal – *varman*.[7] As for the name 'Funan' itself, an attempt has been made to derive this from Khmer *phnom* (anciently *bnam*), 'hill' or 'mountain', enlarging on the traditional notion that there was a series of local rulers who called themselves 'King of the Mountain'.[8] Neither this nor most of the other identifications have received universal acceptance.

It is related in the *History of the Liang Dynasty* that when the king of 'Funan', himself a usurper, died in about 550, a period of disorders ensued. The then king of 'Zhenla', a vassal state to the north, seized the opportunity to turn the tables and make 'Funan' a vassal of 'Zhenla'. According to Coedès,[9] this powerful kingdom, which eventually covered a territory almost equal in extent to that of the later Khmer Empire, subsequently divided itself into a 'Land Zhenla' that included most of Cambodia and the Khorat Plateau, and a 'Water Zhenla', centred on the Delta. 'Zhenla' continued to send embassies to China, and that name remained the one used by the Chinese for the Cambodian state for many centuries. They described this as a wealthy and militarily powerful country with over 30 cities. In the latter part of the thirteenth century, Ma Duan-lin wrote an ethnographic study of the 'outer barbarians', and included material on early 'Zhenla' from the *History of the Sui Dynasty* (AD 581–618) that gives some idea of the magnificence of the Khmer court of those times:

> Every three days the King goes solemnly to the audience-hall and sits on a bed made of five pieces of sandalwood and ornamented with seven kinds of precious stones. Above this bed is a pavilion of magnificent cloth, whose columns are of inlaid wood. The walls are ivory, mixed with flowers of gold. The ensemble of this bed and the pavilion form a sort of little palace, at the background of which is suspended...a disk with rays of gold in the form of flames. A golden incense burner, which two men handle, is placed in front. The King wears a girdle of *ki-pei* cotton, dawn-red, which falls to his knees. He covers his head with a bonnet laden with gold and stones, with pendants of pearl. On his feet are sandals of leather and sometimes of ivory; in his ears, pendants of gold. His robe is always made of a fine white cloth called *pe-tre*...The great officers or ministers number five...There are many inferior officers.
>
> Those who appear before the King touch the earth three times with the forehead, at the foot of the steps to the throne. If the King calls them and orders them to show their degrees, then they kneel, holding their hands on their shoulders.[10]

By combining these Chinese documents – most of them rich in what seems to be historical detail – with the often self-conflicting genealogical information in far later Sanskrit-language inscriptions from the Classic

Angkor period, Coedès, Briggs and others have put together a scenario for the history of the Early Kingdoms period that dominated scholarship for the better part of the twentieth century. In it, there was an early 'Funan' polity, centred in the Delta, possibly with a single capital at Angkor Borei (of which more later), and strongly linked by trade with both India and China. From the mid-sixth century until the establishment of the Angkor Empire in AD 802, 'Funan' had been succeeded as the major power in this part of Southeast Asia by 'Zhenla', led by Khmer kings who had come from the north, beyond the Dangrek Range, into the inland basin of Cambodia. During the 'Zhenla' ascendancy, there was again a single capital, in all likelihood ancient Ishanapura (modern Sambor Prei Kuk) in central Cambodia, but in the eighth century this split, as the Chinese annalists had told us, into a 'Water Zhenla' and a 'Land Zhenla'.

The Delta chiefdoms

To historians Claude Jacques and Michael Vickery, much about this scenario is wrong. As Professor Jacques has said, '…the history of pre-Angkorean Cambodia was, to begin with, reconstructed much more on the basis of Chinese records than on that of inscriptions found in Cambodia itself'.[11] In Professor Vickery's view, not only did 'Water Zhenla' and 'Land Zhenla' never exist, but the Chinese categories of 'Funan' and 'Zhenla' may be misleading and even meaningless, since the best evidence shows that until AD 802, there was never a single, great state in the land of the Khmer, but a number of smaller ones.[12] What these earlier scholars have ignored is the large corpus of inscriptions of the sixth to eighth centuries, many of them in Khmer rather than Sanskrit. These are *contemporary* records, and must be given primacy over the Chinese ones, which are at best second-hand. As outlined by Vickery, here are the stages of cultural evolution in this part of Southeast Asia.[13]

In the last millennium BC, and particularly during the Iron Age, supravillage communities developed inland, with populations of between 500 and 2,000 individuals led by chiefs. These latter had control of overland trade in valuable and rare commodities.

Then, in the first six centuries of the Christian era, in response to a growing Chinese demand for luxury products from Southeast Asia, or transported via this area, a group of ports of trade sprang up, the most important of which were in the Delta (such as Oc Eo, see below). These funnelled or channelled goods that had arrived via a maritime trading network extending to India and even further, to the Mediterranean world; while allied with each other, they never formed a single polity, in spite of their Chinese designation 'Funan'.

The chiefs of these palisaded Delta settlements bore the Mon-Khmer title *poñ*, an office that was inherited matrilineally (passing from the deceased to the sister's son). The population of a core *poñ*-dom formed a lineage or clan, with its own deity whose representative was the *poñ* himself; some, however, had several of these *poñ*, perhaps hamlet chiefs. Living around or near a pond, which might be an artificial one, these large villages or supravillages grew enough rice for self-sufficiency.

There was a hierarchy of *poñ*, probably based on wealth and political influence. As early as the fifth century AD, superior *poñ* started claiming kingship, taking on Indic names and titles, especially a Hindu god's name followed by the honorific suffix *–varman* ('protected by…'), although Khmer names linger. The earliest Khmer king about whose existence we may be sure was Rudravarman ('protected by Rudra [an aspect of the great god Shiva]'), who ruled the Delta *poñ*-doms in the first half of the sixth century; Cambodian tradition gives his capital as Angkor Borei, in the lower Mekong at the head of the Delta. And, even more importantly, during these first five or six centuries of our era, elements of both Hinduism and Buddhism were adopted throughout the Delta.

Hands across the sea

Thanks to the entrepreneurial spirit of traders in the Indian subcontinent, and to the boat-building and navigational skills of seafarers from the Mediterranean to Southeast Asia, over two millennia ago much of the Old World was bound up in what was virtually a single economic system. During the Pax Romana, established by Augustus in 27 BC, some Indian traders sailed to the mouth of the Red Sea, within the confines of the Roman Empire; about the same time, others headed east over the Indian Ocean to the Malayan Peninsula and the rest of Southeast Asia, looking for the tin that they needed to make bronze coinage. Exotic luxury goods began to flow in both directions, as well as to and from China across the Delta.[14]

According to the Indian historian Himanchu Prabha Ray, Buddhism was the potent motivating factor in the expansion of maritime trading networks from India to Sri Lanka, and then to the eastern lands.[15] Unlike Vedic Brahmanism, Buddhism was quite open to trade and to usury – that is, to money-lending and banking; Brahmanic Hinduism had evolved in an agrarian environment, whereas Buddhism had taken root in a milieu of urbanism and growing trade networks. It was and is a congregational religion, and the proselytising *bhikkus* or monks who accompanied the traders on their expeditions were able to provide identity and cohesiveness to these peripatetic merchants.

But, paradoxically, Buddhism and Hinduism arrived together in mainland Southeast Asia and Indonesia, and one reason why they did so is probably, as Professor Ray has said, that while the lay community followed precepts of the Sangha (the Buddhist monastic order) in its search for salvation, its daily life continued to be governed by Brahmanical (Hindu) rituals. Buddhism has always been remarkably tolerant of the Hinduism from which it sprang, but the reverse has never been true, orthodox Hindus considering it a heretical sect. Be that as it may, almost surely learned Brahmins, gurus and *rishis* (ascetic sages) would have been supercargoes on these long-distance voyages to the east.[16]

Indianization

During this early epoch of trading contacts, the most powerful *poñ* chiefs and embryo kings of the Delta, and probably of inland regions as well (including Khorat), deliberately and willingly underwent a process of Indianization to consolidate and magnify their rule. The major source culture, as Monica Smith of the University of Pittsburgh has made clear,[17] was surely the powerful and prosperous Gupta state of northern and central India, which flourished from about AD 320 to 455. After a period in which Buddhism had been virtually a state religion in India, the Guptas returned to a pre-Buddhist Vedic (Hindu) tradition, while reviving the Sanskrit language as the principal one for monumental inscriptions, land-grants, seals and coins. Furthermore, the Guptas were great builders of temples and shrines, and in spite of their pro-Hindu stance, even donors to Buddhist foundations.

The various elites in Southeast Asia could have chosen the Chinese model, for China also was a trading partner, but did not do so. Why not? As the peoples of northern Vietnam later found out, China was an expansionist nation (as the Indian principalities were not); an adoption of Chinese-style imperial bureaucracy would have meant a burdensome and humiliating submission to the Middle Kingdom, and the lessening of their own powers. With China, it was all or nothing. In contrast, the Hindu religion and its trappings offered the benefits of a royal ideology tailor-made for nascent Southeast Asian kings, with no political strings attached.

Here is what Indianization eventually brought to the region:
- The rich and complex Hindu religion, its mythology and cosmology, and its ritual (see p. 80); in particular, the cults of the gods Shiva and Vishnu, with whom local kings could identify.
- The Sanskrit language, the vehicle of Hinduism and one sect of Buddhism, and the source of many loan-words in early Khmer.
- The Indic (Brahmi) writing system, stone inscriptions and palm-leaf books.
- The Hindu temple complex, and an architectural tradition of brick and/or stone based upon Gupta prototypes.
- Statuary representing gods, kings and the Buddha.
- Cremation burial, at least of the upper stratum of society.
- Rectilinear town and city plans.
- Artificial water systems, including rectangular reservoirs (the *srah* and *baray* of Classic Khmer culture), as well as canals.
- Wheel-made pottery, which supplemented but did not supplant the local paddle-and-anvil ceramic tradition.

But certain Indian traits, such as the minting and use of coinage, never 'took': the Khmer realm essentially remained a barter economy until the arrival of the French in the nineteenth century. Perhaps more importantly, India's complex and rigid caste system failed to take hold in Southeast Asia; there were upper-caste Brahmins, especially in the royal courts, but the elaborate bans on inter-dining (eating with persons of other castes) and other concepts of social and ritual purity and impurity never caught on.

Oc Eo and early maritime contacts

21   The extraordinary site of Oc Eo was discovered in 1942 by the French archaeologist Louis Malleret as part of a large-scale project in the Delta of southern Vietnam, but he was not to begin excavations there until 1944. These were suddenly terminated in March 1945, when the Japanese ousted the Vichy-controlled French colonial government in Indo-China. Malleret's research had been carried out under very trying conditions, and the volumes that he subsequently published leave much to be desired.[18] Nevertheless, Oc Eo is key to the understanding of the role of the Delta. Since the end of the

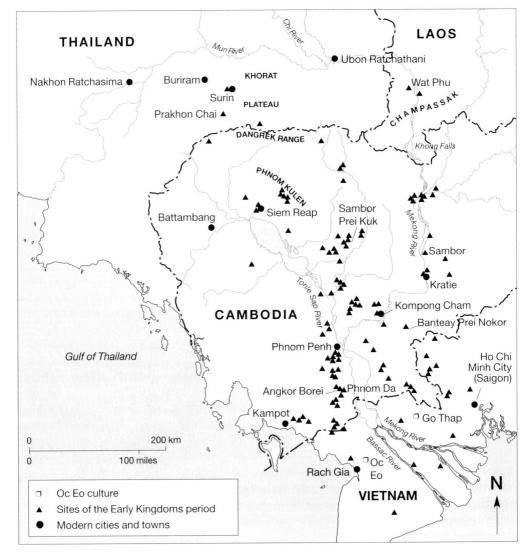

21   Sites of the Oc Eo culture and Early Kingdoms period.

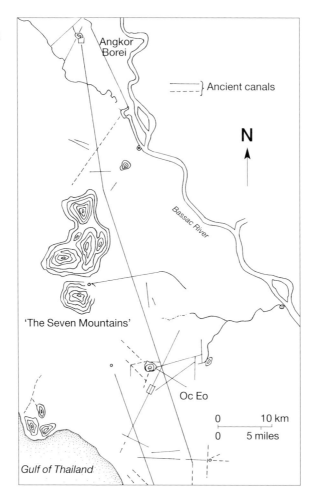

22 The ancient canal system linking Oc Eo and Angkor Borei.

Vietnam War, Vietnamese and EFEO archaeologists have found many more sites of what they call the 'Oc Eo culture'.

Oc Eo lies about 15 km (9 miles) inland from the Gulf of Thailand and 30 km (18 miles) from the Bassac arm of the Mekong. It is placed in the midst of a network of ancient canals that crisscross the flat, low country of the Delta; one of these went from Oc Eo to connect to what must have been the town's seaport, while another runs about 70 km (42 miles) north-northeast to Angkor Borei (of which more below), across the Cambodian border. Aerial photos show a rectangular, planned town oriented to about 27° east of north, bounded by multiple enceintes; the outermost enclosure measures some 1.5 km (0.9 miles) in width and may have once been 3 km (1.9 miles) long, and probably supported palisade walls. The entire town could have covered c. 450 hectares (1.74 square miles) and thus might have contained many thousands of people. Oc Eo is longitudinally bisected by a canal, and there are four transverse canals along which pile-supported houses were perhaps ranged. If so, this would have looked like many historic Southeast Asian urban

22

23

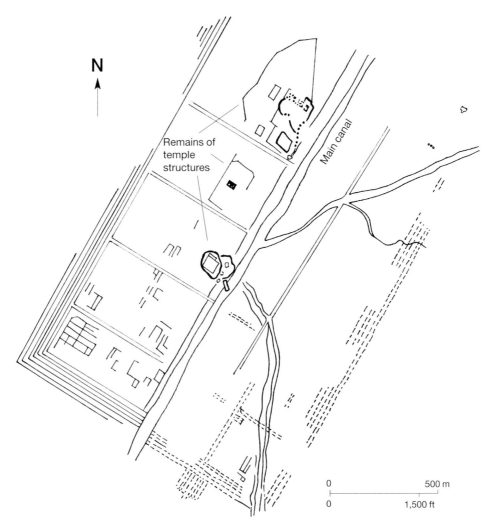

23 Plan of Oc Eo, based on aerial photographs. The rectangular town was bounded by a system of moats and palisaded ramparts; its 'streets' were tributary canals branching off at right angles from the main canal.

settlements, such as seventeenth-century Ayutthaya, or even early twentieth-century Bangkok.

As geographer Paul Wheatley tells us,[19] living at Oc Eo were glass workers, potters, gold-beaters, jewellers, engravers in many media, and craftsmen in bronze, iron and tin; these have left plentiful evidence of their activities in the form of tools, manufactures and trash. Sadly, most of the sumptuous artifacts illustrated by Malleret – which include exotic imports from the Mediterranean and the Indian subcontinent – are not stratigraphically fixed in time, since they were bought from the local villagers who had been looting the site for decades. The earliest surely dated object is a find that has attracted worldwide interest: a small, gold medallion struck in AD 152, during the reign of the Roman emperor Antoninus Pius. This and a few other exotics (which include a coin from the reign of Marcus Aurelius and a rock-crystal seal with an erotic scene) are testimony not to the actual presence of Romans or Greeks in the Delta, but to the east–west, and west–east flow of goods in those days that linked the Mediterranean, Persia, India, Southeast Asia and China through both maritime and overland trade.

Nonetheless, there must have been Indian merchants in Oc Eo and other Delta towns, and with them both Brahmin priests and Buddhist monks. These traders brought with them the kind of coinage in common use in the Indian subcontinent, particularly silver pieces marked with the conch and trident symbolic of the god Vishnu. The earliest known writing in the Khmer area consists of seals and finger rings from Oc Eo marked in Sanskrit with the genitive form of the owner's name or with protective formulae. Locally manufactured pottery, both wheel-made and formed by paddle-and-anvil, was abundant in Malleret's excavations, which turned up very early examples of the spouted *kendi* pots that were produced and used throughout the entire historic period. Exactly how old are all these objects? In lieu of a detailed stratigraphy linked to radiocarbon dates, one can only fix an estimated span of about AD 100 to 600. Regrettably, we cannot be more specific than this.

24 Various artifacts from Oc Eo. *a*, gold medallion of the Emperor Antoninus Pius; *b*, rock-crystal seal; *c*, Vishnuite silver coin; *d–g*, glass beads; *h*, onyx bead or pendant (½ scale); *i*, gold ring-seal marked with owner's name; *j*, gold articulated pendant.

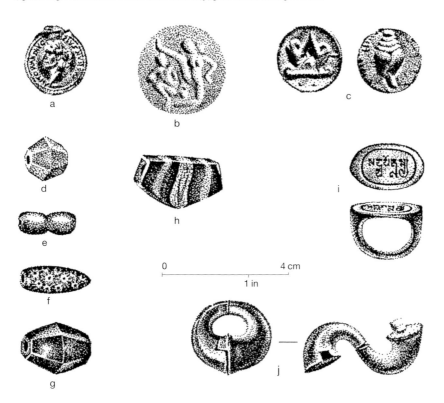

The same dating problem applies to the remains of two temple or shrine foundations excavated within Oc Eo by Malleret. One is a very large foundation of brick. The other ('Structure K') is far more complex – as art historian Philip Rawson tells us, above a brick foundation was 'a rectangular chamber of huge granite slabs mated by mortise and tenon…The chamber was crowned probably by a corbelled roof-vault whose two granite pediments have survived. Near by was a brick building with rooms and a veranda.'[20] To Rawson, who tentatively dates it to the fifth century, the whole complex suggests an Indian temple of the same period. Yet true prototypes are hard to come by in India: most of the really ancient temples are rock-cut sanctuaries, the earliest free-standing examples from the Gupta kingdom of the north being no earlier than Structure K, if the date of the latter is correct.

In 1984 and 1993, Vietnamese archaeologists investigated Go Thap, an important religious centre of the Oc Eo culture, where they uncovered five rectangular grave pits containing cremation burials; three of these were brick-lined.[21] Near the middle of each was a hollow, chimney-like brick structure that contained the ashes along with mortuary goods. Among the latter were many gold leaves with appliqué decoration representing the figures and symbols of Hindu gods, including Vishnu, Shiva, Brahma and Indra. It is reasonable to suppose that such structures were devoted to the veneration of members of the Brahmin (priestly) caste, since the burials had been carried out according to Hindu practice. Presumably the rest of the population continued to inter their dead in the way that their ancestors had done for centuries.

From chiefdoms to kingdoms

By the early seventh century, political power in this part of Southeast Asia had shifted inland from the maritime trading towns of the Delta according to Michael Vickery – to the Cambodian Basin, to Khorat, and to Champassak (southern Laos).[22] An economy centred upon mercantile activities was replaced by an agrarian one based upon the production of rice. Concurrently, among the elite families of these early states, there was a shift from matrilineal to patrilineal descent, so that an especially powerful *poñ* could pass his wealth and lands to his son rather than having it go to a nephew or other matrilineal heir. Even the title of *poñ* itself began to die out (in fact, it disappeared completely after AD 719). It is clear that during the two centuries or so preceding AD 802 – the founding date of the Khmer Empire – there were a number of independent states in Khmer territory, not just the one, or at most two, of the so-called 'Zhenla' of the Chinese annals. Each of these was a highly stratified class society, rather than the tribal one of the old *poñ* chiefdoms.

At the head of each state was the king, who always took the Sanskrit name of a patron deity, followed by *-varman*; this suffix, meaning 'protected by', was ordained by the 'Code of Manu' for Kshatriyas, the warrior caste from which Hindu kings were drawn. The first part of the ruler's name was usually applied to the capital, followed by the suffix *-pura*, 'city'. In Sanskrit inscriptions, the king's title was *raja*, but in Khmer it was *vrah kamratan añ*,

25 Limestone figure of the god Vishnu, from Phum Tuol Khum, sixth to seventh century (Early Kingdoms period). Now in the National Museum of Phnom Penh. His four hands once held a club, an orb, a conch shell and a *chakra* (discus). Ht 1.4 m (4.6 ft).

an honorific that he shared with the Hindu gods since he himself was at least semi-divine. Also in the royal courts were queens, as well as other royal females known as *ge kloñ*. All of these constituted the royal class.

Beneath this class was the hereditary aristocracy, from which the non-royal officialdom was drawn. Among these dignitaries were the *mratañ*, probably superior to the *poñ* whom they gradually replaced. There was also a group of special female officials, high-status women with special duties, both ritual and scribal, to the officiants of the temple establishments.

What we know of the common people comes almost entirely from Khmer-language inscriptions related to the upkeep and holdings of the great religious foundations dedicated to the Hindu gods. The pre-Angkor super-natural world consisted of Hindu gods, their names commonly ending in the Sanskrit *-ishvara*; the most important of these great deities, being closely connected with the royal persona, were Shiva – often in the form of a *linga* (phallus) – and Vishnu, in all his avatars. Very frequently shown in pre-Angkor sculpture is a combined form of Vishnu and Shiva known as Harihara. But there were also Buddhist religious monastic establishments, although these must have declined in importance later on, as they had already done in the Indian subcontinent. Many commoners were involved with the upkeep of the religious complexes; of these, some were known as *khñum*, often translated as 'slave', but 'servant' might be just as apposite. Most of these *khñum* seem to have been assigned to one or another temple foundation, to which they had been donated by a *mratañ* who typically had bought them from a *poñ* with goods like silver or cloth. Linguist Judith Jacob tells us that individual *khñum* often bore pejorative names, such as 'stinking', but some had complimentary ones; for example musicians and dancers had poetic San-skrit names (such as 'Spring jasmine'). Productive lands of all sorts were also donated to the temples, and agricultural *khñum* worked rice fields, orchards, plantations, market gardens and pastures. They took care of coconut and areca palms, and of domestic animals (elephants, buffalos, oxen and goats). The more talented and fortunate among them were engaged in cooking, weaving, grinding, spinning, singing and dancing, playing musical instru-ments, grooming the king's elephant and moulding statues.[23]

Thus, while the king was probably the theoretical owner of everything within his realm, the great temple foundations with their own holdings of lands and people must have functioned as powerful corporations; even small temples had foundations and collected taxes. Typically, the king would 'establish a god', that is, found a temple complex by his munificence, or else make donations of land, goods, and *khñum* to an already existing foundation. By the close of the eighth century, the Khmer landscape was dotted with temples and shrines to the gods.

Angkor Borei

It will be remembered that Angkor Borei, at the head of the Mekong Delta region on the Cambodian side of the border, was connected to Oc Eo by a very long canal. Some scholars have even suggested that it was the capital of the 'Funan' culture, and Oc Eo its port, but since no ancient name is known for Angkor Borei, it is difficult to prove this. There is a tradition that says it was ruled by Rudravarman, but again the evidence is insufficient. Since 1995, Miriam Stark of the University of Hawaii, along with her Cambodian co-director Chuch Phoeurn, has been conducting intensive survey and exca-vation at the site, together with researchers from Cambodian institutions.

Radiocarbon dates and ceramic chronology suggest that it was occupied from at least 400 BC through the Early Kingdoms period.[24] In fact, a modern village and two Buddhist temples are still located on its remains, considerably complicating matters for the archaeologists!

Angkor Borei was surrounded by a double moat, the inner one paralleling a brick-built city wall. Unlike the geometrically planned Oc Eo, the overall plan of the site is irregularly wedge-shaped. There are many water features visible on its surface, both small ponds and more ambitious *barays* (rectangular tanks), the latter often associated with the remains of collapsed brick structures. During the 1999–2001 field seasons, an extensive cemetery was located and excavated; 45–50 burials were found, so closely packed together that some were placed directly atop each other. Radiocarbon dating suggests that the cemetery was in use from the second century BC to the fourth century AD.[25]

There can be little doubt that Angkor Borei, whatever its name, and whether ruled by a *poñ* or *raja*, was a key political and religious centre during the first half of the seventh century, for this site and its immediate area have produced an important body of very early sculpture that has been ascribed by art historian Nancy Dowling[26] to this period. This includes twelve images of the Buddha; two schools of Buddhism are reflected in these images:

- a school that used Sanskrit for its canonical language, associated with a style of representation ultimately derived from the Buddhist imagery of India's Gupta Empire (*c*. AD 320–455); and
- a school associated with Amaravati, an ancient Indian capital, and with Sri Lanka.

It is at this time, and at Angkor Borei itself, that we have the first known inscription in the Khmer language; this appears on three sides of a damaged stone block.[27] The text opens with a date given in the *saka* era[28] corresponding to AD 611, along with the lunar month and lunar fortnight. Then appears the laconic statement 'The *poñ* Uy has given [the following] *khñum* (slaves or servants)', followed by a list of names. It seems that these were assigned to a Hindu god – that is, to a temple foundation – but that the donor allowed them to also serve another individual.

From this we know that Buddhism peacefully coexisted with Hinduism, as it had under the Guptas on the Indian subcontinent. It has long been known that much of the earliest and in some respects the most beautiful body of Hindu sculpture in Cambodia has come from Angkor Borei and the nearby Phnom Da. This art is flowing, three-dimensional, and filled with vitality.[29] While based upon Indian (largely Gupta) prototypes, it is far from a slavish imitation of Indian styles. Particularly frequent are standing, multi-armed images of the protector and saviour god Vishnu, shown with cylindrical mitre; to support his arms, which carry the symbols of his power, his figure is backed by a support shaped like an upside-down magnet. Very similarly posed are figures of Harihara, the two-in-one divinity combining Vishnu and Shiva, respectively the creator and the destroyer of the universe. But most dynamic of all are masterfully *contraposto* representations of Krishna

26 Grey limestone statue of Krishna Govardhana, Early Kingdoms period, sixth century. This statue, from Phnom Da, near the Delta centre of Angkor Borei, represents the young Krishna in the act of raising Mount Govardhana to shelter shepherds and their cattle against rains unleashed by Indra. Ht 118.8 cm (46.8 in).

Govardhana, Vishnu's youthful avatar, who saved shepherds and their cattle from the rains unleashed by Indra's wrath, by sheltering them under a mountain that he had raised with one hand.

Sambor Prei Kuk

At the beginning of the twentieth century, the pioneer French archaeologist Lunet de Lajonquière located many Early Kingdoms sites in Cambodia, particularly in the lower Mekong below Phnom Penh and in Kompong Thom Province, to the east of the Great Lake.[30] Among the latter is Sambor Prei Kuk ('hillock in the forest of Sambor'). Identified by most authorities as ancient Ishanapura, the seventh-century capital of Ishanavarman, Sambor Prei Kuk is truly huge in extent: there are said to be over 170 structures and traces of a town bounded by a rectangular moat and earth levee 2 km (1.2 miles) on a side. But the site has suffered much with the vicissitudes of time and history, and only ten major monuments remain, located to the east of the ancient town.[31]

27

These are of brick with sandstone embellishment – an identifying feature of pre-Angkorian architecture, as well as that of some of the earliest temples in the Angkor area – and all face east, the direction of the god Shiva. There are three principal groups at Sambor Prei Kuk, each on an artificially raised terrace with enclosing walls. Structure S1 within the South Group is a large, rectangular edifice that once had four or five retreating storeys on top, supported by a corbel vault; its door and false doors are framed in sandstone. Within its enormous interior, according to the inscription, was a golden *linga* donated by the king.

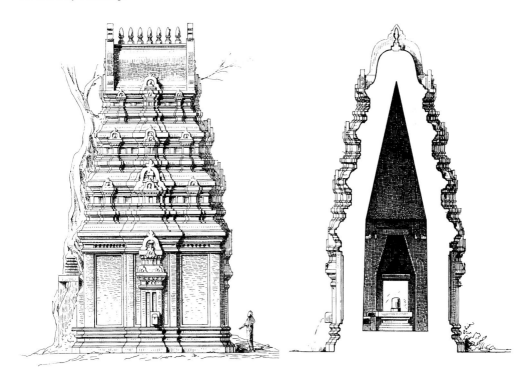

27 Brick temple N18 at Sambor Prei Kuk. Early Kingdoms period, seventh century. Within the cross-section can be seen the temple's cult object, a *linga* on its pedestal.

The exterior decoration here and in other structures at the site consisted of
28   'flying palace' reliefs carved into the brick exteriors, and (over the doorways)
29   elaborately carved sandstone lintels. Early Kingdoms lintels, which Lajonquière classified into three series, are all relatively flat compared to ones from
the Classic period, and show two *makaras* (grotesque water monsters) at
either end spewing out a wavy band from which depend garlands or jewelled
necklaces – suggesting that the door is the entrance to the abode of the gods.
And, like all Hindu temples from the subcontinent to Indonesia, the temple
was in fact the home of a particular god, in this case Shiva, whose vehicle, the
bull Nandin, rested in stone form on a pavilion before the temple door.

Into the dark interior of these thick-walled shrines, only a Brahmin priest
or other officiant, or perhaps the king himself, was allowed to be present.
30   Over the male *linga*, inserted upright into its square, female *snanadroni*, the

28   Carved-brick 'flying palace' ornament on temple N7 at Sambor Prei Kuk.

29   Sandstone lintel from Prah That Thom, Early Kingdoms period, seventh century. The wavy band emanating from the mouths of flanking *makaras* (water monsters), the three medallions, and the swagged necklaces or garlands are typical of the earliest form of Khmer lintel. Length 1.65 m (5.4 ft).

30 Cut-away view of *linga* and pedestal within temple S11 at Sambor Prei Kuk. The cylindrical top of the *linga* symbolizes Shiva; the octagonal middle Brahma; and the square base Vishnu. The receptacle and spout is the *snanadroni*, a symbolic vulva.

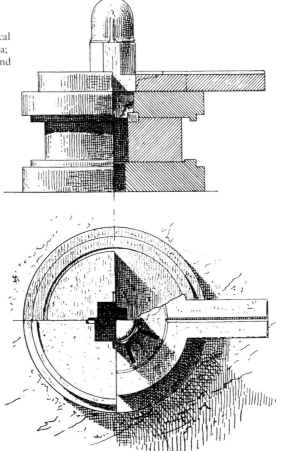

priest would have poured libations of water, milk, clarified butter, and other holy substances. By the time that temple N11 in the North Group was built, perhaps in the eighth century, the lustral fluids were removed to the outside of the temple through a special conduit, an architectural detail with Indian prototypes.

Banteay Prei Nokor

Located to the east of the Mekong River in Kompong Cham Province, and surrounded by an impressive moat with earthen embankment some 2.5 km (1.5 miles) square, Banteay Prei Nokor is considered by many scholars to have been a major capital during the Early Kingdoms period.[32] The site, with about ten early, brick-built towers, has never been properly mapped or explored, but Michael Vickery[33] feels that it may have been the city of Vyadhapura, seventh-century capital of Jayavarman I, while others have suggested an identification with Indrapura, where Jayavarman II reigned before being created 'universal ruler' in 802. The site cries out for excavation.

Wat Phu

Champassak is a beautiful corner of southwestern Laos, a fertile province lying between the middle Mekong and the borders of Thailand and Cambodia. The province's most arresting sight, visible to any traveller on that river from many miles away, is known to the locals as Phu Kao, at the southern end of a small mountain chain. With an elevation of 1,416 m (4,646 ft), this is a vestige of a very eroded sandstone bed that looks as if someone had placed Wyoming's famous Devil's Tower on top of a mountain. The Phu Kao also looks extraordinarily like a massive *linga*, and it surely must have struck the first religious wayfarers from India in the same way. Accordingly, it was mentioned in many inscriptions by later kings as the Lingaparvata ('*linga* mountain'), and a cult grew around it, centred on the important temple complex of Wat Phu, at the foot of the mountain.

Coedès and other scholars have called attention to a passage in the early eighth-century *History of the Sui Dynasty* that may be a specific reference to this cult. In speaking of 'Zhenla' it states:

31 Distant view of the Lingaparvata mountain (Phu Kao), Laos, looking west from the Mekong River. This has always been an object of great veneration in Southeast Asia, and the early site of Wat Phu lies at its foot.

Near the capital is a mountain named Ling-jia-bo-po, on the summit of which a temple was constructed, always guarded by five thousand soldiers and consecrated to the spirit named Po-do-li, to whom human sacrifices are made. Each year, the king himself goes to this temple to make a human sacrifice during the night. It is thus that they honour the spirits.[34]

According to Coedès, a long-time believer in the reality of 'Funan' and 'Zhenla', Champassak was the place where the ruling dynasty of 'Zhenla' originated, and Wat Phu was the first capital of what he took to be a unitary state[35] – a view not accepted by modern scholarship. Professor Vickery even questions the identification of the Phu Kao as the Ling-jia-bo-po or Linga-parvata described in the annals, emphasizing that there are a number of hills in Cambodia that could have had that honour.[36] Nonetheless, it must be reiterated that nowhere else in Southeast Asia does there exist anything like the extraordinarily phallic form of the Phu Kao. Furthermore, the Shivaite cult centred on the *linga* was always strong here, being worshipped as the god Badreshvara; in fact, even today thousands of pilgrims come to Wat Phu from southern Laos for a Buddhist–Hindu ceremony held in February, during which young girls in white pray to Shiva and buffalos are sacrificed.[37] As for the human sacrifice mentioned in the Chinese annals, this was not entirely absent in Cambodia before the French Protectorate – for instance, right up until the mid-nineteenth century, humans were crushed alive under the gate foundations of every fortified enclosure, of which they became the guardian spirits.

The sanctuary of Wat Phu is enormously impressive.[38] A long causeway leads from magnificent rectangular *barays*, between two beautiful, identical buildings of laterite and sandstone (both of them built and endowed by Suryavarman II in the twelfth century), west to the foot of the hill. There it ascends to the remains of much older and much-ruined temples, rock-cut shrines and reliefs, and a sacred spring originating in a rock overhang. The most unusual feature is a crocodile form indented in a rock, which the photographer Michael Freeman notes has the same dimensions of a man, and so might have been the place of sacrifice described in the annals.

What the tourist might not realize is that there is an ancient town of the Early Kingdoms period associated with this holy site. The 'Old City' lies 4 to 5 km (2.5 to 3.1 miles) due east, immediately above the banks of the Mekong, which has probably cut part of it away. Like Angkor Borei, it is surrounded by a double enclosure, in this case of earthen walls, but it is rectangular in ground plan like Oc Eo, and orientated to an east–west axis. Divided into more or less equal halves by a north-south earthen dyke, the town may have covered over 3 square km (1.2 square miles). A Lao-French archaeological project directed by Marielle Santoni of the Centre Nationale de Recherches Scientifiques has been mapping and excavating the 'Old City' since 1991, and has found the ruins of about thirty pre-Ankorian temples that had been built of brick, along with residential and workshop remains.[39] The religious structures, unfortunately mishandled by looters, show many of the same stone details that are seen in Sambor Prei Kuk (frames for real and false doors, sills, decorated lintels, and so forth); they are usually associated with rectangular pools.

Two inscriptions were discovered in 1991, incised on the bases of Nandin monuments (Nandin is the bull 'vehicle' of Shiva). These show that King Mahendravarman had dedicated the statues to his father and his uncle in AD 590. It will be remembered that this potentate ruled in Ishanapura, but he had extended his sway into this part of Laos and over one of Southeast Asia's holiest centres. This must have considerably enhanced his prestige, for among these early kingdoms, while other hills and mountains in Cambodia and even in the Delta may have been thought to be 'Lingaparvatas', the one above Wat Phu was certainly the original, the *real* Lingaparvata, the *linga* of the great god Shiva himself.

31

The bronzes of Prakhon Chai

It is true that the major concentration of sites and inscriptions of the Early Kingdoms period lies in the Delta and in central Cambodia, but these early chiefs and kings controlled both sides of the Dangrek Range separating the Cambodian Basin from the Khorat Plateau. Early Kingdoms inscriptions in Khmer have been found just west of Nakhon Ratchasima, in the far western headwaters of the Mun River, and almost certainly the entire Mun drainage, and probably most of the rest of Khorat, was ethnically Khmer by that time.

In 1964, under what have been described as 'mysterious circumstances', a very large hoard of bronzes was found in a burial chamber underlying a Buddhist temple precinct in Prakhon Chai, a settlement about midway between the Angkorian site of Phnom Rung and the town of Surin, in southern Khorat.[40] Since the deposit immediately entered the antiquities market, no one knows how many pieces there once were (estimates range from 20 to 300), but ten of these were large – up to 1.5 m (5 ft) – and incredibly beautiful examples of the 'lost wax' casting process. There are both standing and seated Buddhas, but the majority relate to the Mahayana branch of Buddhism. These latter depict the four-armed Bodhisattvas: Avalokiteshvara ('the compassionate one') and Maitreya ('the friendly one', the Buddha of the future). Probably all were once gilt, and some still have inlaid details of silver, black stone or glass.

32

Art historians place the entire Prakhon Chai group in the seventh to ninth centuries of the Early Kingdoms period, and relate them to the stone sculptures of Angkor Borei and Phnom Da. In lieu of real context, all one can say is that these bronzes must have resulted from the patronage and endowment of a powerful Khmer ruler with strong ties to Mahayana Buddhism, at a time when Buddhism was on the wane in both India and mainland Southeast Asia.

32 Bodhisattva Maitreya, from Prakhon Chai, Buriram Province, Thailand. Early Kingdoms period, eighth century. Copper alloy with inlays of silver and black stone. This image is of the Buddha of the future, who will come to purify the world; here he wears the traditional Khmer *sampot* or kilt. Ht 96.5 cm (38 in).

Hinduism

Perhaps more accurately called 'Brahmanism', Hinduism is an ever-changing complex of myths, beliefs, practices and philosophical speculation that has been likened to a river: meandering, splitting into numerous channels, yet always coming back together, and always drawing upon the sources from which it sprang.

The sources

The most ancient of these is the *Rig Veda*, an oral body of hymns that may be traced to the Aryans, a pastoral, early Indo-European people who had erupted into northwest India from a homeland on the steppes. In its present form, the Vedic texts probably date to about 1200 BC. They speak of a semi-nomadic culture in which sacrifice of cattle and horses was important, as well as purification and the offering of fire to the gods. It was these Aryan invaders that introduced into the Indic world the rigid ordering of humans into four hereditary, endogamic classes. Three of these were 'twice-born': at the top were the priests (Brahmins), followed in rank by the warriors (the Kshatriyas, from which the royal houses were later to be drawn), and then the commoners (Vaishyas, which included the merchants). Far below these were the serfs (Shudras), condemned to work for the 'twice-born'. From these classes sprang all of the myriad castes of the subcontinent, excepting the so-called 'untouchables', peoples inherently contaminated by the impurity of their calling – such as tanners of animal hides, refuse collectors, etc.

Parenthetically, while there were certainly Brahmins in the temples and royal courts of mainland Southeast Asia (there still are), and although Khmer kings may have thought of themselves as Kshatriyas, the Hindu caste system was and is basically unknown throughout its history.

Over thirty gods (*deva* for male ones and *devi* for females) are named in the Rig Veda hymns, and many or most of them are the personification of natural forces. The king of the gods, cognate to Zeus of the Greeks, was Indra with his thunderbolt. The duty of Agni, the fire god, was to carry the sacrificial offering from humans to the gods. Although these two play a relatively minor role in developed Hinduism, the opposite is true for Rudra, 'the howler', a deity of mountains and of the wilderness who was later considered to be an important manifestation of the great god Shiva (see below). Also appearing in the Vedic texts are the sun, Surya, the moon, Chandra, and storm gods, Marut. The universe, according to the Rig Veda, is an equilibrium between good and evil, as symbolized by two opposing fluids. Soma is the elixir of life, associated with divine semen and with the Moon, but it is balanced by an equal amount of poisons. Present in developed Vedic religion is the important role of asceticism and meditation, pursued in post-Vedic India by Brahmin sages known in Sanskrit (the language of the Rig Veda) as *rishis*.

There are two other great, basic sources for Hinduism: the epics, both composed between 300 BC and AD 300. The earliest of these may be the *Mahabharata*, the world's longest epic poem (with about 100,000 verses); its narrative unfolds on the north Gangetic Plain and relates the cosmic struggle between two sets of royal cousins:

- **Kauravas**, the sons of Darkness, who usurped the rulership; and
- **Pandavas**, the sons of Light, exiled by their cousins.

The culminating point of the *Mahabharata*, which is a virtual encyclopedia of mythology, epic history and religion, is the eighteen-day Battle of Kurukshetra, marking the beginning of the present Hindu era in the year 3102 BC. During this tremendous conflict, magnificently commemorated in one of Angkor Wat's reliefs, the Pandava hero Arjuna is counselled by his charioteer Krishna, in the verses known as the *Bhagavad Gita*, the 'Song of God'.

The other epic is the *Ramayana* (*Reamker* or *Ramakerti* in Khmer), well known in the Western world through modern translations. It relates the exciting story of Rama, the King of Ayodhya. Rama's beautiful wife Sita had been abducted by the evil, ten-headed demon Ravana, King of Lanka (modern Sri Lanka). To regain his wife, and aided by the monkey king Sugriva, Rama dispatched an invasion army of simians headed by the monkey general, Hanuman. Sita was eventually restored to her husband, but first had to pass through a series of cruel ordeals to demonstrate her faithfulness. In all of the Indianized states of Southeast Asia, Rama – actually an avatar of the god Vishnu – has always been considered the exemplary king, Sita the exemplary wife, and Ayodhya the exemplary city.

The *Puranas* are the third great source for the Hindu religion, one continuously drawn upon by the kings, priests, gurus and sculptors of Southeast Asia. They comprise a huge repository of mythology, composed over many centuries (between AD 250 and 1350).

Hindu cosmology

In Hindu thought, time is circular, and not linear as in the western world. Their cosmologists conceived of great cyclic eras called *kalpas*; each *kalpa* is but one day of Brahma, the

33 Relief on a boulder at Kbal Spean, in the Kulen hills, representing the creation of the universe. Vishnu reclines on a serpent; from his navel sprouts a lotus bearing the god Brahma. Below the relief are multiple *lingas*.

Creator, and is equivalent to 4,320,000,000 human years. In turn, each *kalpa* is divided into four *yugas* of progressively diminishing length and merit, the best of which was the first (the Krta Yuga), and the worst is the fourth, our own Kali Yuga that opened with the Battle of Kurukshetra. Creation takes place at beginning of each *kalpa* when the god

33

Vishnu rests on a serpent lying on the waters of the primal ocean. Brahma, the Creator, is born from a lotus growing from Vishnu's navel (visitors to Khmer sites will often see this depicted on temple lintels). At the end of each *kalpa*, the world is destroyed by fire, invoked by the dancing of the god Shiva.

Hindu concepts

Over the centuries, many speculative and mystical texts collectively called the *Upanishads* were composed as commentaries on the Veda; these focussed on the nature of reality, and of the self. Absolutely basic to the Hinduism of the Upanishads, and to the Buddhism that sprang from them, is the idea of *samsara*, reincarnation: that every living thing is reborn after death, and that *what* one is reborn into is determined by one's *karma*, the cumulative effect of one's good and bad actions. To break out of the endless cycle of rebirths, knowledge is sought and renunciation practiced by adepts dedicated to a life based upon poverty, celibacy, and meditation. These are the *rishis*, the ascetic sages one may see throughout India today, and practitioners of *yoga*.

Also shared with Buddhism is the concept of Dharma; this is the moral order of the universe, what ought to be, as given in the Vedic texts. In Hindu thought, the universe is balanced between good and evil, between the gods and their enemies,

the demons (*asuras*), and between the human world and the world of gods. The gods live on Mount Meru, a mythological peak in the Himalayas. This is a three-dimensional *mandala*, a cosmic diagram, and is golden and bejewelled, with perfumed breezes – a true heavenly home of supernatural beings, who are attended by nymph-like celestial dancers (*apsaras*). Surrounding Mount Meru are seven seas of different liquids; from its summit flows the Ganga (the Ganges), the ultimate holy river of the Hindus, and an ever-renewing source of purification.

The ideal Hindu temple is a recreation of Mount Meru, a home for a particular god or group of gods. The *deva* or *devi* resides in the form of an image cared for by a Brahmin priest. The god must be awakened daily, bathed, fed with offerings, and allowed to rest. As Gavin Flood states, 'Devotion (*bhakti*) to deities mediated through icons and holy persons provides refuge in times of crisis and even liberation…from action (*karma*) and the cycle of reincarnation.'

Hinduism is essentially a male-oriented religion, and females are essentially unclean and dangerous. The ideal is male asceticism. But *kama*, sexual desire and love, is a powerful force for both gods and humans, and the greatest of the gods have divine consorts.

The supreme gods

By any definition of the word 'god', there are hundreds of them in the various Hindu texts, above all in the Puranas, but only a handful played a major role among the Indianized kingdoms of Southeast Asia. It is important to emphasize that each of these deities is in fact part of a complex: that each god had more than one aspect, and that some functions, including creation and destruction, were often shared with other gods. A particularly important aspect of certain supernaturals has been conceptualized as an animal mount or 'vehicle' on which he or she travels.

Brahma, depicted with four arms and four faces, and with the goose as a vehicle, is a creator god, but his importance as a focus of worship became very minor through the centuries. The really great gods in the Indian and Indianized worlds were and are Shiva and Vishnu – almost all non-Buddhist temples in the land of the Khmer were consecrated for the worship of one or the other of them.

Shiva, who began as the wild god Rudra in the Rig Veda, can be recognized by his unruly locks, the animal skin that he sometimes wears, and by his three eyes; in Hindu thought, one eye is the Sun, another is the Moon, and the third eye is Fire. His vehicle is the ox, Nandin, and he may hold a trident in one hand. Shiva is the destroyer of the world (but at times he acts as its creator and preserver), and he is the main god of asceticism; he dwells not on Meru, but on his own mountain, Kailasa, along

with his consort Parvati, or Uma. Symbolized by the *linga*, the stone replica of his phallus, Shiva was the object of an intense royal cult among the Khmer rulers.

Vishnu, whose mount is the half-eagle, half-man Garuda, is considerably more benign than Shiva, functioning as the saviour and preserver of the universe. In his four arms he carries his attributes: a wheel-like discus or *chakra*, a conch, a club, and the earth visualized as a ball. He also had a consort, the goddess Lakshmi. In his ten earthly avatars (reincarnations), Vishnu was the benefactor of mankind at critical moments. One of these avatars was as Rama, the ideal of princes. But an even more important one was as Krishna, a man/god created to rid the world of monsters. When he was born, Krishna was hidden among the swineherds and raised as one, to keep him from being slain by his evil uncle. Krishna is the embodiment of youthful male sexuality, beguiling milkmaids by his charms.

The Churning of the Sea of Milk, famously depicted in Angkor Wat, took place at the Creation of the Universe, and was the work of Vishnu. For 1,000 years the *devas* and the *asuras* had been contending to

34

pl. XI

34 Heads of the *Trimurti*, the three greatest Hindu gods. Left, Brahma. Centre, Shiva. Right, Vishnu. Early tenth century, found on Phnom Bok. Ht 45–49 cm (17–19 in).

35 Rock-cut shrine of the Hindu *trimurti* ('trinity') at Wat Phu, with a multiheaded and multiarmed Shiva in the centre, Brahma on the left and Vishnu on the right. Possibly tenth century.

produce the divine elixir *amrita*, but without success by either side. Vishnu resolved the matter by having them work together: using the serpent Vasuki as a rope and a mountain as the pivot, for another 1,000 years they churned the sea to manufacture not only the elixir, but also Lakshmi, the three-headed elephant Airavata (Indra's vehicle), and the lovely *apsaras*, among other prodigies.

Along with Shiva and Vishnu at the summit of the Hindu pantheon one must place the Great Goddess (Devi), who goes under different names and performs different functions, and who has her own devotees. Some aspects of the goddess are benevolent and nurturing, while others are far less so. As the ferocious Durga, she attacks and slays the Buffalo Monster. While her cult was important in the Indonesian Archipelago (in Bali, it still is), the Great Goddess played only a minor role in the Khmer area.

Buddhism

The historical Buddha

Buddhism arose about twenty-five centuries ago from the world of Brahmanic Hinduism. The historical Buddha, Siddartha Gautama, was born about 480 BC (a much-disputed

36 (*left*) Limestone figure of the Buddha standing on a lotus flower, from Wat Phnom near Udong. The simple robe and absence of jewelry indicate the Master's renunciation of the world. Early Kingdoms period, seventh century. National Museum of Phnom Penh. Ht 97 cm (38.2 in).

37 (*above*) Sandstone head of the Buddha, from Wat Kromlok, Angkor Borei, sixth(?)–seventh century. Ht 28 cm (11 in).

date) in the small Shakya kingdom, on the border of what is now Nepal; hence, he is also known as Shakyamuni, 'sage of the Shakyas'. According to tradition, his father was king; the young prince was raised in luxury, eventually married, and had a son.

At age twenty-nine, Gautama was taken on a chariot ride, and saw successively a worn-out old man, a sick man and a corpse. Horrified by the misery, he changed his behaviour and adopted a life of renunciation, asceticism, and Yogic meditation, so as to find how humans could be liberated from suffering. Near the point of starvation, he realized that the path to Enlightenment was not to be one of extreme self-denial, but a

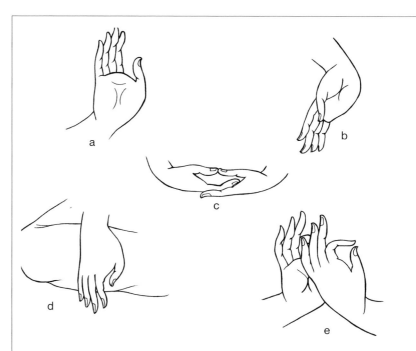

38 The *mudras*, symbolic hand gestures of the Buddha. *a*, Fearlessness Gesture; *b*, Compassion Gesture; *c*, Meditation Gesture; *d*, Calling the Earth to Witness Gesture; *e*, Teaching Gesture.

'Middle Way' between asceticism and the world. On his path to enlightenment, he was waylaid by the Satan-like figure of Mara, who tried to deflect him from the right way; rejecting this, Buddha 'called the Earth Goddess to witness' his own merit.

36
37

After deep meditations, the 35-year-old Buddha achieved Enlightenment at Bodhgaya, a place to the south of the Ganges. During the rest of his long life, he preached many sermons, which have been preserved along with commentaries as the 'Pali Canon' (Pali, another Indic language, is the language of Buddhism, as Sanskrit is that of Hinduism). At his death he passed into deathless *nibbana*, that state of extinction of all Self that is the ultimate goal of the 'Middle Way'; after cremation his ashes and relics were divided among the disciples,

and buried under *stupas*, funerary mounds. Gautama's message was one of compassion, humaneness and the striving for self-release from the bonds of desire and from the endless cycle of rebirths. It might be summed up by his famous admonition, 'Work out thine own salvation with diligence.'

The Four Noble Truths

- The truth of *dukkha*: all forms of existence are subject to *dukkha* (suffering, unsatisfactoriness, disease, imperfection).
- The truth of the cause of *dukkha*: *dukkha* is caused by desire.
- The truth of cessation of *dukkha*: eliminate desire, and *dukkha* will cease to exist.
- The truth of the path: the Eight-Fold Path is the way to extinguish desire.

The Eight-Fold Path

- Right understanding
- Right thought
- Right speech
- Right bodily conduct
- Right livelihood
- Right effort
- Right attentiveness
- Right concentration.

The Sangha

In all schools of Buddhism, there are 'The Three Jewels': the Buddha, the Dhamma (Buddha's teaching), and the Sangha, or community of monks and nuns. All Buddhists consider monasticism a superior way of life, and enormous respect is paid by all lay persons – kings and commoners alike – to those wearing the robes of a monk, even to young novices. Ordination of a monk is a two-stage process. Boys as young as seven or eight may enter lower ordination, while senior ordination takes place at age 20. Monastic rules are strict and multiple (as many as 227 for monks, 311 for nuns).

Since monastery members do not work, and have very few material possessions, they are totally dependent on alms given to them by persons wishing to acquire merit. In this way the Sangha is closely tied to the laity of a community, whose children they educate and for whom they conduct life-cycle rituals. Much of a monk's long day is taken up with meditation and study. This, at any rate, is the ideal. Nonetheless, throughout the history of mainland Southeast Asia, monasteries have become involved in large commercial enterprises and have acted as land-holding corporations, much like their Hindu counterparts.

A Buddhist monastery consists of a number of buildings: a meditation hall, shrine hall, Dhamma hall, refectory, and so forth. The sacred space of the most sacred hall is marked out by boundary stones called *sima* or *sema* (in Thailand and Cambodia, these are often the only witnesses to the presence of now-disappeared Buddhist establishments, since the latter were of wood and other perishable materials). In early Buddhism in the Indian subcontinent, depiction of the Founder in sculpture was forbidden – he was shown only as an empty throne, or as footsteps. By the first centuries of our era this had changed, and there developed a set iconographic canon for portraits of the Buddha. Deep meaning was conveyed by his posture and hand gestures; for example, a figure seated crosslegged with the right hand pointing down signifies 'calling the Earth to witness (his triumph over Mara)'. Soon an elaborate set of iconic hand gestures called *mudras* evolved, so that devotees could 'read' these images, and this system spread not only into Hindu art but also into the developing carving styles of Southeast Asia.

38

Mahayana Buddhism

If Hinduism can be thought of as a river, Buddhism is a tree, with major branches. The major branch, known as *Mahayana*, split off in the first century AD. 'Mahayana' means 'the Great Vehicle', to contrast it with *Hinayana*, 'the Lesser Vehicle'. Hinayana, better called *Theravada* Buddhism, has remained close to the original Pali Canon, and is still the majority faith in Sri Lanka, Burma, Thailand, Cambodia and Laos. But Theravada is mainly concerned with meditation and concentration and with the Sangha; Mahayanists say that it is really an agnostic philosophy rather than a religion. Mahayana Buddhism is centred not just on the historical Buddha, but on a host of supernaturals of whom the most important are the *Bodhisattvas*, 'beings of wisdom' on their way to becoming Buddhas, benevolently performing acts of kindness and generosity for the good of humankind.

Gautama Buddha himself, according to Mahayanists, had lived many lives before he was born as the Enlightened One. There is a large body of elevating but quite lively tales describing his previous existences, and these Jataka stories are often depicted by wall paintings in Buddhist temples throughout mainland Southeast Asia. The Bodhisattva *Maitreya* ('the Friendly One') is the Buddha of the Future, who will come to purify the world, and to teach the Dhamma when Gautama Buddha's teachings have fallen into disuse. Often depicted in Khmer stone and bronze sculpture of the Early Historic period, Maitreya may be recognized by the *stupa* in his headdress.

Perhaps even more important to Khmer culture history is *Avalokiteshvara* (also known as *Lokeshvara*), the Bodhisattva of infinite compassion and mercy, the most universally revered of all Mahayanist deities, who guards and protects the world between the death of the historical Buddha and the appearance of Maitreya. He is the earthly manifestation of the eternal *Amithaba* Buddha, whose figure appears in his headdress. Visitors to Angkor will never forget the multiple, smiling faces of Avalokiteshvara gazing out from the many towers of the Bayon, in the middle of Angkor Thom, the city of Jayavarman II, Cambodia's great Mahayanist king.

Tantrism or *Vajrayana* is an important aspect of Mahayana, particularly in Northern Buddhism as it is practised in countries like Nepal, Tibet and Mongolia, but it also had reflections in ancient Cambodia. It is a kind of practical discipline to reach enlightenment and release that uses *mantras* (oral formulas) and *mandalas* (cosmological diagrams), as well as symbols such as the *Vajra*-sceptre and the *Vajra*-bell, to attain its ends. Female deities, some of Hindu origin, play an important role in Tantrism, and there is a strong emphasis on male–female polarity and union with the absolute through physical consummation.

It is important to keep in mind that all of these traditions – Hinduism, Theravada Buddhism, and Mahayana Buddhism – have been interwoven throughout history. Gautama Buddha, for instance, is held by Hindu thinkers to be an avatar of the god Vishnu, and even in today's Cambodia, the gods Indra, Vishnu and Shiva (under Khmerized names, of course) are considered to be protectors of Buddhism. In the fifteenth century, following the fall of Angkor, Theravada Buddhism has replaced Hinduism and Mahayanism, but these two have never totally disappeared from the Khmer consciousness.

I (*right*) Synthetic-aperture radar image of Angkor acquired on 30 September 1994, from the space shuttle Endeavor. The Great Lake and its environs are at lower left, and the Kulen hills at upper right.

II Banteay Srei, view north across the moat surrounding the central Group. This compact, Shivaite complex was dedicated in AD 967.

III Sandstone pediment on the South 'Library' of Banteay Srei. The demon king, Ravana, shakes Mount Kailasa to disturb the meditations of Shiva, seated here with his consort Uma.

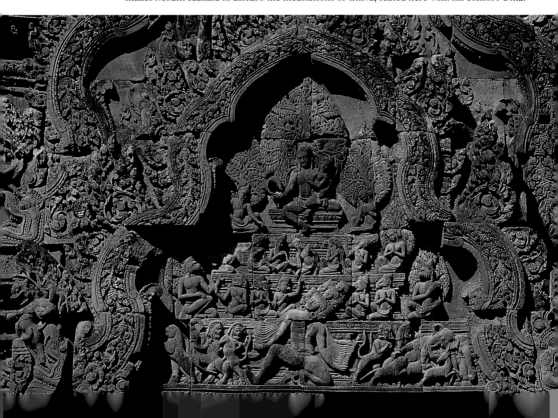

IV One of the *devatas* (goddesses) on the north shrine of Banteay Srei. Second half of the tenth century. These graceful figures, which gave the site its modern name ('Citadel of Women'), served as guardian figures, along with their male counterparts the *dvarapalas*.

V Limestone panel with guardian figure (*dvarapala*), set into a brick temple-tower in the Lolei complex, Hariharalaya. Classic period, end of the ninth century.

VI South face of *Gopura* III at Preah Vihear, a Classic site spectacularly located on the edge of the Dangrek escarpment, overlooking the Cambodian Plain. Late ninth to mid-twelfth centuries.

VII Brick-carved relief of the goddess Lakshmi (Vishnu's consort) and attendants. Prasat Kravan, Angkor. Classic period, early tenth century.

VIII Angkor Wat, aerial view looking northwest by west. This great temple complex was dedicated to the god Vishnu by Suryavarman II in the first half of the twelfth century, but was converted to Buddhist practice in the Post-Classic. Contemporary Buddhist *wats* can be seen at the left and near the top centre.

IX View of Angkor Wat, from the west. The highest tower marks the central shrine dedicated to the god Vishnu. Classic period, first half of the twelfth century.

6 · The Classic Angkor Period: From Kingdom to Empire

The term 'classic' as a category of cultural development was first applied to describe the highest development of Maya civilization in Mesoamerica. Here it will be used to describe ancient Khmer culture at the time of its apogee, between AD 802 and 1327. While some of the following traits of Classic Angkor civilization predate it, and some persist into much later periods, all of them together cluster into a time span of slightly more than five centuries:

- A universal monarch as head of an imperial state.
- The capital of the empire almost always based in Angkor.
- Hinduism and/or Mahayana Buddhism as the state religion.
- Religious architecture primarily in stone (sandstone and laterite) rather than wood.
- State and ancestral temples.
- Worship of the *linga*.
- *Prasats* (shrine towers) housing images of the gods, often arranged in quincunx and supported by stepped pyramids.
- Massive and extensive public waterworks, including canals and vast reservoirs (*barays*).
- A network of highways, causeways and masonry bridges.
- Inscriptions in Sanskrit, as well as Khmer.
- Iconography primarily Hindu, mainly derived from the epics and from the Puranas.

In this chapter we shall describe the historical trajectory of this great civilization, and in the next its anthropology.

The founding of the Khmer Empire

Until AD 802, the entire Khmer political landscape consisted of a number of independent kingdoms, all more-or-less in a constant state of warfare not only with external enemies (such as the Cham, in what is now central Vietnam), but with each other. All of this was to change with the man known to us as Jayavarman II, but referred to by his descendants and political heirs by the posthumous name of Parameshvara ('supreme lord'). Although there are no contemporary inscriptions associated with this key figure, his career has been traced in later texts by epigraphers such as Claude Jacques.[1] It was this king who founded the Khmer Empire.

The history of Jayavarman ('protected by victory') is contained on a four-sided stela found at Sdok Kak Thom ('SKT'), a site in southeast Thailand

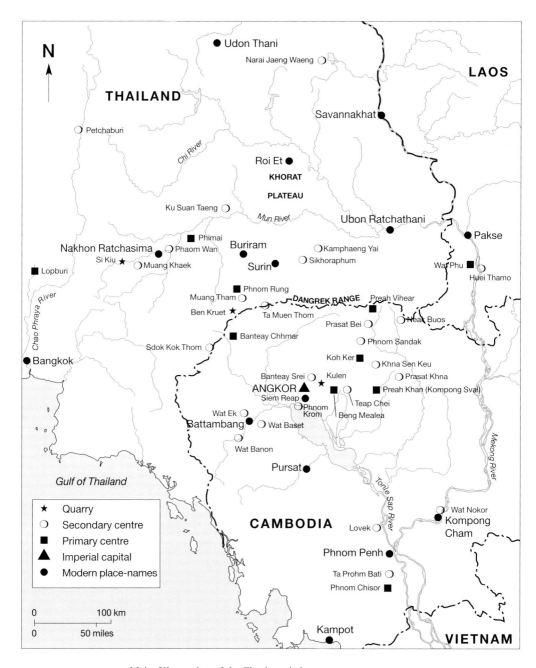

39 Major Khmer sites of the Classic period.

close to the Cambodian border.[2] The very long text in Sanskrit and Khmer dates from about AD 1052, and is the record of a prominent family that claimed it had supplied the *purohita* or royal chaplain to each ruler in a long line of kings, beginning with Jayavarman II (three other families claimed likewise!); in fact, the SKT inscription contains the only near-complete list of Angkorian rulers in existence, covering about 250 years. Jayavarman II, according to SKT, was said to have come from a land called 'Java', where he may have been held prisoner; Jacques doubts whether this was actually the island of Java (the Malay Peninsula has been suggested), but its location remains unknown. Once in Khmer territory, he first ruled over Indrapura, possibly located northeast of Phnom Penh near Kompong Cham.

From there Jayavarman began his relentless, expansionist military campaigns, conquering Vyadhapura (across the Mekong from Phnom Penh), followed by Sambhupura – perhaps modern Sambor, on the Mekong above Kratie. At some point he was at Wat Phu in Champassak, where he must have paid homage to the super-sacred Lingaparvata that towers over the area. More significantly, he established himself at Hariharalaya – of which more subsequently – in the plain between Phnom Kulen and the Great Lake, after which he founded Amarendrapura, probably not far from SKT in the far west of the country.

For the present-day Khmer of the Angkor region, Phnom Kulen is 'Litchi Mountain', but to their distant ancestors it was Mahendraparvata, the Mountain of Indra, the King of the Gods.[3] On and near this eroded, flat-topped plateau was quarried all of the sandstone from which the temples and palaces of Angkor were built, and all of its statues fashioned. It is also the ultimate source of the Siem Reap River, which drains most of the plateau before reaching Angkor, where it was the main acquifer for the mighty waterworks of the great city – including the major *barays*. During the Classic era and probably later, the river was identified with *Ganga*, the Ganges, as Phnom Kulen itself must have been with the mythic Himalayan mountains of Meru and Kailasa. Now a protected national park, Phnom Kulen was a very holy place, indeed.

It was here, according to the SKT text, that the founding event of the Khmer Empire took place. In AD 802, Jayavarman II, who had probably settled on Mahendraparvata to escape his many enemies, was declared *chakravartin*, 'universal monarch', in a rite conducted by a Brahmin priest. Here is what the Khmer-language text says:

> Then H. M. Parameshvara [Jayavarman] went to reign at Mahendraparavata… Then a Brahmin named Hiranyadarma, wise in magic science, came from Janapada, for H. M. Parameshvara had invited him to conduct a ritual so that Kambujadesa [Cambodia] would not be dependant any more on Java and that he would be a sovereign *chakravartin*.[4]

But while the Brahmin was in effect crowning the king, his *purohita* Shivakaivalya was conducting a parallel rite for the supernatural being known in Khmer as the *kamraten jagat ta raja* (*devaraja* in Sanskrit), 'the god who is king'. Contrary to generally accepted opinion, Jacques makes clear that this was definitely *not* the mortal sovereign, nor even an image or *linga* of the god Shiva, but a special type of incorporeal Cambodian protective deity; perhaps it even partook of the essence of the localized, ancestral fertility spirits, the *anak ta* or *neak ta*, that predate the Indianization of Khmer culture.[5] In this sense the 'god who is king' would have been the supreme *anak ta* of Cambodia.

Dynastic succession in Cambodia

Accession to kingship in ancient and even modern Cambodia has always been a perplexing subject for foreign observers, as it seldom follows rules familiar to Westerners. A recent study by Michael Vickery has shown why this is so.[6] In the first place, the genealogies that we have in the inscriptions, mainly of the Classic period, are complex and partly faked. Secondly, in Vickery's analysis, the royal houses of Cambodia formed 'conical clans', defined as clans in which all members are ranked hierarchically in terms of their relationship to the common ancestor, real or putative, who may merge with a god. This is suggested by the practice, from Early Kingdoms times, of ranking gods and earthly chiefs in a single hierarchy, and of constructing genealogical pyramids. The consequences of such an organization are:

• When such a clan becomes a state apparatus, state offices are distributed according to clan rank, and the highest-ranking member becomes king.

• Succession is not necessarily from father to son. For royalty and the aristocracy, descent is 'ambilateral': it may be counted through females, as well as males.
• Very often the rules prescribe that kingship passes through individuals of the same generation before descending to the next.
• The system may be very unstable, with various branches attempting to pass the kingship from father to son, instead of relinquishing it to the next branch.

Much of the dynastic turmoil of Cambodian history, including bloody fratricidal wars, has been the result of this seemingly chaotic system. In its mitigation, one must point out that it must have ensured a high level of competence in those who finally achieved the throne. Finally, as we know from the modern history of the Cambodian royal house, the practise of polygamy has created further problems in the succession, as princes with a single father but different mothers compete among themselves for the throne.

Where exactly on Phnom Kulen did this pivotal double rite take place? The evidence points to a concentration of about seventeen temples in the southeastern part of the plateau that are largely built of brick and that date to Jayavarman II's time. At their centre is a very plain, three-tiered temple-pyramid constructed of laterite blocks, known as Prasat Rong Chen, accessed by recessed stairs on the east and west.[7] Now about 10 m (30 ft) high, it was once topped by a brick sanctuary that housed a *linga* set on a cruciform stone base. In spite of its simplicity, this structure is believed by most authorities to have been where the founder took over the reigns of a new empire – only two years after his European counterpart, Charlemagne, had been crowned Holy Roman Emperor. The SKT stela continues the story thus:

> Then H. M. Parameshvara returned to reign in the city of Hariharalaya, and the *kamraten añ ta raja* [the 'god who is king'] went there also.[8]

Hariharalaya: a proto-Angkor

Modern tourists on a visit to Angkor of more than a day or two are usually taken first to a cluster of three early temple complexes near the village of Roluos, about 10 km (6 miles) east of Siem Reap, on the flat plane to the north of the Great Lake. It was here that Jayavarman II descended from his mountain and established his imperial capital at Hariharalaya, named for Harihara, the combined godhead of Shiva and Vishnu; and it was here that the great warrior-sovereign died, in about AD 835.[9]

The king was succeeded by his son Jayavarman III, who began the building of shrines in Hariharalaya, but whose achievements were hugely overshadowed by that of *his* successor Indravarman I, one of the truly great Khmer rulers, who acceded to the throne in 877 and died *c.* 889. This man was not, as one might expect, the son of a king, but probably the nephew of Jayavarman II's queen.

The mini-city of Hariharalaya ('the Roluos Group') is almost entirely a creation of Indravarman's decade-long reign, and established norms that were to guide architects and urban planners throughout the Classic Angkor period. His most astonishing feat, begun five days after his coronation rite, was the construction of an immense rectangular water-catchment basin or *baray* known as the Indratataka or 'Sea of Indra'. Some 3.8 km (2.3 miles) long and 800 m (2,625 ft) wide, at least when the earthen dyke on its north side was finished, the Indratataka could have held 7.5 million cubic metres of water at the height of the monsoon season. Nothing like this had ever been seen before in the land of the Khmer. But, as we shall see, there is still a debate about just what all this water was for.

Like most subsequent Khmer rulers, Indravarman built both an ancestral temple and a state temple within his capital, Hariharalaya. The first is known today as the Preah Ko ('Sacred Bull', named for the kneeling stone image of Nandin, Shiva's mount, found within its precinct). Consecrated to the gods in 880, and placed on an enclosed terrace of laterite, Preah Ko's six brick-built towers were dedicated to the memory of Indravarman's parents, maternal ancestors, and the dynasty's founder Jayavarman II and his wife. These were represented by statues of various forms of Shiva and his consorts, the gods representing the deified ancestors. Preah Ko, incidentally, is celebrated for the beauty of its male guardian figures (*dvarapala*) and female divinities (*devata*), and for the graceful qualities of the sandstone lintels, their supporting colonettes, and the 'false doors' that embellish these towers.

It is not unlikely that Indravarman's wood-built palace stood within Preah Ko's precinct, but his state temple – Bakong – lay just to the south of Preah Ko. This stepped pyramid is truly a major public work, placed within a massive double moat – in many respects, the precursor of Angkor Wat and Angkor Thom, the great royal complexes of later centuries. Symbolically this was a temple-mountain, the earthly version of Mount Meru, the abode of the gods. In an innovation, the 'mountain' is faced with sandstone quarried on Phnom Kulen, but the eight towers that surround it are still built from brick and

40

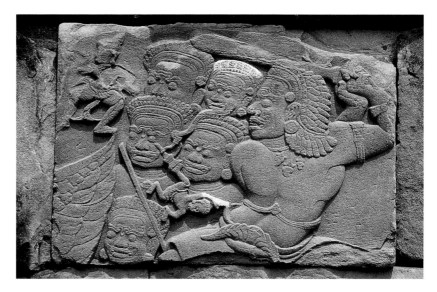

40 Fragment of sandstone relief from the Bakong, the state temple of Indravarman I in Hariharalaya ('Roluos Group'). Ninth century. A group of *asuras* (demons) is engaged in battle; a battle standard has been broken. The style shows strong Javanese influence.

embellished with stucco. The stone tower atop the pyramid is perhaps a later reconstruction of the original dating to the time of Suryavarman II, but both it and its predecessor would have housed a stone *linga* emblematic of Shiva, and the main entrance is to the east, the sacred direction of that royal divinity. Within Bakong's moats, one can imagine many other buildings thronged with religious specialists, and even today a large and active Theravada Buddhist establishment with school and devotional halls remains within the precinct.

How extensive was the domain of Indravarman I? The only evidence bearing on this comes from inscriptions, but it surely reached the foothills of the Dangreks and across into Khorat (at a site near modern Ubon in the Mun Valley of northeast Thailand, a pious Buddhist invoked the king's name in the year 886).[10] Indravarman was a pivotal figure in Khmer history, and fully deserved the epithets that were heaped upon him: 'lion among kings', 'prince endowed with all the merits', and so forth.

The 'Glory-bearing City': the founding of Angkor

With the death of Indravarman, a period of armed conflict ensued, sparked by a struggle for succession that apparently involved two of his sons; Jacques believes that there were even naval battles on the Great Lake.[11] In all events, the victor was Yashovardhana, who took the name of Yashovarman ('protected by glory') at his coronation in 889 or 890. Yashovarman I's first act was to build 100 *ashramas* (hermitages or ascetic retreats) throughout his domain; since these were constructed of wood, they have all perished, only the associated inscribed stelae remaining. But these probably give a good account of the extent of the Khmer Empire in those days, for they are found from all across Cambodia, north to Phnom Rung in Khorat, and northeast to Wat Phu in Champassak.

His next act was to embellish his father's capital of Hariharalaya, finally completely enclosing the Indratataka Baray, and constructing a large ancestral temple, Lolei, on an island (*mebon*) in the midst of this huge, artificial lake, now largely silted up. The Lolei temple consists of four impressive   pl. v
brick towers placed on a brick platform, itself located within a laterite enclosure. According to the beautiful texts incised on its sandstone doorjambs,   41
Lolei was dedicated to the spirit of his father Indravarman as personified by the god Shiva. Next, Yashovarman I took a step that in its significance for the history of Southeast Asia rivals the famous declaration of Jayavarman II on Phnom Kulen. He made the decision to transfer the capital of the Khmer Empire northwest from Hariharalaya to Angkor proper, where it remained (with one brief lapse) for over five centuries. There were probably several compelling reasons for this move – economic, sociopolitical, military, and probably religious (undoubtedly he was advised by Brahmin gurus about where and when this should take place), but suffice it to say that the Angkor region is strategically located about halfway between the hills of Kulen and the margins of the Great Lake, on the right bank of the Siem Reap River – not only an abundant source of water for whatever hydraulic schemes the ruler might be contemplating, but also a waterway as holy to the Khmer as the Ganges was and still is to Indians.

41 Sandstone lintel in the Lolei temple complex, Hariharalaya. Ninth century. A *garuda* grasps a vegetal scroll ending in *naga* heads; above, rampant lions alternate with seated ascetics.

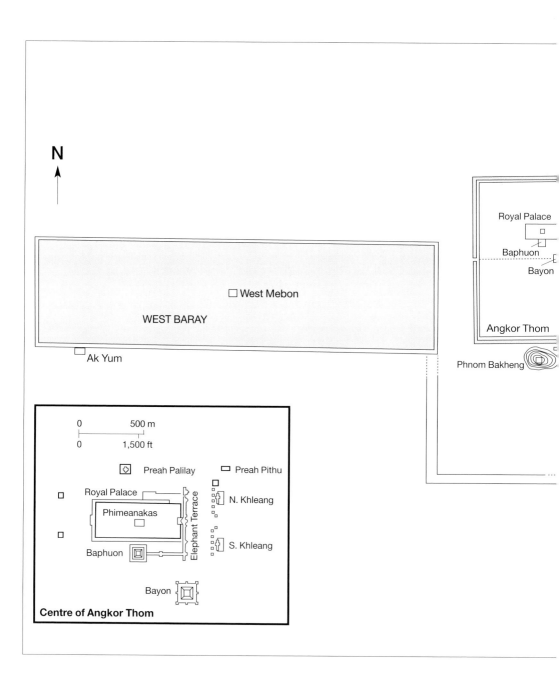

N

Royal Palace

Baphuon

Bayon

West Mebon

WEST BARAY

Angkor Thom

Ak Yum

Phnom Bakheng

0   500 m

0   1,500 ft

Preah Palilay   Preah Pithu

Royal Palace   N. Khleang

Phimeanakas

Baphuon   S. Khleang

Elephant Terrace

Bayon

Centre of Angkor Thom

42 Map of Angkor, showing the two great reservoirs (*barays*) either side of the central Angkor Thom and Angkor Wat.

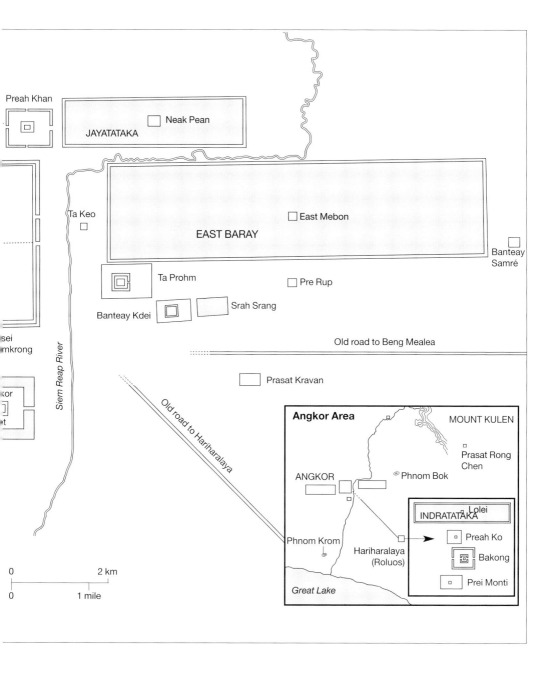

Preah Khan

JAYATATAKA
Neak Pean

Ta Keo

EAST BARAY
East Mebon

Banteay
Samré

Ta Prohm
Pre Rup

Banteay Kdei
Srah Srang

sei
mkrong

Siem Reap River

kor
t

Old road to Beng Mealea

Prasat Kravan

Old road to Hariharalaya

Angkor Area

MOUNT KULEN

Prasat Rong
Chen

ANGKOR
Phnom Bok

Lolei
INDRATATAKA

Preah Ko

Phnom Krom

Hariharalaya
(Roluos)
Bakong

Prei Monti

Great Lake

0   2 km

0   1 mile

But geomancy may have had as much to do with Yashovarman's siting of his city – Yashodharapura, 'Glory-bearing City' – as anything else. He chose to make its centre Phnom Bakheng, a 67-m (220-ft) high hill with ovoid outline and an artificially flattened top. On this prominence he constructed his state temple, making this a new Mount Meru. Standing on the summit of Phnom Bakheng and looking 14 km (8.4 miles) northeast by east, the king could make out the Shivaite temple complex that he had constructed atop the 235-m (771-ft) high Phnom Bok; this was crowned with a gigantic, 4-m (13-ft) high *linga*. And, continuing in exactly the same line of sight, from Phnom Bok could be seen Prasat Rong Chen on Phnom Kulen, the temple-mountain on which the empire had been founded.[12]

The Bakheng temple, seemingly dedicated in 907, is more complex than any that had heretofore been attempted in the country of the Khmer.[13] Within a walled enclosure is a five-tiered, stepped pyramid supporting a summit platform on which rest five stone towers in the form of a quincunx, a mandala echoing the appearance of the golden peaks on Mount Meru; within the shrine at the centre of the quincunx was the *linga* of the god Shiva in the guise of Yashodhareshvara, 'the Lord of the one who bears glory'. A large number of smaller shrines are arranged geometrically on and around the structure's tiers,

43 Air view of Phnom Bakheng, looking east. Beginning of the tenth century. The five shrines on the summit are arranged in quincunx, replicating the five peaks of the mythical Mount Meru in the Himalayas. The whole temple-mountain lay in the exact centre of Yashodharapura, Yashovarman I's capital city.

making a total of 108, a magic number in Hindu thought. The entire Phnom
Bakheng complex was approached from the east by officiants of the cult, who
would have passed two stone guardian lions at the foot of the hill, and after
their ascent walked between two 'libraries' to the foot of the pyramid itself.

A word should be said about the so-called 'libraries', which become a characteristic feature of Khmer religious complexes, and are prominent in later
monuments like Angkor Wat. According to art historian Hedwige Multzer   pl. VIII
o'Naghten, the evidence that small, usually paired structures of this type
ever housed manuscripts is slight.[14] They may have done so, but on the testimony of iconographic and epigraphic data, their principal function seems to
have been two-fold: 1) as the location of a fire cult devoted to Agni, the Fire
God of the Vedic tradition, and 2) the worship of the 'Nine Planets', com-
prising the Sun and Moon, Rahu (an eclipse deity), Ketu (god of all comets
and meteors), along with either the five visible planets or the directional gods.

Each of the major *chakravartin* who ruled the Khmer Empire felt it necessary to build an important public waterworks, an ancestral temple, and a state
temple, usually in that order.[15] Yashovarman followed in this tradition. Even
before the construction of Lolei and Bakheng, he ordered the digging of a
reservoir, this time on an almost cosmic scale. This waterworks was the
Yashodharatataka or East Baray, to the northeast of the great, square capital,
7.5 km (4.7 miles) long by 1.8 km (1.1 miles) wide, eight times larger than the
Indratataka Baray. Claude Jacques and Michael Freeman estimate that it
would have taken 6 million man-days to build its embankments alone.[16]
According to them, it was placed by the king under the protection of the goddess Ganga (logically, since it was fed by the Siem Reap River), and managed
by the abbots of four *ashramas* located south of the *baray*, facts that have to be
taken under consideration when facing the problem of the use to which these
huge waterworks were put (see Chapter 7). Today, the East Baray is totally
dry and devoted to rain-fed, rice-paddy cultivation.

Interlude at Koh Ker

The great Yashovarman died in about AD 900, to be succeeded by his son
Harshavarman I. When Harshavarman ('protected by joy') passed on 23
years later, his brother Ishanavarman II took the throne. As Lawrence Briggs
so nicely put it, 'both of these kings received their full mead of praise in the
inscriptions'. Here is one such text:

> He [Yashovarman I] had a well-beloved son, Sri Rudraloka [Har-
> shavarman I], who caused the joy of the universe and whose feet
> were lighted by the splendour of the garlands of rubies covering
> the diadems of the kings of the four cardinal points. Clever at arms,
> resplendent with glory, [firm as a] pillar in meditation, active to
> serve others, endowed with a powerful energy, closed to evil.
>
> Then his younger brother…, victorious, surpassing Kama [the
> god of love] by his beauty, dissipating the fogs, possessing all the
> talents, was a moon among kings.[17]

While little is known of the latter's brief kingship, to the reign of Harshavarman are credited two magnificent structures in Angkor. One of these is Baksei Chamkrong, a small but lovely temple-pyramid immediately northeast of Phnom Bakheng. The other is Prasat Kravan ('the cardamom sanctuary'), a three-towered, brick-built temple dedicated to the god Vishnu and sensitively restored by B.-P. Groslier. Carved into the brick surface of its interior walls are reliefs of Vishnu on his mount Garuda, Vishnu in his dwarf avatar taking three strides to create the world, and representations of his consort Lakshmi.

pl. VII

The next *chakravartin*, Jayavarman IV (reigned *c*. 928–41), caused a sudden downturn in the fortunes of Yashodharapura, the imperial city. For still unknown reasons this ruler decided to transfer the capital from Angkor to Koh Ker (Chok Gargyar), some 90 km (56 miles) to the northeast.[18] Although Koh Ker is situated in a relatively poor region of Cambodia, lying not far southeast of the city were uplands rich in iron and copper ores, and even gold. Now reached only by very primitive roads and still somewhat dangerous to visit because of old land mines, Koh Ker is distinguished by its state temple: Prasat Thom, an impressive, seven-storey, stepped pyramid that once had an enormous *linga* on its summit, set within a now-ruined Shivaite shrine. To the east of the pyramid are the remains of Jayavarman's extensive, moated palace, and to the south the Rahal Baray, a tank 1,200 m (3,940 ft) long and 560 m (1,840 ft) wide, laboriously cut from the living stone.

Yet what really distinguishes Koh Ker is the large number of magnificent freestanding statues found by the École Française d'Extrême-Orient

44 Massive limestone statue of fighting monkey-men, from Koh Ker (National Museum of Phnom Penh). These are the two monkey brothers, Sugriva and Valin, who were generals in the *Ramayana*. Their rivalry eventually resulted in the death of Valin. Classic period, second quarter of the tenth century. Ht 1.94 m (6.7 ft).

(EFEO) in its ruins. The sculptors of Koh Ker had easy access to high quality sandstone, and were able to create works of art of a monumentality and sense of movement seldom seen in other epochs. Many of the greatest masterpieces seen in public collections in Cambodia and abroad, such as the renowned statue of fighting ape-men, were their work.[19]

44

Disruption and rebirth

Three or four years of imperial disintegration followed the death of Jayavarman IV in 941, as one after another king broke away from the central administration during the weak reign of Harshavarman II; this was a period during which no major monuments appeared in either Cambodia or Khorat. A major turnabout took place with the accession of Rajendravarman II in 944, who wisely and probably forcefully returned the capital to Yashodharapura (Angkor). As one inscription has it:

> He restored the holy city of Yashodharapura, long deserted, and rendered it superb and charming by erecting there houses ornamented with shining gold, palaces glittering with precious stones, like the palace of Mahendra [Indra] on earth.[20]

The Khmer Empire was reborn as its ruler Rajendravarman ('protected by the king's Indra') brought back all the various breakaway kingdoms under the imperial sway. However, the administrative centre of *his* capital was to be centred not in the area around Phnom Bakheng, but south of the East Baray, where he dedicated Pre Rup – the state temple – in 961; this was a Shivaite complex built of brick and sandstone, in the classic quincunx form.[21] Its near twin, the East Mebon (also consecrated to Shiva), was constructed directly north of Pre Rup on an island in the midst of this great *baray*. Rajendravarman, while tolerant of the cult of the Hindu gods, was a devout Mahayana Buddhist, and to him is credited the small Buddhist temple of Bat Chum. But the truly great Buddhist foundations were not to appear at Angkor for another three centuries.

Quite clearly Rajendravarman regarded the old Baksei Chamkrong as his ancestral temple, for only four years after his accession he restored this elegant temple-pyramid and placed a golden statue of Parameshvara (Shiva) in the shrine on its summit. The lovely calligraphic inscriptions that he caused to incise on the temple's doorjambs invoke the spirits of all previous Khmer kings, including the hermit Kambu, mythic ancestor of the Kambuja or Cambodians (see Chapter 3). Present-day tourists will also note traces of graffiti in black ink on these jambs, left by Japanese or Chinese pilgrims who visited the shrine during the seventeenth century.

These temples are all impressive achievements, but few ancient monuments anywhere in the world can match the breathtaking beauty and elegance of the renowned complex of Banteay Srei, begun towards the end of Rajendravarman's reign, but not dedicated until shortly after his death in 968.

pls II–IV

Banteay Srei

Many modern visitors to Cambodia (this author included) consider Banteay Srei (the so-called 'Citadel of Women') to be the highest achievement in art and architecture of the Classic Angkor civilization.[22] This relatively tiny temple complex is situated 23 km (14 miles) northeast of Phnom Bakheng – not far from the western end of Phnom Kulen, where the very hard, reddish sandstone used in its buildings, pediments and sculptures was quarried. Also within convenient distance was the largest ancient laterite quarry ever discovered. In 1923, Banteay Srei was the target of a meticulously planned but ultimately unsuccessful looting expedition by the famous French author and intellectual André Malraux. Not long after, it was restored by the EFEO using the then-new technique of *anastylosis*.

It was commissioned by the Brahmin *guru* Yajñavaraha, a grandson of Harshavarman I and tutor to the crown prince. He must have been a man of immense taste and knowledge. Like all Shivaite temples, Banteay Srei is approached from the east by a causeway; passing through a *gopura*, one crosses the moat surrounding the main part of the complex. On this island are wonderfully ornate shrines and two 'libraries'. Within the central shrine was the principal cult object, the *linga* known as 'the Great Lord of Three Worlds'. Everything here is in miniature: all of the doors of the shrines and other buildings are only 1.30 m (4.25 ft) high.

The glory of Banteay Srei is the beauty of its sculpture and decoration. Youthful guardian figures (*dvarapala*) and lovely young goddesses (*devata*) are carved in three-quarter relief on door flanks and exterior walls. Above the doors and false doors are pediments and

45   Perspective reconstruction of Banteay Srei, looking northeast. This diminutive but most beautiful of all Classic temple complexes was dedicated in AD 967 to the god Shiva, and stayed in use for almost three centuries.

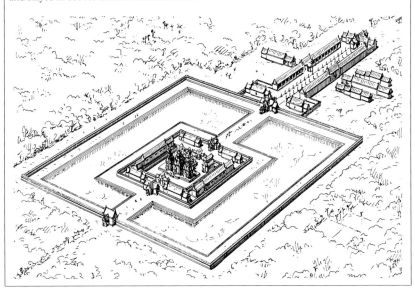

lintels with intricately carved scenes taken from the epics and Puranas, for example the ogre-King Ravana shaking Mount Kailasa to disturb the mediations of Shiva; or the same villainous god stealing Rama's wife Sita; or Krishna killing his evil uncle Kama. All of these display an intimate and extraordinarily extensive familiarity with all the myriad details of Hindu religion, mythology and literature. While these sculptures could never be mistaken for supposed 'prototypes' in mainland South Asia, they are by no means the production of a provincial or marginal tradition. As art historian Thierry Zéphir has said, 'The art created at Banteay Srei at the instigation of Yajñavaraha, the temple's founder, constitutes one of the major contributions of Khmer art to the artistic heritage of the world.'[23]

46 Façade of sanctuary in Group I, Banteay Srei. Classic period, AD 967. Built in roseate sandstone, this miniature temple is richly embellished with Hindu-inspired carvings.

The next ruler, Jayavarman V, was a pious Buddhist like his father Rajendravarman, whom he succeeded following his death, yet he still payed homage to Shiva and Vishnu, for Mahayanism is a remarkably tolerant, syncretic faith. This particular Jayavarman is noted for the construction of his state temple, Ta Keo, near the west bank of the East Baray. A massive, sandstone temple-pyramid some 22 m (72 ft) high, with summit shrines laid out in the standard quincunx pattern, Ta Keo has a somewhat forbidding aspect since (according to a perhaps fictitious story contained in an inscription) it had suffered an inauspicious lightning strike during its construction, and thus was never completed. It certainly does have very little decoration. Jayavarman V passed away about AD 1000; here ended a long and remarkably peaceful epoch of Angkorian history, as well as the ascendancy of his own family. In 1001, a transient ruler named Udayadityavarman I took power, but he probably had only one year in office; in the words of Louis Finot, Udayadityavarman ('protected by the rising Sun') was 'a phantom of a king, who flitted across the throne'. What ensued was one more period of turbulence, violence and a mighty struggle for the supreme throne among rival kings.

'Protected by the Sun': the triumph of Suryavarman

The principal contenders to become *chakravartin*, 'universal monarch', were two rival princes, Jayaviravarman and Suryavarman ('protected by the Sun'), who each controlled part of the empire, the former based in Angkor, and the latter in eastern Cambodia. Within the space of nine years of what must have been a very bloody struggle, Suryavarman I had triumphed. In 1011, having subdued the entire empire, he called 4,000 of his officials to the capital to swear an oath of allegiance, sealed with blood. The ultimate sanction for breaking it was to be 'reborn in the thirty-second hell as long as the sun and the moon shall last' – the first recorded instance of a loyalty oath that was still being sworn in the Cambodian royal palace in the twentieth century.[24]

During his long reign (until 1049), Suryavarman I proved to be one of Classic Angkor's greatest builders and innovators, as well as an outstanding military leader. The Royal Palace, and the 6-m (20-ft) high laterite walls that enclose it, were largely his creation. This huge complex – 600 by 250 m (1,968 by 820 ft) on a side – remained the centre of the imperial administration for centuries after, a Khmer version of Rome's Palatine Hill. Within its walls Suryavarman built the Phimeanakas, his relatively modest state temple, famed for a probably legendary story recounted by Zhou Daguan at the end of the thirteenth century. According to Zhou, a nine-headed *naga* snake-woman dwelt in its golden tower, and every night the king mounted there to sleep with her – an improbable scenario that recalls the female *naga* origin myth described in Chapter 3.

Among his other public works in Angkor, perhaps the most stupendous is the West Baray, a perfectly rectangular, east–west reservoir no less than 8 km (5 miles) long and 2.2 km (1.4 miles) wide. Today partly silted up on its eastern end, it once held an estimated 48 million cubic metres of water; it is so huge that it can be seen from outer space. The function or functions of this

pl. XVI

pl. I

and the other waterworks of Classic Angkor will be handled in the following chapter.

Lawrence Briggs once called Preah Vihear 'the most remarkable site of any large temple of Indo-China'.[25] The construction of this magnificent Shivaite sanctuary began about 893, and several later rulers altered and embellished it. But according to abundant inscriptions, Preah Vihear as we see it is largely the work of Suryavarman I. It lies right on the escarpment of the Dangrek Range that divides the Khorat Plateau from the lowland Cambodian Plain to the south, on the edge of a triangular promontory. On a clear day, one may see all the way to Phnom Kulen. The sanctuary is stretched out over 800 m (2,625 ft) in successive courts, connected by causeways; as one proceeds towards the south, one gradually rises up via connecting stairs and causeways, passing through a succession of *gopuras* or entrance pavilions, until reaching the final shrine, on the edge of a 500-m (1,640-ft) drop to the plain below. Ironically, the builders of Preah Vihear turned their backs on the stupendous view, since the final building is essentially blind.

Suryavarman greatly extended the empire's frontiers, subduing not only southern Laos to the northeast, but to the northwest the city of Louvo or Lavo (modern Lopburi in the Chao Phraya River Valley of Thailand). In fact, Louvo became an important Khmer provincial capital for this and subsequent reigns, until finally overwhelmed by Thai incursions in later centuries.

On the death of Suryavarman I in 1049, he received the posthumous name of Nirvanapada, 'the king who has gone to Nirvana'. This does not, however, imply that he was a Mahayana Buddhist at heart, for he was a thoroughgoing Shivaite throughout his reign, endowing many temples to that god.

47

pl. VI

47 Aerial perspective of Preah Vihear. This Shivaite temple complex, spectacularly located on the edge of the Dangrek escarpment on the Cambodian-Thai border, was built over a period of three centuries beginning in AD 893.

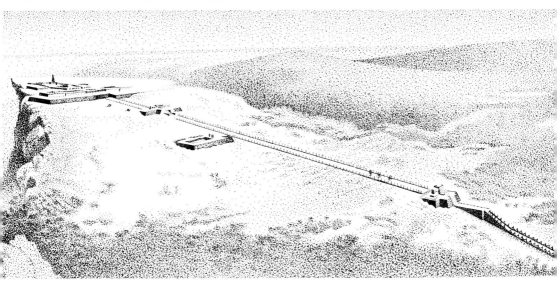

The Baphuon and the building of Phimai

During the reign of the next *chakravartin*, Udayadityavarman II (1050–66), territorial revolts occurred once again, as they were to do throughout so much of Cambodia's war-torn history. This time the major revolt was put down by the monarch's loyal war leader Sangrama, who killed the insurgent general in a single combat carried out with bow and arrow. Udayadityavarman II is fulsomely described in one inscription:

> He excelled in seducing women to his will by his beauty, warriors by his heroism, sages by his good qualities, the people by his power, Brahmins by his charity.[26]

One of Angkor's most impressive temple-pyramids – the state temple known as the Baphuon – was erected during his tenure, but suffered massive alterations at the end of the fifteenth century when it was extensively reworked into a Theravada Buddhist sanctuary. Located immediately south of the Royal Palace enclosure, the Baphuon is distinguished by a large number of lively relief carvings that mainly depict scenes from the *Mahabharata* and *Ramayana* epics. Its modern history has been equally unfortunate.[27] Due to faulty construction techniques, the building collapsed during the monsoon season of 1943. After the Second World War the EFEO authorities, directed by B.-P. Groslier, dismantled it with the intention of rebuilding it from scratch, but the Khmer Rouge put an end to these works, and the temple fell into even worse disrepair. The current EFEO restoration programme is expected to be completed in 2004.[28]

Udayadityavarman's other grand project was the raising of the dykes around his predecessor's West Baray, and the building of an island temple – the West Mebon – in its midst. Above the surface of the waters contained within this structure was a colossal, reclining bronze statue of the god Vishnu, depicted at the moment when the present universe was created. Probably seen by the Chinese traveller Zhou Daguan over two centuries later,[29] the upper half of this astonishing work of art was discovered and excavated in 1936 by EFEO archaeologists. Incidentally, the celebrated Sdok Kak Thom (SKT) stela was written for the glory of Udayadityavarman II's *purohita*.

The year AD 1066 may mark the Norman Conquest of England for Westerners, but for the Cambodians it was the year when Udayadityavarman II died

48

48 Colossal bronze image of the god Vishnu, from the West Mebon, in the centre of Angkor's West Baray. This is a fragment of one of the largest bronze figures ever cast in Southeast Asia, a statue that was mentioned by Zhou Daguan. It depicts the reclining deity in the moment of world-creation; depressions on the face probably once held silver or gold inlays. Second half of eleventh century. Ht 122 cm, width 222 cm.

49 The temple of Phimai, in Thailand's Khorat Plateau, view from the southwest. Late eleventh to late twelfth centuries. This great centre on the upper Mun River was connected to Angkor by a major highway. Its main tower closely resembles the towers of Angkor Wat.

and the power passed to his brother Harshavarman III. Little is known about the latter's fourteen-year reign, but again it was a time of internal disruption, and apparently also of a defeat by that long-time enemy of the Khmer, the Cham (of whom more later). Of far greater significance than this king was his successor Jayavarman VI (1080–1107), who seems to have earlier been a vassal prince native to the Mun Valley of the Khorat Plateau, and who had apparently led a revolt against Harshavarman. In Angkor itself, this Jayavarman accomplished little more than the embellishment of the Royal Palace, but in his native Khorat he was largely responsible for one of the greatest temple sites in Southeast Asia: Phimai, the ancient Vimayapura, in the upper reaches of the Mun River.

Occupied fairly continuously since the Iron Age, by the time of Jayavarman VI Phimai had become a small, planned, rectangular city (later enclosed by a laterite wall dating from the time of Jayavarman VII and by an outer moat), and crisscrossed by a network of avenues and streets that is still detectable on aerial photographs. So important was this provincial city to the empire that it was connected to Angkor by one of the greatest roads of antiquity, a highway that ran about 300 km (180 miles) southeast to the imperial capital.[30]

Beautifully restored by Thailand's Fine Arts Department, the Phimai temple complex lies along the city's north–south axis, and – unusually for a Khmer sanctuary – faces south. There are two concentric temple enclosures, each with cruciform *gopuras* (entrance pavilions) placed at the cardinal points; the main one on the south is reached across a 'bridge' of rearing stone *nagas*. The central sanctuary, built from a pinkish sandstone, is dominated by a pineapple-shaped tower that must have inspired similar architecture at Angkor Wat, and was to be adapted in the *prangs* or towers of far later Thai sacred structures. Jayavarman VI was clearly a Buddhist, and although some of the lintels and other details of Phimai exhibit Hindu iconography, others are patently

49

Mahayana Buddhist in content; at its very centre was a figure of the Buddha in meditation, seated beneath the protective hood of a *naga*.

Analysis of data obtained in 1996 by an AIRSAR (Airborne Synthetic Aperture Radar) flight over Phimai revealed that a very large *baray* once existed to the south of the ancient city, aligned exactly with Phimai's urban plan.[31] Like the similar reservoirs at Angkor, it had an island in its middle, topped by a temple.

Suryavarman II, builder of Angkor Wat

In AD 1113 Suryavarman II came to the throne through force of arms, overthrowing his great-uncle, the aged ruler Dharanindravarman I, an elder brother of Jayavarman VI. There can be little doubt that he was one of the greatest Khmer rulers, for to him is ascribed the largest and one of the most magnificent religious structures of all time, the world-renowned Angkor Wat, begun in his reign but not completed until after his death in about 1150 (see special section).[32] Here is a partial list of his other accomplishments:

pl. VIII
50, 51

- In AD 1116, Suryavarman II re-established diplomatic relations with China, according to the Chinese historian Ma Duan-lin, and in 1128 was recognized as a 'vassal' by the emperor of the Middle Kingdom.
- During 1144–45, he invaded Champa, defeated the Cham king, and captured and sacked the capital, Vijaya.
- He extended the Khmer Empire to dominate the Khorat Plateau as far as Lopburi, and even further north in Thailand; to the borders of Pagan in Myanmar; and south into the northern part of the Malay Peninsula.
- The construction of Beng Mealea, a huge and yet little-known complex about 40 km (24 miles) east of Angkor; situated near the base of Phnom Kulen, it may have been the prototype (along with Phimai) for AngkorWat.
- The final form of the Shivaite temple of Phnom Rung, in southern Khorat on the royal road between Phimai and Angkor. It was built under the patronage of the local ruler and military leader, a relative of Suryavarman. Spectacularly situated atop a small, extinct volcano, Phnom Rung's sanctuary is reached by ascending a series of causeways, stairs, and *naga* bridges.[33]
- Banteay Samre, a Vishnuite temple with enclosure near the southeast corner of Angkor's East Baray.

While justly famed for the building programme that he sponsored, it is apparent that his military campaigns in Vietnam laid the groundwork for the troubles that later came close to destroying the empire. Between 1123 and 1136, Suryavarman attacked the Dai Viet of northern Vietnam over and over by land and by sea, but he was no more successful in overwhelming them than the Chinese had been. His hold over Champa was always shaky, and merely confirmed the long-standing enmity between the Khmer and the Cham. Eventually, these latter were to have their revenge.

As we know from Angkor Wat, Suryavarman was a thoroughgoing devotee of Vishnu: on his death around 1150 he received the posthumous name of Paramavishnuloka, 'who has rejoined the realm of the supreme Vishnu'.

Angkor Wat

Situated in the southeastern quadrant of Yashovarman I's city, Angkor Wat is surrounded by a 200-m (656-ft) wide moat; bordered by sandstone blocks, the moat measures 1,500 m (4,922 ft) from west to east, and 1,500 m (4,265 ft) from north to south. On the approximately square 'island' bounded by this water, Angkor Wat itself covers about 21 hectares (500 acres), and is bounded by a laterite wall. As a masterpiece of monumental architecture and planning, it is only approached in magnificence and perspective by Beijing's Forbidden City, and by Bernini's colonnade facing St Peter's in Rome.[34]

The complex consists of a series of concentric, rectangular enclosures, covered galleries or terraces, with open courts between, tied together by cruciform galleries. The main entrance is from the west, by a wide causeway built from massive sandstone blocks. Crossing a cruciform terrace (apparently a rather late addition to the complex), one ascends a staircase and passes through the outermost of three successively higher galleries or enclosures. This is the Third Gallery, renowned for its bas-reliefs. Eventually one rises by stone steps to the highest level – this is the heart of the complex, the great, conical towers laid out in quincunx, an earthly reflection of the five heavenly peaks of Mount Meru. The central tower or shrine was the abode of the god Vishnu, for Angkor Wat was thoroughly Vishnuite before it was converted into a Buddhist temple (*wat*) during Angkor's latter days; it once contained a statue of the god, but this has never been found.

It had long been the custom in Cambodia to place an offering deposit of gold leaf and small jewels in a pit below the image of the god to whom a particular temple was dedicated, but many of these deposits have been looted over the centuries. However, in 1934, EFEO archaeologists discovered a laterite slab with a cavity

50
pl. VIII
pl. IX

50 Plan of Angkor Wat.

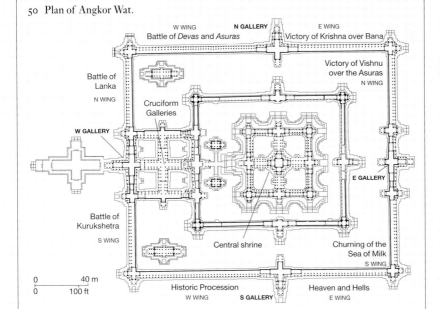

51 Angkor Wat, seen from the west. First half of the twelfth century. This temple complex was dedicated to the worship of Vishnu. In the Third Gallery, seen below the five central towers, are the famous bas-reliefs depicting mythological and civic scenes.

containing two pieces of crystal and two gold leaves far beneath where the Vishnu statue must have been – here as elsewhere it was deposits such as these that spiritually 'energized' a temple, much as a battery will provide power to a portable electronic device.

Most of the bas-reliefs of the Third Gallery are of the greatest beauty, excepting those along the gallery's northeast angle, which are poorly executed productions of the sixteenth century. Not counting the reliefs in the corner pavilions, they extend almost 700 m (about 2,300 ft) and measure about 2 m (about 6.6 ft) high, the longest continuous bas-reliefs in the world. There are literally thousands of figures drawn from the Hindu epics, the Puranas, and courtly and military life in the days of Suryavarman II. Here are the main themes:

- The Battle of Kurukshetra, as recounted in the *Mahabharata* – the epic struggle between the Pandavas and their cousins the Kauravas.
- A historic procession overseen by

Suryavarman, who is labelled with his posthumous name of Paramavishnuloka. This includes state ministers, Brahmins, ladies of the royal palace, and a military parade of cavalry, infantry and commanders mounted on war elephants (including the king), as well as Thai mercenaries.
- The Heavens and the Hells, with torture of sinners in the land of Yama (God of Death).
- Churning of the Sea of Milk. This, a chapter in the Hindu story of Creation, is one of the masterpieces of Khmer art. It describes how the *devas* (gods) and the *asuras* (demons) churned the ocean under the aegis of Vishnu, to produce the divine elixir of immortality.
- Victory of Vishnu over the *asuras*. This is one of the late reliefs.
- Victory of Krishna over the *asura* Bana (another late production).
- Battle between the *devas* and the *asuras*, with the 21 gods of the Hindu pantheon, on their respective mounts.

52 View east down a gallery of Angkor Wat. To the left of this corbel-roofed colonnade is the great processional relief of Suryavarman II. At the base of each column are seated *rishis* or holy men.

- The Battle of Lanka, from the *Ramayana*, with the victory of Rama's monkey army over the demon king, Ravana. This theme is also found in the corner pavilions.

Apsaras or celestial nymphs were also produced by the Churning of the Sea of Milk, and over 1,800 of them are carved into the walls of Angkor Wat; they give a good idea of the beauty, dress and ornament of the myriad dancers, concubines and other young women who lived at Suryavarman's court. Almost no part of the monument is without repetitive decoration, much of it lightly spread 54
55

53 Suryavarman II giving orders to his ministers, from the western wing of the southern gallery of the reliefs in Angkor Wat. The king is seated on a low throne covered with rugs, and surrounded by courtiers bearing umbrellas, fans and fly whisks.

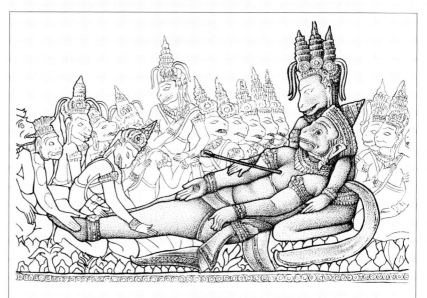

54 Valin dying in the arms of his wife, detail of a relief in the Southwestern Corner Pavilion, Angkor Wat. In this episode from the *Ramayana*, the monkey general has been pierced by Rama's arrows. The females of his court and other monkeys grieve for him.

like embroidery over the surface, the work of thousands of artisans.

Ever since its 'discovery' by the Western world, there has been a lively debate over the meaning of Angkor Wat. Of course, today it is a working Buddhist temple or *wat*, as it has been since at least the fifteenth century. To Hindu rulers like Suryavarman, its dedication to Vishnu necessitated that it face west, the direction of that god. But that is also the direction of the setting sun and of death, and Coedès among others has argued that this was a funerary temple or mausoleum, built to house Suryavarman's ashes.[35]

A different approach to this problem has been taken by the art historian Eleanor Morón Mannikka of the University of Michigan.[36] Using the plans published in 1949 by Guy Nafilyan,[37] she has shown that the ancient builders had achieved an extraordinary degree of accuracy and consistency in planning Angkor Wat, almost surely because of religious concerns. In Mannikka's account, the complex functioned as a solar observatory: on the day of the spring equinox, to an observer standing at the southern edge of the first projection on the causeway, just in front of the western entrance gate, the sun rose directly over the lotus crowning the central tower. From the same spot, on the day of the summer solstice the sun rises over Phnom Bok, a temple-crowned hill 17.4 km (10.9 miles) to the northeast. Mannikka and her collaborators have suggested additional sighting lines related to lunar observations, but these are less convincing.

In Hindu cosmology, the apparent movement of the sun through the year is counterclockwise; the bas-reliefs of the Third Gallery seem to conform to this:

1. The spring equinox is in the *east*, and corresponds to the Churning of the Sea of Milk, representing creativity and new life.
2. The summer solstice is in the *north*, and it is at the north pole on

55 Four of the 1,876 *apsaras* that are carved into the walls of Angkor Wat. These celestial maidens were believed to have been created from the Churning of the Sea of Milk.

the cosmic Mount Meru where all the gods live, as they are seen on the relief of the Battle of *Devas* and *Asuras*.

3. The autumn equinox is in the *west*, as the sun travels towards the place of its setting; this corresponds to the horrifyingly destructive Battle of Kurukshetra.

4. Finally, the sun reaches the winter solstice in the *south*, the realm of the death god Yama.

Having determined the exact length of the cubit used by Angkor Wat's architects, *gurus*, and astronomers, Mannikka claims that various measured dimensions along the west to east axis represent the number of years in each of the *yugas* or eras of the present creation, beginning at the moat with the Kali Yuga (our own, the worst), and ending at the central shrine where one completes the first and best of them, the Krta Yuga or Golden Age.

Many of her findings are still controversial, but it should be remembered that similar astronomical and cosmological considerations were, and remain, part of the planning of all Hindu temple complexes, whether in the Indian subcontinent or elsewhere.

Disaster

The famous Chinese curse, 'may you live in interesting times', was only too true of the three decades of turmoil and trouble that ensued on the death of Suryavarman II. The next 'universal monarch' on the Angkor throne was Yashovarman II, but he may have been an usurper, as was the rebel bureaucrat who assassinated him in 1165.

In 1177, the Cham king Jaya Indravarman (himself a usurper to the throne of Champa), taking advantage of the confused situation, decided to invade the Khmer Empire by land and by sea. Guided along the Vietnam coast by a shipwrecked Chinese sailor, his fleet navigated the difficult Delta waterways and proceeded up the Tonle Sap River into the Great Lake. After the capital, Yashodharapura (Angkor), had been taken, and its *parvenu* ruler slain, it was thoroughly sacked of its treasures, and many of its wood-built structures burned to the ground. In fact, the unpublished excavations by B.-P. Groslier in the Royal Palace compound found huge, charred, structural timbers buried under later layers.[38]

The empire had always been beset by centrifugal tendencies, and provincial kings within it once again asserted their independence, as they had so often done in the past. It looked as though the days of glory were past.

Rebirth of the empire: Jayavarman VII

56   Jayavarman VII, arguably not only the greatest of all the Khmer kings but also the greatest personage in Cambodian history, had once been a prince in voluntary exile, biding his time in Vijaya, the Cham capital.[39] Long before he came to the throne at about age fifty, he had been deeply influenced by his chief wife Jayarajadevi, a devout and even mystically-inclined Mahayana Buddhist; but the pacific message of the Buddha seems not to have diminished his prowess on the battlefield. When this remarkable woman died during his reign, he married her sister Indradevi.

At some point in his life, Jayavarman reached a decision to end the period of anarchy that had prevailed since the Khmer defeat by the Chams, and in 1181 he turned the tables on them by crushing them in land combat near and within the capital, and in a mighty naval battle on the Great Lake – one inscription speaks of a 'lake of blood'. These battles are wonderfully recorded in the reliefs of his state temple, the Bayon. He was then consecrated as the new *chakravartin*, but as a Buddhist seems to have dispensed with a Brahmin *purohita* and ended the cult of the *devaraja*, at least for the duration of his reign.

This outstanding monarch not only reestablished and even extended the empire, but entered on a building programme in Angkor and throughout his realm that was truly unprecedented in its scope. His capital – a city within a city, so to speak – was Angkor Thom ('Great Angkor'), a huge square 3 km (1.8 miles) on a side, bounded as usual with a moat and a laterite wall. Zhou Daguan describes how he saw it about one century later:

56 Portrait head of Jayavarman VII, from Preah Khan of Kompong Svai. Classic period, end of twelfth or beginning of thirteenth centuries. The monarch, a Mahayanist Buddhist, is depicted in meditation. Ht 42 cm (16.5 in).

57 Giant head from one of the causeways leading to Angkor Thom.

58 The South Gate of Angkor Thom. Below the face-tower, on either side, are elephants in lotus-ponds; giants holding *nagas* form the balustrades of the causeway leading to the gate.

58　It has five gates, each with double portals. Two gates pierce the eastern side; the other sides have one gate only. Outside the wall stretches a great moat across which access to the city is given by massive causeways. Flanking the causeways on either side are fifty-four divinities [*devas* and *asuras*] resembling war-lords in stone, huge and terrifying. All five gates are similar. The parapets of the causeways are of solid stone, carved to represent nine-headed serpents [*nagas*]. The fifty-four divinities grasp the serpents with their hands, seemingly to prevent their escape. Above each gate are

57　grouped five gigantic heads of Buddha, four of them facing the four cardinal points of the compass, the fifth head, brilliant with gold, holds a central position. On each side of the gates are elephants, carved in stone.⁴⁰

59　　At the very centre of this great urban compound is the Bayon, Jayavarman VII's state temple.⁴¹ The focus of the worship in this labyrinthian complex was Mahayana Buddhist, although a gamut of Hindu deities had representation in its multiple galleries and shrines. The Bayon's most striking feature is

pl. xv　the smiling face of Avalokiteshvara – the Buddha of compassion and mercy – that looks out towards the four directions both here and on Angkor's gates; this may well be the visage of the king himself, since it so strikingly resembles the face of statues accepted by most as Jayavarman in meditation.

　　What most visitors remember about the Bayon are its extensive and detailed bas-reliefs realistically depicting not only the great battle with the Chams, but also charming details of everyday life. From a purely aesthetic

59　The Bayon, view looking north. This great Mahayana Buddhist temple complex at the centre of Angkor Thom belongs to the reign of Jayavarman VII, and is notable for its fifty-four face-towers and many relief scenes of everyday life and warfare. The central tower once housed a gigantic seated Buddha, but many other Mahayana and Hindu supernaturals were worshipped here.

60 Detail of the Elephant Terrace, Angkor Thom. This monumental procession of Jayavarman VII's war elephants fronted on the parade grounds just to the east of the Royal Palace.

viewpoint, it must be admitted that these are no match to the Angkor reliefs, but it is mainly upon these, along with Zhou Daguan's eyewitness observations, that any anthropological reconstruction of the city and empire must depend (as will be seen in the next chapter).

Within Angkor Thom, Jayavarman restored the old Royal Palace and its surroundings, and erected the splendid Elephant Terrace that fronts it on the east, as well as the so-called Terrace of the Leper King (this famous statue is actually of Yama, god of Death, and the terrace the probable royal cremation ground).

60

pl. xvii

As every major *chakravartin* had to have his *baray*, so Jayavarman had his: the Jayatataka reservoir, northeast of Angkor Thom, measuring 3,500 by 900 m (11,500 by 3,000 ft). In the centre of this 'Sea of Victory' he placed the Neak Pean, an island temple within an island, dedicated to the Bodhisattva Avalokiteshvara; here pilgrims could come to bathe in its sacred pools, and partake of curative waters from its fountains. Jayavarman was much concerned with the health and welfare of his subjects, and founded 102 hospitals in various parts of the empire. Midway in size between a pool and a *baray* is the Srah Srang ('Royal Bath'), a lovely body of water south of the East Baray. Begun in an earlier reign, Jayavarman renewed the Srah Srang with sandstone and laterite access stairs; the view over it at sundown from the main platform on the west, dominated by *nagas* and guardian lions, is truly memorable.

As a Buddhist monarch, Jayavarman was a major patron of the Sangha, the community of monks, and at Angkor he built three cities in miniature for them, each surrounded by a moat and laterite wall. One was Ta Prohm, aptly

61 Relief of goddesses holding fans, a section of a hidden wall below the Terrace of the Leper King, Angkor. Classic period, reign of Jayavarman VII, early twelfth century.

described by Claude Jacques as a 'temple-monastery',[42] halfway between the Srah Srang and Angkor Thom. Its immense size and importance is made clear in an inscription that says that 12,640 persons – probably many of them monks – were employed within its walls, supported by the labour and produce of 79,365 people in the various villages belonging to Ta Prohm. Wisely left by the EFEO authorities in its original, jungle-covered state, this is one of Angkor's favourite tourist venues.

pl. XVIII

Preah Khan, immediately west of the Jayatataka, was even larger; Jacques calls it a kind of university rather than a mere monastery[43]; in this case, 97,840 villagers provided support, perhaps for as many as 15,000 residents. Originally built upon the site of Jayavarman's land victory over the Cham invaders, it is now under conservation by the World Monuments Fund. Preah Khan is architecturally and iconographically complex, in part Buddhist, in part Vishnuite, and in part Shivaite. There are even temples and shrines to former kings and to state heroes. The smallest of these was Banteay Kdei, west of the Srah Srang, no match to the other two, but interesting because a community of monks has continued to use it into the present day.

62

One of his many constructions beyond Angkor is the enigmatic and little-known Banteay Chhmar, in what is now an extremely poor part of Cambodia lying to the northwest of the country near the Thai border. It was first explored by the early archaeologists Aymonier and Lunet de Lajonquière, who characterized it as perhaps the most ruined, the most vast, the most chaotic, and the most indecipherable of all Khmer cities. According to George Groslier, who partly mapped it in the 1930s, it may be even larger than Angkor Wat.[44] To the east of its enormous temple complex, believed by

62 A hidden shrine in the Preah Khan complex, with modern offerings to a Classic-period goddess.

Groslier to have been the funerary temple of the crown prince, he discovered a *baray* over 1.6 km (1 mile) long, with an island temple in the centre. Distinguished by its reliefs of many-armed Avalokiteshvaras and of Khmer court life, Banteay Chhmar has been badly pillaged in recent times for the Thai antiquities market.

The hand of Jayavarman VII can be seen all over his empire, which now covered a large part of mainland Southeast Asia: it reached towards the north across all of Khorat to the area around Vientiane (the present capital of Laos), to the east and northeast into central Vietnam (Champa) and the border of Dai Viet in northern Vietnam, in the west across Thailand to the Burmese border, and south to the Malay Peninsula. Across these vast lands he established not only highways, bridges and hospitals, but also a series of sandstone 'Houses of Fire' that some have seen as rest stations for travellers, but which Jacques interprets as a special kind of temple.[45]

No later inscription records the death of this powerful *chakravartin*, but it must have taken place about AD 1215. Jayavaraman VII was succeeded by the little-known Indravarman II, who may have continued the Mahayana Buddhist and other building projects of his predecessor until his own decease in 1243.

Reaction and iconoclasm

With the mighty Jayavarman gone, the empire began once more to face threats. This time, however, they came from the outside, rather than from internal dissidence. Champa broke away from Khmer rule, only to face a threat from the Vietnamese, who were one day to overwhelm them. From the north came the Thai, down into Khorat and into the valley of the Chao Phraya River. What this meant to the survival of the Khmer Empire and Khmer culture will be explored in Chapter 8.

A vast reaction against Buddhism and the Sangha took place at Angkor some time during the thirteenth century. Some scholars have thought that this might have been triggered by dissatisfaction with the long Mahayanist rule of Jayavarman VII, yet that monarch was not only tolerant to Hinduism, but had installed shrines to the Hindu gods within the Bayon. Whoever was responsible for the iconoclasm, it must have been a king, for the extent of the vandalism staggers the imagination: every single Buddha image in Angkor was systematically broken up or defaced, including the great seated Buddha in the Bayon's central shrine. This meant, for example, the chipping out of an estimated 45,000 images along the crests of 8.5 km (5.1 miles) of walls surrounding the monastic complexes of Preah Khan, Ta Prohm and Banteay Kdei; the conversion of relief-carved Buddhas into *rishis* (ascetics) or even *lingas*; and the erasure of some stela texts. In 2001, during test excavations within Banteay Kdei, a team from Tokyo's Sophia University unexpectedly encountered a vast deposit of 272 statues of the Buddha that had been smashed and buried in deep pits.

Here was iconoclasm on a scale that was not to be matched until the entry of Mehmet II into Constantinople in 1453. Such intolerance of one religious tradition for another was unprecedented in Southeast Asia, and has yet to be

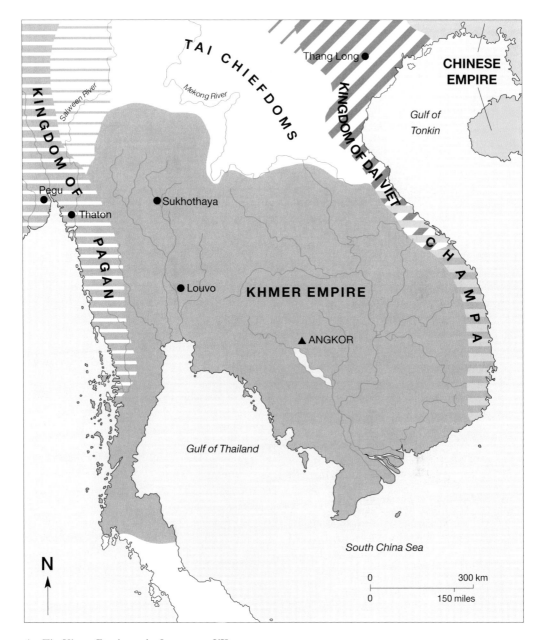

TAI CHIEFDOMS

CHINESE
EMPIRE

Thang Long ●

Mekong River

Gulf of
Tonkin

Salween River

KINGDOM OF PAGAN

Pegu ●

● Thaton

●Sukhothaya

● Louvo

KHMER EMPIRE

▲ ANGKOR

KINGDOM OF DAI VIET

C H A M P A

Gulf of Thailand

South China Sea

N

0   300 km

0   150 miles

63 The Khmer Empire under Jayavarman VII.

explained, since both Buddhism and Hinduism had easily coexisted for many centuries.

The instigator could have been Indravarman II, but in the literature it is Jayavarman VIII (1243–95) who is most often blamed. Yet when the Chinese diplomat Zhou Daguan was in Angkor only a year after the latter's abdication, he was vastly impressed by the magnificence of the capital; furthermore, Zhou noted the fact that most of its population were Buddhists, and that saffron-robed monks were to be seen everywhere. Then who did it? Claude Jacques thinks it possible that one or more kings may have sat on the throne between Jayavarman VII and Indravarman II (whose accession date is unknown); the culprit may have been one of these, but the mystery is yet unsolved.[46]

Professor Jacques points out that Angkor was 're-Hinduized' during the time of the iconoclasm. Since to create an entirely new capital was impractical, the unknown ruler would have kept living within Angkor Thom, with its mighty walls, but the state temple at its centre – the Bayon – had to be converted into a purely Hindu temple. For Angkor Wat, as the temple of Vishnu, he had a new western approach constructed, a broad causeway of massive flagstones, reaching a cruciform terrace, all raised upon cylindrical columns; in earlier times, the western approach crossed Angkor Wat's great moat via a wooden bridge.

On the eve

In 1296 Indravarman III (Srindravarman) was crowned *chakravartin*. Although a son-in-law of the aged Jayavarman VIII, this ruler was a Buddhist, and it was he who had forced the old man to abdicate. In the opinion of Coedès and others, he may even have been a Theravada Buddhist, rather than a Mahayana one. For us, at any rate, the most significant event of his reign was the arrival in the capital during the month of August, 1296, of a Chinese commercial embassy, which included the remarkable Zhou Daguan, whose chronicle is our best source for reconstructing the life of Classic Angkor (see Chapter 7).

The empire was by this time greatly reduced, but Zhou's testimony shows that Yashodharapura, 'The Glory-bearing City', still was a vibrant and flourishing capital – far from the civilization in decline seen by some authors.

Yet the seeds of decline were certainly present after Indravarman III's abdication in 1308, and during the reign of Shrindrajayavarman (1308–27), the last and little-known monarch of Classic Angkor. The first inscription in Pali, the literary vehicle of the Theravada branch of Buddhism, commemorates the founding of a *vihara* (monastic 'dwelling') in 1309. The termination date for the Classic period may be taken as 1327, when the very last Sanskrit inscription was cut into stone, commemorating the accession of one Jayavarmadiparameshvara. By this time, the Khmer Empire, beset by Thai enemies, was effectively dead.

This does not mean that Angkor was suddenly abandoned to the encroaching forest, for there is mounting evidence of an occupation that continued for several centuries more. Khmer civilization was not ended in 1327, but what ensued was something different. Monks now thronged the Vishnuite terraces and courtyards of Angkor Wat (which now really *was* a Buddhist *wat*), and wood-built halls for communal Theravada worship by the Sangha and faithful gradually replaced the masonry temple complexes and tower-shrines of the Hindu and Mahayana Buddhist traditions. This Post-Classic era will be examined in Chapter 8.

7 · The Life and Culture of Classic Angkor

The reconstruction of a long-disappeared civilization from surviving records, whether historical or archaeological, is no easy task. This is especially true for the city of Angkor and its empire, where until recently almost all research has been focussed on architecture, art and dynastic history, and where field archaeology and systematic survey have really just begun.

The sources

There are five major sources for the study of Classic Angkor: 1) the late thirteenth-century account of Zhou Daguan; 2) the visual testimony of the bas-reliefs of Angkor Wat, the Baphuon, the Bayon and Banteay Chhmar; 3) inscriptions of the Classic period, particularly those in the Old Khmer language; 4) contemporary archaeological research, including remote sensing; and 5) French accounts of nineteenth-century Cambodia on the eve of the Protectorate.

Zhou Daguan (Chou Ta-kuan), a native of Zhejiang, China, arrived in Angkor in 1296 as a member of an embassy from the Yuan (Mongol) Dynasty court in Beijing. The purpose of the expedition sent by the 'Son of Heaven', was 'to recall these people to their sense of duty'(as Zhou so typically puts it). On internal evidence, he seems to have been a kind of commercial attaché, and he may have spent most of his time in the Chinese community within the Khmer capital. In all events, Zhou passed less than a year there, returning to China in 1297. Shortly thereafter, he composed his *Memoirs on the Customs of Cambodia*, a unique and indispensable eyewitness account of the splendours and curiosities of the city and its inhabitants, from King Indravarman III down to the lowliest slave. Unfortunately, we have only a part of the lost original, so many topics on which we would like more information are missing in what survives.[1]

It must be remembered that Zhou probably never learned much of the Khmer language, and some of what he says about local customs was surely given to him by his fellow countrymen residing in Angkor. Nonetheless, he brings this civilization to life in an unforgettable (and sometimes even humorous) way.

There are 1,200 square m (12,900 square ft) of bas-reliefs in Angkor Wat's famous Third Gallery, but for a view into the administration and military organization of the empire, those in the south gallery are the most revealing of all. In addition, the horrific Battle of Kurukshetra – a sort of cosmic Stalingrad – depicted in the west gallery gives many details of Khmer battlefield

51

equipment and tactics. And, of course, the myriad divine maidens carved all over Angkor Wat furnish a very good idea of the costume and headgear of what palace women might have looked like.

The Bayon is also replete with reliefs depicting the naval and land battles fought by Jayavarman VII against the Cham foe, as well as the many camp followers and other support staff associated with the royal army. Of even greater anthropological interest are the lively scenes of Khmer daily life carved on the walls of the Bayon's south gallery, and the many representations of palace architecture to be found throughout this complex monument. Less well known, as they are less well studied, are the bas-reliefs of Jayavarman VII's enormous temple complex in northwest Cambodia, Banteay Chhmar, which show the usual battle scenes, as well as the monarch relaxing among his harem women.

The real problem with using any or all of these carvings to reconstruct Classic Angkorian culture is that they have not been well published in accurate and accessible form. While the architecture of these temples has been drawn in magnificent detail, the reliefs often appear only in substandard reproduction. This is particularly true of Banteay Chhmar (now, alas, badly looted), but also of the myriad reliefs of the Bayon. Even in publications depicting the Angkor Wat galleries *in toto*, the photographs are not well lit and are too small in scale to be as useful as they might be. Unhappily, there is

64 The reliefs of the Bayon's South Gallery are a rich source for the ethnography of twelfth-century Angkor. In this market scene, men carry away what seem to be baskets filled with mounds of cooked rice (or possibly loaves of palm sugar).

no real published corpus of either drawings or photographs for the reliefs of any Classic Angkor temple, with the exception of Banteay Srei.

As for the inscriptions, these are all basically religious in context; but considerably more information is given by the texts in Old Khmer than by those in Sanskrit (the latter are essentially poetic prayers to the Hindu gods, effusively eulogizing the king or other donors to temples). Many Khmer-language inscriptions contain valuable data on such topics as land ownership, class structure, social and political networks, and religious foundations. It must be admitted, however, that these are often ambiguous in meaning and thus difficult for even specialists to interpret. For just one instance, we shall see that controversy continues to rage over the meaning in Classic times of the Old Khmer word *khñum* – did it mean 'slave', 'servant', both of these, or something else entirely?

Modern archaeology began in Cambodia during the 1950s and 1960s with B.-P. Groslier, until snuffed out by the Indo-China War. Happily, at present there are a number of active archaeological 'digs' going on in the old Khmer domain, not just in Angkor, but in key sites like Angkor Borei, with attention being paid not only to architecture but also to more mundane aspects such as settlement pattern and ceramic analysis. For the very first time, there now exists an accurate base map for most of Angkor. At the same time, such space-age techniques as airborne radar survey and multiband, satellite imagery are being applied to the city as a whole. pl. 1

It is now apparent that many aspects of the Classic Khmer sociopolitical system, as well as much of the rest of the culture, passed down in fairly intact fashion through the centuries following the Classic period. This is particularly true of the administration of the Khmer state, above all the royal house. Thus, one can gain many insights into Classic Khmer political, social and religious organization from the detailed accounts of the Kingdom of Cambodia as it was when the French Protectorate was first established in 1863. Especially useful for this purpose are the perceptive, sympathetic observations and descriptions of Jean Moura (1883) and Étienne Aymonier (1901), both outstanding scholars.[2]

The divisions of Classic Khmer society

Given the army of bureaucrats, servants, slaves, guards, religious specialists and others in attendance upon the ruler and his family – including a sizeable corps of pages – the royal compound may have resembled a small city in its own right. Membership in the huge royal family was recognized only out to the fifth degree of relationship, and except for those genealogically closest to the king, these persons had little authority except that conferred by the monarch.[3]

There was no hereditary, ranked nobility in Cambodia, either ancient or modern. On the other hand, in Classic times and later, there was a sizeable group of what the French would later call 'mandarins'; these were the royally appointed bureaucrats who administered Angkor and its empire, most of them chosen from members of the great, landholding families. While in office, these generally received the Classic Khmer title *khloñ*; during the early nineteenth century, such officials were designated by the word *okña*. This bureaucratic class was enormous, and existed on all levels of administration, from the capital down to the smallest village.

It will be remembered that the Indian Vedas and other early scriptures – particularly the Laws of Manu – divided society into four major, endogamous castes (*varna* in Sanskrit): the priestly Brahmins, the Kshatriya warriors, the merchant Vaishyas, and the lowly, labouring Shudras. But caste in the Indian sense never really took hold in either Cambodia of the Early Kingdoms period or in Classic Cambodia. There were always Brahmins, to be sure, and these were probably the dominant element in the religious bureaucracy, especially in the royal court, but intermarriage of Brahmins with Kshatriya members of the royal family was not uncommon. The king, in fact, seems to have combined the secular, military role of a Kshatriya with the religious functions and ideology of a Brahmin. It is generally agreed that among the Classic Khmer, the *varna* were not castes but something like aristocratic guilds of specialists within the Royal Palace; the occupational titles may have been entirely honorific and theoretical (on the order of 'Keeper of the Bedchamber' and the like in European royal palaces).[4] Thus, we have a '*varna* of the fly whisk bearers', who seem to have been military officers and generals. In all cases, membership in a *varna* was something that could be bestowed by a king in recognition of outstanding service of one sort or another.

The majority of the Classic population apparently consisted of peasant rice farmers, subject to regular corvée labour and to occasional military service, and obligated to provide goods and services to the religious foundations, to landlords, to the mandarin bureaucracy, and to the king. Many of these laboured on the estates of large landholders, while others were attached to specific temples; and some were dedicated to providing the palace with certain types of products. Some of these sound like serfs, but little is known about serfdom in ancient Cambodia.

Now we come to the thorny problem of the *khñum*, usually translated as 'slave'. On the eve of the French Protectorate, there were two categories of slaves (see Chapter 8): 1) debt slaves, a theoretically temporary category, and 2) slaves for life, who were far less numerous, and who were either those who had been sold by their parents during childhood, or aboriginal Mon-Khmer tribesmen captured in the eastern highlands (these were treated abominably by the Khmer majority). The Classic inscriptions describe three kinds of slaves: 1) slaves legally acquired, 2) slaves who are inherited, and 3) religious slaves.[5]

Zhou Daguan describes only the unfortunate aboriginal slaves:

> If young and strong, slaves may be worth a hundred pieces of cloth; when old and feeble, they can be had for thirty or forty pieces. They are permitted to lie down or be seated only beneath the floor of the house. To perform their tasks they may go upstairs, but only after they have knelt, bowed to the ground, and joined their hands in reverence. Their master they call *pa-t'o* [Old Khmer *patau*, father]; the mistress is addressed as *mi* [*me*, mother]. If they have committed some misdemeanour, they bow their heads and take the blows without daring to make the least movement.

If a slave should run away and be captured, a blue mark would be tattooed on his face; moreover, an iron collar would be fitted to his neck, or shackles to his arms or legs.[6]

Zhou's 'slaves' were certainly true slaves in every sense of the word; that is, they were chattels, to be disposed of as the owner saw fit. According to him, the affluent had 100 or more slaves, the less well off 10 to 20, but only the very poor had none. Yet, as Claude Jacques reminds us,[7] of the many individual *khñum* mentioned in the Classic stone inscriptions, a considerable number have names suggesting a less than servile status. Many bear the Sanskrit names of gods, and were probably *vrah khñum*, so-called 'religious slaves', but in all likelihood 'slaves of the gods', not of humans; they would have been village peasants who lived around a temple and entered its service on alternate fortnights. Perhaps loaned by rich proprietors, they would have worked for the temple, but were recompensed by their master. While the donor gained spiritual merit by his generosity, the servants working for the god would have benefited likewise, and achieved the honour of seeing their names engraved in stone. There are also large numbers of artists (musicians, dancers, and the like) mentioned in donation texts as *khñum*, but whose names suggest higher status than what Zhou is describing.

Thus, Jacques questions the old model of Classic Khmer society as one of an aristocratic minority opposed to an enormous mass of slaves. The reality is that while the *khñum* could never be aristocrats or bureaucrats (no individual *khñum* ever belonged to a *varna*), the term covered a wide spectrum of society from peasant commoners to the most abject tribal chattels living in degradation on the ground floor with the animals.

Administration of the city and empire

The king

The all-encompassing potentate at the head of the Khmer state was the king (*raj* in Sanskrit, *stach* in Old Khmer). As Aymonier put it, when speaking of the royal power in nineteenth-century Cambodia:

> The State is the King, whose power is limitless, and who is the absolute leader of the country, of its armies, of all its political and administrative affairs. The sovereign appoints and dismisses all dignitaries, great mandarins and provincial governors; he establishes and shares out taxes in fixed shares, and disposes to his liking the kingdom's revenues, of which he is the great usufructor. Supreme judge, he has the power of life and death, of mercy, of revision of judgements…Unique legislator, his ordinances have the force of law; he makes and revises codes, he promulgates them in solemn audience.[8]

Although in theory the Classic monarch was the all-powerful supreme landowner and representative of the gods on earth, it is generally agreed among modern scholars that in actuality he was far from a megalomaniac despot (an idea arising from the mistaken notion that the *chakravartin* was considered by his subjects to be a *devaraja* or 'god-king'). As historian Ian Mabbett has shown,[9] within the bureaucratic administration of the empire there were complex affiliations and crosscutting loyalties that made it virtually impossible for all power to be consolidated at any one point; and while some kings (like Suryavarman I and Jayavarman VII) were obviously far more effective than others, their position may often have been in part symbolic. Nonetheless, the king was always a vastly impressive personage in both his private and public appearances. Zhou describes his raiment thus:

> Only the ruler may wear fabrics woven in an all-over pattern. On his head he carries a diadem much like those worn by the *vajradhara* [one of the names of the Eternal Buddha]; at times he lays aside the diadem and weaves into his hair a garland of fragrant blossoms reminding one of jasmine. Round his neck he wears some three pounds of great pearls. On his wrists, ankles, and fingers he wears bracelets and rings of gold, all set with cat's eyes. His feet are bare. The soles of his feet and the palms of his hands are stained red with henna. On leaving the palace he wears a golden sword [the Preah Khan, about which more in Chapter 8].[10]

103

Even in the nineteenth century, when his domain had been severely reduced, Aymonier was able to describe the religious aura that surrounded the Cambodian king:

> Inviolable, [after coronation] he is henceforth the object of a cult pushed to adoration. No one is permitted to address a word to him or to lay a hand on his sacred person; only his principal wives, by softly caressing his feet, dare to awaken him on urgent matters.[11]

Like many traditional oriental potentates, the ruler gave frequent audiences (twice daily, according to Zhou), and even heard the pleas of humble petitioners who felt that they had not received justice in lower courts. Here is Zhou's description of a typical audience:

> No list of agenda is provided. Functionaries and ordinary people who wish to see the Sovereign seat themselves on the ground to await his arrival. In the course of time distant music is heard in the palace, while from the outside blasts on conch-shells sound forth as though to welcome the ruler…Two girls of the palace lift up the curtain with their slender fingers and the King, sword in hand [this is the Preah Khan], appears standing in the golden window. All present – ministers and commoners – join their hands and touch the earth with their foreheads, lifting up their heads only when the sound of conches has ceased. The sovereign seats himself on a lion's skin, which is an hereditary royal treasure. When the affairs of state have been dealt with, the King turns back to the palace, the two girls let fall the curtain, and everyone rises. From all this it is plain to see that these people, though barbarians, know what is due to a Prince.[12]

65 Mythical lion in gilt bronze, now guarding the chapel of the Emerald Buddha in the Grand Palace, Bangkok. This is one of twelve such lions believed to have been brought to Thailand during the nineteenth century from Angkor, at a time when western Cambodia was governed by Siam. Classic period, twelfth to thirteenth centuries.

The lion skin was surely an import from India, for this noble animal was and is unknown in Southeast Asia (the stone guardian lions that flank the 65 entrances of many Classic-period temples bear little resemblance to living lions). As for the audience window, Zhou tells us that it was golden, flanked

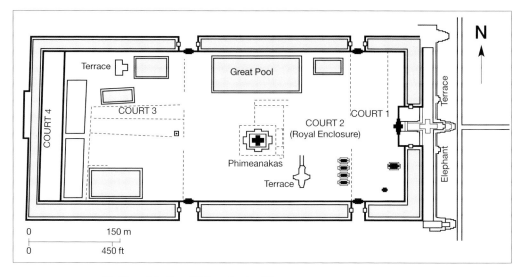

66 Plan of the Royal Palace, Angkor Thom.

by mirrored square columns, and with a 'frieze of elephants' below. Basing himself upon Zhou's statements and upon his own extensive excavations in the area, B.-P. Groslier was convinced that this audience hall rested on the spectacular Elephant Terrace.[13]

pl. XVII

There are extremely few portraits of Khmer kings of any epoch, which is curious considering the improbably exaggerated encomiums to them that appear at the beginning of most Sanskrit inscriptions. One of the few exceptions is the relief representation of the enthroned Suryavarman II at Angkor Wat. Surrounded by his seated courtiers, the king wears a diadem like that described by Zhou, as well as ear pendants, a broad collar, armlets and anklets, all undoubtedly golden. With crossed bands on his chest and wearing an elaborate *chawng kbun* or *sampot* (hipwrapper), his stylized portrait recalls similarly attired figures of gods, particularly the royal divinity Vishnu. Like that god, the king's upper lip is adorned with a pencil-line moustache. Suryavarman is seated on a throne supported by legs ending in *naga* (cobra)-heads. Around and behind him, subordinates hold multiple umbrellas, long-handled fans, and fly whisks, all symbols of high rank and respect.

56

With Jayavarman VII, we come into the realm of real, not idealized, portraiture. There are several sculptural masterpieces that depict this enigmatically smiling ruler seated in Mahayanist meditation, without any regal accoutrements; his hair is drawn back into a chignon, and he has the usual delicate moustache. Just as beautiful are the portrait sculptures of his beloved first wife, Jayarajadevi, in the guise of a Mahayanist female divinity. Two reliefs at Banteay Chhmar show Jayavarman 'at home', so to speak: wearing a loose-fitting jacket, in one scene he is seated in the second storey of his palace, with wives or concubines placed behind him, and in the other he reclines, while at his feet what may be a principal wife raises her hands in homage to her lord.

Since they were constructed of wood with tile roofs, little remains of the various palaces that were occupied by Khmer kings throughout their history. As a rule, they were placed not far north of the state temple of a particular reign. The Royal Palace in the northwestern quadrant of Angkor Thom was the home of a succession of rulers, including Jayavarman VII and Zhou Daguan's Indravarman III. Laid out as an east-west rectangle, and surrounded by a 20-m (65-ft) wide moat and a high, laterite wall, it encloses 13.8 hectares (34 acres). As Zhou tells us, the principal entrance was on the east, fronted by the renowned Elephant Terrace – a kind of reviewing stand for pl. XVII the king and the court. Visitors with business in the palace would have mounted stairs, crossed a cruciform platform, and passed through a *gopura* into the outer court, which may have been relatively accessible to the public. Two other entrances were on the north side, and two matching ones on the south.

Like many Southeast Asian palaces, the one in Angkor Thom became increasingly private as one moved west through inner courts. The royal ancestral temple, the Phimeanakas, lay at the approximate centre of the complex, probably adjacent to the private apartments of the king (readers will recall from Chapter 6 Zhou's account of the nocturnal visits of the ruler to the *naga* princess who was said to dwell in the golden tower on this structure's summit).[14] The next court west was probably reserved for the royal harem. Zhou tells us that the king had five wives, one of whom dwelt in the central part of the palace, and the others in the cardinal directions (echoing the traditional quincunx layout of Khmer temples). In addition, there were 3,000 to 5,000 'concubines and palace girls', separated into unspecified categories; these 'were seldom seen beyond the palace gates'.[15]

To support this royal establishment, there was an enormous service staff. Zhou mentions that at least 2,000 women worked in the palace, all of whom were married and commuted to work from houses located throughout the city; these day workers had high, shaved foreheads, with a vermillion mark placed there and on each temple. Entry to the palace was forbidden to all those of lesser rank. It is likely that the innermost court on the west was given over to kitchens, storage, and other service activities. Add to all of this the royal bureaucracy, and one can appreciate the justice of historian Ian Mabbett's words:

> Inevitably, a ruler lived spider-like at the centre of a huge web of activities, surrounded by an army of clerks, cleaners, attendants, cooks, porters, messengers, carters, valets, maintenance workers, engineers, and so forth.[16]

There are many depictions of Cambodian palaces in Classic-period reliefs, 67 especially those of the Bayon. Zhou was suitably impressed with the Royal 68 Palace, with its carved lintels and its enormous wooden columns – of which charred remains have been found in recent excavations. He tells us that the roofs of the central royal dwelling were covered with lead tiles (some of these have actually been found by EFEO archaeologist Christophe Pottier),[17] while other parts of the palace were covered with yellow-glazed pottery tiles. Not

67 Male courtiers bearing fans and offerings ascend to the second storey of the palace, while women wait below. A *kendi* (spouted vessel) rests on a stand. From a relief in the Bayon.

68 Palace activities in the time of Jayavarman VII. In this scene from the Bayon, the king, holding the Sacred Sword, gives audience to ministers or royal princes. To his right two female dancers perform to the accompaniment of a harp, fiddles and male singers.

least of its amenities were its five or more stone-lined pools, one of which –
the Great Stone Basin – measures 150 by 50 m (492 by 164 ft). These may
have been as much for the delectation of royal bathers and the palace women
as for religious ablutions. All in all, this was probably the grandest and most
splendid royal residence ever built in Southeast Asia, the fitting centre of its
greatest empire.

The Classic Khmer king may have lived in luxury but he had heavy
responsibilities: the undertaking of royal works (including the great *barays*),
the establishment of royal foundations and charities, the maintenance of the
Dharma (order, tranquillity, and the rule of law), and the leadership of his
armed forces whenever necessary. He was trained for this role from boyhood
by a *Vrah Guru*, the Brahmin entrusted with his instruction; the Hindu
Dharmasutra and the *Arthashastra* texts decree that the education of a prince
should begin in his eleventh year, and end when he reaches 16.

The state bureaucracy[18]
Classic Angkor was the centre of an empire, the huge territory of which was
divided into provinces. Although Zhou claims that there were more than 90
of these,[19] most scholars consider this doubtful. Among his many other bene-
factions, Jayavarman VII distributed 23 images of the Mahayanist deity
Jayabuddhamahanatha throughout his empire, and these must more accurately represent the number of such divisions at the end of the twelfth
century, when the Khmer Empire had reached its apogee. There are two
words for 'province': *praman* and *visaya*, probably both synonymous. Each of
these was in turn divided into villages (*sruk* or *grama*). At every level there
were mandarin bureaucrats (*khloñ*, 'chiefs') representing the central administration, and who ensured that revenues (rice, goods, corvée labour, and the
like) flowed smoothly upwards through the system. Most or all of these were
appointed by the king, not elected: Angkor was no republic or democracy.

The *khloñ visaya* was the provincial chief, overseeing the fiscal officers
responsible for tax collections, as well as property transactions and the fixing
of boundaries. Each village had its headman (*khloñ sruk*), in reality a royal
agent; the actual representatives of the Cambodian village were the *gra-
mavrddha*, the village elders, who acted as a link between the local and central
administrations. Ian Mabbett provides this minimalist definition of a *sruk*:
'the division of a territory where a religious foundation [temple] is set up and
a community grows'. The vast majority of such local temples were probably
of perishable wood and other materials, and have either disappeared from the
Cambodian landscape or else have been replaced by Buddhist pagodas.

According to historian Sachchidanand Sahai, there were three kinds of villages:

- those attached to temples by the king or by individuals;
- those assigned to individuals by the king; and
- those that supplied particular commodities to the royal storehouse.

An ambitious individual from a prominent family could buy a tract of
unoccupied land or obtain it from the king, then found a *sruk* with royal
approval. Large proprietors possessed many villages, but the number held by

69 Bronze official seal in the shape of a squirrel. Classic period, twelfth to thirteenth centuries. Length 17.4 cm (6.9 in).

some great religious establishments staggers the imagination – the vast twelfth-century Ta Prohm monastery within Angkor received the revenue of 3,140 villages.

Lesser functionaries were such officers as the *khloñ vala*, the leader of corvée-men or soldiers; the *khloñ vnam*, the superintendent of a temple; and the *khloñ sru*, chief of the rice-fields. Within the village were local judicial courts (*vrah sabha*), and there was always a keeper of records – an office that continued down to the nineteenth century.

Between the central and local administrations was the institution known as *tamrvach*. This was a corps of peripatetic royal inspectors, divided into four categories – first, second, third, and fourth *tamrvach*, possibly each in a different cardinal direction. Such roving agents undoubtedly allowed the king to keep his finger on the country's pulse and to be given ample warning about any troubles or even rebellion that might be brewing outside the capital. It is no accident that the 4,000 men who swore a loyalty oath in 1011 to Suryavarman I were all *tamrvach*.

Because almost all the Classic inscriptions deal with matters that are fundamentally religious in nature, such as the endowment of temples and foundations, we have much information on the central religious hierarchy, but little about the secular one. The picture is also somewhat clouded by the situation that certain religious officers also played important civil roles: the *vrah guru*, for instance, not only educated the crown prince and sacrificed for rain, but he also controlled the administration of some temple lands.

The religious authorities and functionaries in the royal court were certainly almost entirely of the Brahmin caste, although some of the priests in the provinces and villages may not have been so. Most of them may have received the honorific Khmer title of *sten an*, reserved for learned men. We have already run across the *purohita* (see Chapter 6). In peninsular India, this

Sanskrit word indicated a family priest or chaplain; in Classic Angkor, this important individual was the chaplain and chief priest of the king and, at least according to the self-serving SKT stela, was a hereditary officer charged with maintaining the cult of the *devaraja*. The Sanskrit title of *hotar* or 'sacrificer' occurs frequently in the texts; this is also supposed to indicate 'royal chaplain' – but the exact scope of the term is unclear since while the royal *purohita* of the *devaraja* was a *hotar*, there were other *hotars*. Most of these may have had important administrative roles.

There were many religious functionaries who received the Sanskrit title of *acharya*, a learned priest who acted as teacher and spiritual guide; or of *pandita*, someone versed in sacred lore; or of *upadhyaya*, a teacher and preceptor learned in the Vedas. As with many Classic Khmer titles, there is little information on whether these were or were not interchangeable. Zhou Daguan mentions three categories of religious specialists in the Angkor of his day: 1) the *pandita* (probably applied here to learned Brahmins in general, distinguished by the white thread worn across one shoulder), 2) the Buddhist monks in their saffron robes, living in monasteries and 3) those who he describes as 'Taoists', but who apparently were Shivaite priests in charge of the cult of the *linga*.[20] Added to these were the bearded *rishis*, the ascetic holy men who, while they would have lived apart from the world of human affairs, may have been consulted on theological matters.

70 The god Shiva depicted as a very high-ranking Brahmin priest, from an Angkor Wat relief. He wears a beard (the sign of an ascetic), bears the sacred white thread over his left shoulder, and holds prayer beads in the right hand.

In the Classic reliefs, all Brahmin priests and dignitaries can be distinguished by their high chignons, by moustaches and goatees, and by the sacred cord over the left shoulder. As for the lay administrators, these, according to Zhou, either were of princely rank, or had gained office by offering their daughters as royal concubines. As can be seen in Suryavarman I's magnificent procession in the Angkor Wat reliefs, and in Zhou's account, when in public the rank of these bureaucrats was correlated with insignia as follows:

> The highest dignitaries use palanquins with golden shafts and four parasols with handles of gold; those next in rank have a palanquin with golden shafts and two gold-handled parasols; then come those entitled to one palanquin with gold shafts and one golden-handled parasol; and finally those with only a golden-handled parasol. Further down the line come those permitted only a silver-handled parasol, and there are others who use a palanquin with silver shafts... All parasols are made of red Chinese taffeta...[21]

In contrast with these, the great Suryavarman received the honour of fourteen parasols.

Law and order in ancient Angkor

As in the rest of the Indic world, the Angkor state and empire were governed by rules laid down in the Code of Manu, a great compendium of Brahmanic law probably composed in the fourth century BC. Of course, modifications had to be made to a legal system that had been devised for the rigid four-caste system of Vedic India. Every juridical act was theoretically inscribed on stone as well as on plaques of gold, silver or copper. The Khmer king was the defender of law and order in Cambodia. His law courts, present on every administrative level right down to the village, instituted criminal proceedings against transgressors and guaranteed the integrity of landholdings and the settling of boundary problems. Not even religious institutions such as temples were immune, since they as well as private individuals could be sued over land.

In theory, the king owned all land in the empire, but in practice he did not. As M. C. Ricklefs has pointed out, his main function was to serve as umpire in unresolved land disputes, and to sanction transfers of rights to religious foundations and private individuals; 'outside of the capital, the countryside must have been largely under the control of these individuals.'[22]

Persons accused of crimes were taken before examining magistrates called *sabhachara*; these were peripatetic investigators of the court. Witnesses were called, testimony sworn, and written depositions taken. Often, fines were assessed, but punishment for serious infractions of the law was severe. Zhou tells us that '...outside the West Gate [of Angkor Thom]...a ditch is dug into which the criminal is placed, earth and stones are thrown back and heaped high, and all is over.' Lesser crimes were dealt with by amputation of the feet, hands, or nose. Thieves caught in the act were imprisoned and tortured, with this interesting exception:

If an object is missing, and accusation brought against someone who denies the charge, oil is brought to boil in a kettle and the suspected person forced to plunge his hand into it. If he is truly guilty, the hand is cooked to shreds; if not, skin and bones are unharmed. Such is the amazing way of these barbarians.[23]

The central administration in Angkor must have had fairly detailed information for purposes of taxation and corvée labour of all the empire's inhabitants, for according to Zhou a census was taken during the ninth Cambodian month, when everyone (or, more likely, all heads of families) was called to the capital, and passed in review before the Royal Palace.[24] Such census registers were kept in Aymonier's day, and revised every three years. If only we had the registration books from Classic Angkor, we would be in a better position to talk of the ancient population.

The economy

Agriculture and the riddle of the barays

Rice production was the ultimate foundation of Classic Khmer civilization. The kingdom was essentially a thoroughly agrarian state in which the balance between food producers and non-producers was perhaps similar to that of Cambodia today – 80 per cent to 20 per cent, a figure typical of modern Third World countries. Most of this food reached the non-producers through an all-encompassing revenue system in which the lion's share went to the king, to the royal house, to the upper bureaucracy, and to the major religious functionaries and foundations. Yet we have precious little information on rice agriculture from any of our sources – no mapping of ancient rice fields, no production figures, and only slender data on consumption. The main puzzle, however, is the role that the *barays* played in Khmer subsistence, and (if they were in truth used for irrigation) the carrying capacity of the various lands within the Khmer Empire. B.-P. Groslier was convinced that the city of Angkor was a *cité hydraulique*, a 'hydraulic city' with an enormous population dependent upon the production of rice fields irrigated through the *baray* system.[25]

Jacques Dumarçay, an adherent of the 'hydraulic city' model, observes that there were two kinds of reservoirs in the Khmer domain: 1) those using an excavation or natural depression, such as the moats surrounding Angkor Thom, the Royal Palace, and temple complexes and 2) the *barays*, in which water was retained above ground behind elevated, earthen dikes.[26] In his scenario, *barays* first appear at Wat Phu (Champassak) towards the end of the eighth century, and subsequently are found at Angkor, Phimai, Beng Mealea and Koh Ker (they are known at Banteay Chhmar and Preah Khan of Kompong Svai; as well as at Sukhotai, Thailand, during its Khmer occupation). Except for Beng Mealea and Banteay Chhmar, they seem to be characteristic of capitals. As we have seen in the last chapter, Jayavarman II constructed the first really large *baray* – the Indratataka – in Hariharalaya (southeastern Angkor). As the years passed, this began silting up, according to Dumarçay, so that when Yashovarman I took the throne, a truly massive reservoir on an unprecedented scale – the East Baray – was constructed. But sand eventually commenced filling this, too, and the dikes of the great West Baray were thrown up, creating a reservoir 8 km (5 miles) long. As silting afflicted this huge impoundment, the dikes were raised several times. The Jayatataka Baray to the east of Preah Khan was the very last of these mighty reservoirs. As even this *baray* became unusable, the Khmer adapted their stone bridges, with their narrow corbel arches, as dams to feed the postulated system of irrigation canals.

It should be stated that Roland Fletcher has raised serious doubts about the siltation model for explaining the progression of *barays*, for these reasons:

1. Yashovarman I built the East Baray as soon as he had finished the north wall of the Indratataka.
2. The claim that the raising of the dikes of the *barays* was due to siltation cannot be valid. The level of the water in a *baray* is set entirely by the height of the intake points; in the case of the West Baray, these are at ground level, so that the height of the dikes cannot relate to water level inside it, which was about 5 m (16.4 ft) at maximum.[27]

Nevertheless, there was truly an amazing amount of water retained in Angkor's four *barays*, as these approximate figures show (based on an average depth taken to be 3 m, or 10 ft):[28]

Name	Area (millions of square m)	Volume (millions of cubic m)
West Baray	16.0	48.0
East Baray	12.4	37.2
Jayatataka Baray	2.9	8.7
Indratataka Baray	2.5	7.5

Of course, if Dumarçay is correct, not all of these *barays* would have been functional at the same time, and their depths would have fluctuated through time.

The source for the entire water management system of Classic Angkor – *barays*, moats and canals – was Phnom Kulen. At first, for the Indratataka, streams running down from the eastern end of the plateau supplied the water, but as the capital was moved to Angkor proper, the Mekong River – the symbolic Ganges – became the sole supplier, being diverted and canalized by Angkor's hydraulic engineers.

Assuming that the primary purpose of the *barays* was to provide irrigation water for the rice fields in and around the city, including its suburbs, Groslier calculated that this hydraulic system might have supported 600,000 inhabitants. Adding to that an estimated 429,000 persons fed by flood-retreat agriculture carried out on the margins of the Great Lake, plus another 872,000 supported by 'dry rice farming', Groslier claimed that greater

Angkor might have contained approximately 1.9 million inhabitants.[29] These are astonishing figures, for it would have made Angkor the world's largest city in its time.

Now for the opposition.[30] Groslier's critics have pointed out that, although the construction and maintenance of *barays* are referred to in the inscriptions, these fail to say anything connected with their possible economic function. Similarly, Zhou Daguan makes no mention at all of the *barays* in regard to rice cultivation. What he *does* describe is flood-retreat farming on the seasonally changing margins of the Great Lake (see Chapter 2); and there, and along the Mekong, and in the Delta, this highly effective technique must have provided most of the rice consumed by the Khmer in Classic times. Parenthetically, Zhou was astonished by so-called 'floating' rice, which probably then as now played only a slight part in total production. Either by his day the *barays* had fallen into disuse as irrigation reservoirs, or they had never been used for that purpose in the first place. Which of these explanations is the true one? Here is where the debate lies.

These are some of the objections that have been raised by opponents of the 'hydraulic city' theory:

1. The placement of the *barays* would actually have impeded water flow to the rice paddies below them. Furthermore, construction of every new *baray* would have dried up any down-slope *barays*.
2. Instead of bringing in fertilizing minerals and organic substances to the paddies, the *baray* waters would have been acidic, bereft of organic material.
3. By re-measuring and recalculating all of Groslier's claimed figures, and accepting his huge estimated population, geographer Robert Acker concluded that hydraulic agriculture could have fed only 7.8 per cent of Angkor's inhabitants.

Acker's counter-suggestion was that these mighty reservoirs had two functions. One was flood control, to protect both rice fields and temples from inundation during the monsoon season. The other was religious and cosmological, emphasizing the king as re-creator of Mount Meru and its surrounding oceans.

Recent archaeological evidence, however, has shown that B.-P. Groslier was partially right – the *barays* really *were* used in agricultural irrigation. Surveys by Christophe Pottier of the EFEO have revealed inlets and outlets in the eastern dikes of both the East and West Baray. There are huge disperser canals off the West Baray, off the moat surrounding Angkor Wat, and probably also off the East Baray. The West Baray canal runs about 40 km east until it reaches the 25-km (15-mile) long, south-trending, Damdek Canal; this latter could have watered the whole edge of the lake shore when flood levels receded. Coring carried out by Roland Fletcher of the University of Sydney proves that the West Baray canal did indeed carry high energy water flow. In fact, new information obtained by Pottier and Fletcher from the northern half of Angkor shows that the whole landscape is crisscrossed with a complex grid of north-south and east-west channels and also is crisscrossed by northeast-southwest channels which would have moved water directly down-slope.[31]

About the cosmological significance of the *barays* there can be little doubt. But it is now realized that they had multiple functions, the most significant of which seems to have been maintaining water in the flood-recession fields between Angkor and the Great Lake throughout the dry season.

Fishing and hunting

Notwithstanding a century of archaeological excavations in Angkor and other Classic Khmer sites, there is a general absence of reports concerning faunal remains – the basic data for any reconstruction of ancient fishing and hunting practices, not to mention the role of domestic animals. The reliefs of both Angkor Wat and the Bayon show all kinds of freshwater fish in what is probably the Great Lake – many of them improbably exaggerated in size – but no actual scenes of them being caught. We can probably assume that netting of fish in the lake and in the rivers was carried out on the same scale and with the same techniques as it is today (described in Chapter 2).

Hunting may have been the special province of the tribal peoples of Cambodia, who were masters of this skill. Zhou states that it was mountain people who hunted elephants for their tusks, with spears; he also avers that rhinoceros tusks were highly valued, but how this extremely dangerous beast was hunted is not described.[32] In the Bayon and on the sculptured panels of the Baphuon, hunters with bow and arrows shoot deer as well as birds. Several scenes show birds as the prey of hunters with blowguns. This weapon was most likely made of bamboo, and propelled a poison dart; the blowgun is believed to be of Malaysian origin, and is widespread among aboriginal peoples of Southeast and South Asia.

71

71 A pair of hunters shoot birds with blowgun, from a relief on the Baphuon in Angkor Thom.

Commerce

As a Chinese commercial attaché, trade is a subject upon which Zhou speaks with undoubted authority. Because it was generally the women, not the men, who had charge of trade, Chinese merchants – of whom there must have been many in Angkor – took care to get a Khmer wife. Markets were held every day from 6 am until noon; there were no shops, merchants instead spreading their wares on matting layed upon the ground. As in earlier times, the Classic Khmer economy basically operated without money:

> In small transactions barter is carried on with rice, cereals, and Chinese objects; fabrics are next employed, and, finally, in big deals, gold or silver is used.[33]

Like Third World countries today, vis-à-vis the developed countries, there must have been a serious trade imbalance between the Khmer lands and China, since Chinese merchants brought in a virtual cornucopia of fine manufactured goods, in return for Cambodia's raw materials. Here are the respective lists of goods traded, as given by Zhou, in the order of preference by the recipients:[34]

Cambodia	**China**
Kingfisher feathers	Gold and silver
Elephant tusks	Silk fabrics
Rhinoceros horns	Zhenzhou tin goods
Beeswax	Wenzhou lacquered trays
Aquilaria wood (an incense)	Quanzhou celadon ware
Cardamoms	Mercury
Gamboge (a resin)	Paper
Lacquer	Saltpetre
Chaulmoogra oil (medicinal)	Sandalwood
Pepper (*Piper nigrum*)	Angelica-root
	Musk
	Linen
	Huang-cao cloth
	Umbrellas
	Iron pots
	Copper trays
	Freshwater pearls
	Tung oil
	Bamboo traps (?)
	Basketry
	Wooden combs
	Needles
	Mingzhou rush mats

The kingfishers that provided the top luxury item on the Cambodian export list were trapped along forest ponds and streams by skilled hunters, holding a captive female in one hand as a lure, and a net in the other. Their iridescent blue feathers were applied to the ceremonial headdresses of the

Chinese Empire's elite right up until the 1911 revolution. And powdered rhinoceros horns continue be sought by ageing Chinese males to restore their flagging libidos.

Based on this information, there must have been a sizeable Chinese merchant colony not only in Angkor, but in the provincial capitals as well – a state of affairs that has been typical of both mainland and insular Southeast Asia for at least a millennium. The hearts and minds of the Khmer may have been in India, but their pocketbooks were in China.

Taxation and revenue

The Classic Khmer state was an immense revenue-gathering machine, and every individual in Cambodia except religious functionaries, priests, monks and slaves was subject to taxation, which was paid in kind, since there was no system of coinage.[35] The king was the supreme receiver of taxes – there was a Khmer formula that went *svey vrah rajya*, 'he eats the kingdom', meaning that he enjoys the fruits of his own realm, but officials on every level participated in the system. The storehouses of the Royal Treasury were in the charge of high-ranking officers and are known to have contained, in addition to gold and precious jewels, such products of the land as rice, honey and beeswax, clarified butter, sugar, spices, camphor and cloth. The king also benefited by revenues from his immense landholdings, as well as from at least part of the booty gained from military victories.

There seem to have been taxes on everything – on land, on rice, salt, wax and honey, and so forth. Land taxes were based on paddy size and productive capacity (i.e. whether the fields were low-lying, river-side, or dry-season). There was even a market tax, but it is not known whether this was based on goods sold, on the vendors themselves, or on the stalls that they rented. Payments could be made in all kinds of goods, including not only rice but also slaves, buffalos, elephants, and especially cloth.

Drawing upon Hindu precedent, Brahmins were exempted from taxation by virtue of the theory that they transferred one sixth of their spiritual gains to the king, a notion that was extended to exempt the great private religious foundations, themselves the recipients of vast revenues from land grants. From the over 3,000 villages that it owned, the monastic complex of Ta Prohm grew rich enough to support 18 high priests, 2,740 officials, 2,202 assistants, and 615 dancers, along with a host of monks, commoners and 'slaves'. In its treasury were:

A set of gold dishes weighing 500 kg
A silver service of equal size
35 diamonds
40,260 pearls
4,540 gemstones
523 parasols
512 sets of silk bedding
876 Chinese veils [mosquito nets?]

But this was probably trifling compared to what was in Jayavarman VII's Royal Treasury!

Communications and transportation

In spite of a century of Angkorian research, the study of the great system of highways that tied together the provinces of the Classic Khmer Empire has hardly begun. Ironically, this was the purported goal of André Malraux before his arrest in 1924 on looting charges,[36] and is the theme of his 1930 novel *La Voie Royale* ('*The Royal Way*'). According to George Groslier,[37] and in the atlas of Lunet de Lajonquière,[38] there is visible evidence for six major arteries in the system, as follows:

- Angkor to Kompong Thom, the road running along the flood limit of the Great Lake: 150 km (90 miles).
- Angkor to Preah Khan (Kompong Svai) via Beng Mealea: 100 km (60 miles).
- Beng Mealea to Wat Phu, via Koh Ker: 210 km (130 miles).
- Beng Mealea south to the Great Lake: 40 km (25 miles)
- Angkor to Phimai, crossing the Dangrek Range: 210 km (130 miles).
- Angkor to the Sisophon region, and possibly to Banteay Chhmar: 90 km (56 miles).

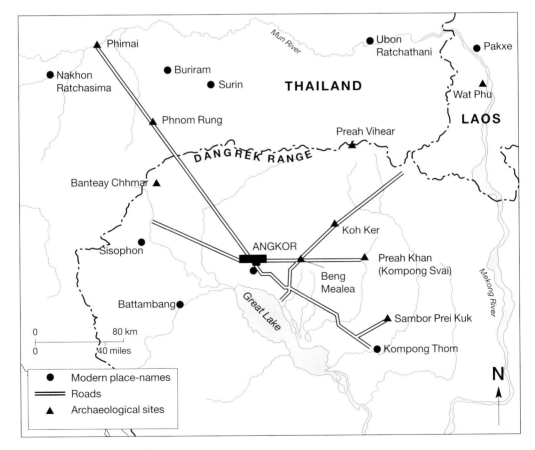

72 The road system of the Khmer Empire.

73 Classic-period bridge (*spean*) at Spean Prap Tos, Cambodia. This still carries motor traffic.

These would add up to a total of about 800 km (497 miles); Groslier would append to this list a road running from Angkor Thom south to the Great Lake of about 20 km (12 miles). There must have been a host of secondary roads; for instance, the villagers in the Surin area of the Khorat Plateau are constantly running across vestiges of such roads; they avoid planting anything on these or disturbing them, lest the spirits become angry.[39]

The principal highways vary in height from 2 to 6 m (6.6 to 19.6 ft), and in width from 10 to 25 m (32.8 to 82 ft), always raised well above the inundated rice fields and floodwater crests. As Groslier notes, they acted as dikes, leaving a series of pits, ponds and pools that probably served to quench the thirst of humans and beasts, as baths, and as a source of water for kitchens. These roads crossed rivers and streams over massive bridges constructed of laterite, up to 160 m (525 ft) long; over fifty of such bridges are known, and even today some carry traffic. Their arches were corbelled, and thus relatively restricted in width; because of this, the bridges could also act as weirs, backing up waters in retention pools that could be used to irrigate downstream paddies, and draining upstream fields as needed. A recent study of Classic Khmer stone bridges by EFEO archaeologist Bruno Bruguier shows that all are located within a radius of about 100 km (60 miles) of Angkor, and he suggests that 'they were probably built to make it easier for the army to move or respond to strategic imperatives rather than to foster economic develop-

73

ment.' Most of the smaller bridges, though, must have been built of wood; in fact, there was once a major wooden bridge on the axis of Angkor Thom's Gate of Victory, but only part of the stone abutments remain.[40] And shown on a Bayon relief is a floating bridge composed of timbers tied together with ropes, capable of transporting elephants whose cargo had been removed.

Along these highways, at regular intervals, Jayavarman VII established a total of 121 'Houses of Fire'. Past scholars have seen these as rest houses for pilgrims, but Claude Jacques suggests that they were shrines, perhaps for a fire ritual; all have the same plan, a long hall with a tower to the west and a forepart to the east.[41]

As for land transport, Zhou Daguan has this to say:

> Palanquins are made from one piece of wood, curved in the middle, 74
> with the two ends rising vertically, and carved with flowery motifs
> plated with gold and silver. At the distance of one foot from each
> end a hook is fastened and to these hooks a large piece of material,
> folded loosely, is attached with cords. The passenger sinks into this
> litter and two men bear him away. A palanquin is followed by an
> object resembling the sail of a ship, but wider, which is made of
> parti-coloured silks. This is carried by four men who follow at a
> run. For long trips travellers often ride elephants or horses; others
> use carts identical with those in other countries. The horses have no
> saddle, but the elephants have benches [howdahs] on which to sit.[42]

74 Relief carving of a high-ranking lady being carried in a roofed palanquin, from Angkor Wat. She is seated in a kind of suspended hammock; the palanquin's poles end in *naga* heads.

This is a highly accurate description. There are many relief representations of very high-ranking personages being carried in such palanquins, which were really a kind of mobile hammock. It is difficult to believe that there was only one pole involved, rather than two, in those palanquins that had elaborately roofed superstructures. In all events, many bronze hooks and finials in the shape of *nagas* have survived in museum collections. There were also wooden litters borne by four or more porters, but their use was less for humans than for transporting ritual objects like statues, *lingas* and the Sacred Fire.

Elephants would only have been for the king and the top tier of the Angkor hierarchy, or for military commanders. There are representations of elephants with special harnesses and side packs, engaged in the transport of large jars and (in one case), stone *lingas*. They must have been used extensively in the moving of large construction stones. The problem with elephants is that they can only carry one to two persons comfortably, and can barely travel more than 24 to 40 km (15 to 20 miles) a day. They require constant watering along the route, not only to drink but also for bathing. Because of this, Clovis Thorel (botanist with the Garnier expedition to the Mekong) noted that in crossing riverless plains during the mid-nineteenth century, the mandarins were obliged to establish 'caravanseries with wells spaced apart at certain distances'.[43] For warfare, for processional displays, and for his own transport, the king must have maintained a huge herd in royal elephant stables. Since a domestic elephant will drink about 50 gallons of water per day, at least one of the functions of the *barays* and immense pools of Angkor and the provincial capitals must have been to supply this necessity.[44]

On the testimony of the reliefs, the two-wheeled, rural carts of today's Cambodia are remarkably similar to those of Classic Angkor. Drawn by two yoked oxen or buffalos, they must have been the principal way that goods and

75 Bronze palanquin fittings, twelfth century, Cambodia. Hooks, ht 22.9 cm (9 in); ring, ht 15.2 cm (6 in). These would have been for the carrying poles of a suspended cloth litter.

people were transported throughout Khmer history. In Classic times, they were far more ornate, and could be roofed against sun and rain. In fact, there are several examples of baroquely carved carts with miniature palaces on top, and with four and even six wheels (these apparently for the king or holy images only). Horse-drawn chariots were constructed on similar lines, and seem largely to have been employed in battle.

Humans, mostly probably of the slave class, transported many goods (as well as carrying the palanquins and litters of their masters). The 'coolie pole' with its double burden was in use, as well as a single pole borne on the shoulders of two men to move a large, suspended cargo.

Architecture and the building trade

By Classic times, most sacred structures were almost entirely built of laterite and sandstone, rather than the timbers used in wooden structures that must have been their prototypes. Claude Jacques has pointed to the ideology behind this:

> …anything that was not to honour the gods was built of perishable material – even the kings' palace…because men are mortal and will cease to exist some day,…so too are the materials relating to his life. The gods, however, are immortal and thus stone was used to honour them forever.[45]

Yet woodworking traditions can be seen throughout Angkor's stone temples – in door frames, false doors, columns, balustered windows, and in all sorts of decorative details.

Although the originals have disappeared, architects Jacques Dumarçay and Pascal Royère have been able to reconstruct Khmer use of wood in architecture from relief scenes, from tiles excavated near ancient structures, and from the spaces left by the embedding of beams in stone structures.[46] The main technique was 'sagging beamwork', based upon the principle that a horizontal beam gives way at shearing points located at one-fifth of the length; accordingly, designers had to bring all the weight of the roof between the points of support and the shearing points of the tie beams (horizontal beams). Compared to Indian and Chinese timber architecture, this is relatively unsophisticated; but it can become complex when the plan is cruciform, as it often was in Classic times.

The terracotta tilework on roofs consisted of alternating vertical rows of convex and concave tiles, these being glazed yellow or green on the more important structures. These rows ended on the eaves with upturned, *naga*-like tiles. Rarely, on some temple structures, stone elements or bricks were laid over timber beamwork.

In mainland Southeast Asia, the use of bricks in temple architecture is certainly far older than the use of stone; it begins with the simple brick shrines of Oc Eo, and reaches a kind of pinnacle with the splendid towers of Sambor Prei Kuk in the Early Kingdoms period. Many of the earliest temples of Angkor are likewise of brick. Clay deposits suitable for brick manufacture are

pl. VII

pl. v   everywhere, so that brickyards could be near the structures for which they were intended. Lime mortar was unknown; instead, in such fine buildings as Prasat Kravan and Lolei, a high quality and effective binder was used, made of the sap of a liana to which palm sugar had been added. Brickwork was never left visible, always being covered with a thick coat of stucco (lime from shells, mixed with sand). The carved brick reliefs on and in such buildings were merely armatures for the artists in stucco.

The Phnom Kulen hills were the source for all the sandstone used in Angkor's architecture and sculpture, including the beautiful roseate stone of Banteay Srei. The closest sandstone quarries were about 30 km (18 miles) from Angkor; in contrast, laterite was ubiquitous, and thus could be quarried next to the construction site, yet Khmer building supervisors preferred to obtain it from deposits closer to Phnom Kulen. There is such a laterite quarry 4 km (2.4 miles) long near Banteay Srei. There were two methods for extracting sandstone: 1) cutting blocks from working faces, and shifting them on rollers, and 2) driving wooden wedges into hollowed-out recess lines, then soaking them in water to split the rock along horizontal planes.[47] An easily visited Classic-

76   period quarry of the first type is located at Si Khiu, on the modern highway from Bangkok to Nakhon Ratchasima on the Khorat Plateau.[48]

For the transportation of a sandstone building block, the stone masons bored a pair of spaced holes on either end of the upper surface, then drove wooden pegs into them, wetting them to make them swell; after that, ropes or cords could be tied to the pegs for lifting and moving (such holes can be seen on the huge blocks of the main causeway leading in to Angkor Wat). Elephant as well as human power must have been enlisted in the colossal job of getting these stones to the site. Dumarçay and Royère calculate that 1,318 blocks of up to 3 cubic m (105 cubic ft) in size were used to build just one of the angle towers on the upper terrace of the Ta Keo pyramid.[49] Before it was put in place, each block had to be prepared, and an Inner Gallery relief in the Bayon pictures workers employing a sling device to grind stones against each other, during the erection of a temple to Vishnu.

All Khmer stone architecture was mortarless, the stones being held in position by friction, by special cuts (like mortise and tenon), or by clamps of bronze or iron. Forcing wedges of sandstone were employed to give additional solidity to masonry, but sometimes shoddy construction techniques and poor foundations have resulted in the partial collapse of some buildings over the centuries.[50] The only vault known was the corbel, adopted from its use in early Indian temples; corbelling was initially carried out in bricks, and later in stone. Incidentally, these vaults were always hidden from view by coffered wooden ceilings – unlike the practice in the Maya civilization of Mesoamerica, where they were always visible.

In peninsular India at this time, the architects, artisans and workmen engaged in the building of temples were organized into groups resembling guilds, and such must have also been the case in Cambodia. Most important were the architect and the master of works, and we know the name of one Khmer architect – one Gunapativarman (a Kshatriya name), who was rewarded by Udayadityavarman II, as this inscription testifies:

By order of the king, he was [promoted to the dignity of] Vishvakarman, chief of the artists…On the occasion of the completion
of these works [the Eastern Baray and the Baphuon], the king gave
him a land from his own domain, exempt in the future from all disputes…Having assembled Brahmins and princes as witnesses, the
king ordered the president of the Court to set out the five bound-
ary-markers of this terrain…In consideration of the virtues of this
Vishvakarman, the king had this domain with the family inscribed
in the celebrated caste [*varna*] of the People in Charge of the
Golden Cups.[51]

Everything had to be carried out with the assistance of learned Brahmins,
however, for the Classic Khmer temple complex was a symbolic replica of the
greatest *mandala* of all, Mount Meru, the three- or five-peaked home of the
thirty-three gods of the Hindu pantheon. Probably working from plans on
paper, the perimeter of the monument had to be laid out on 'pure soil', meaning that an excavation had to be made to a considerable depth and then filled
with layers of sand. Also required was the preparation of places for sacred
foundation deposits, necessary to spiritually activate the temple. In the case
of huge and complex monuments like Angkor Wat, Banteay Chhmar, and the
Bayon, the amount of labour and planning needed to make suitable earthly
homes for the gods staggers the imagination.

The *baray* was a necessary adjunct for the great temple that was built next
to it – in fact, it was situated on the axis of the monument on which it
depended. Symbolically representing the Primordial Ocean surrounding

76 Limestone quarry of the Classic period at Si Khiu, on the Khorat Plateau of northeastern
Thailand.

Mount Meru, the *barays* also acted as reflecting pools for these structures – in their waters, the heavenly temple-mountain would appear linked with its inverted, beneath-the-surface image, as the 'original' Mount Meru was cosmologically conceived.

In her study of Khmer sacred architecture, Hedwige Multzer o'Naghten has stated:

> If to organize space consists in transforming a chaotic and disturbing universe into a comprehensible and accessible world, the Khmer project managers and the kings who directed them have marvellously succeeded.[52]

One group of specialists whose responsibility was the organization of space on a grand scale was that of the surveyors, about whom we know little or nothing. Be that as it may, over a period of centuries they were able to lay out the entire city of Angkor on a grand plan orientated to True North; they were even able to place the city of Preah Khan in Kompong Svai on exactly the same latitude as Angkor Thom, and connect them by a road about 100 km (60 miles) long. All of this would have required accurate surveying instruments and a practical knowledge of astronomy.

Arts and crafts

Sculpture

As George Groslier wrote in 1923, 'Sculpture is incontestably the great art of Cambodia, that which confers on it a matchless prestige.'[53] All Khmer sculpture, he tells us, was religious in nature and associated with the architecture of one or another great temple complex.

Yet this was a totally anonymous art: no works are signed, and we do not have any of the names of the talented sculptors who produced the many thousands of Classic Khmer statues to be seen in the world's museums, in the Conservation d'Angkor in Siem Reap, or remaining *in situ* in Cambodia's monuments. Were these artists and artisans drawn from the ranks of the *khñum*, commoners, Brahmins, or from all of these? We have no idea.

The most prestigious Classic sculptors must have been assigned the carving of three-dimensional statuary – freestanding figures of gods and deified humans who were usually placed on pedestals – as well as the magnificent narrative reliefs of Angkor Wat, the Bayon, and Banteay Chhmar. Even though the main cult object in a monument's principal shrine was typically a *linga*, secondary sanctuaries (and sometimes the main shrine itself) housed such statues.

The statuary that survives is almost entirely in sandstone, but in ancient times wooden sculptures may have been numerous, at least in the shrines of the countryside; however, it is only from very late in the Classic period and during the Post-Classic that significant numbers of wooden images in the Theravada Buddhist tradition have come down to us. The process of producing images from blocks of sandstone can be reconstructed from unfinished examples, as art historian Thierry Zéphir has shown.[54] The artist first

77   Statue of Shiva and his consort Uma, from Banteay Srei (now in the National Museum of
Phnom Penh). Classic period, *c.* AD 967. This was carved from a very hard and dense grey-
green limestone, with the body surfaces polished to a high lustre. Ht 60 cm (23.6 in).

roughed out the form, then refined it to obtain the desired lines and volumes, following strict canons; the latter may have initially followed Indian proto-types, but gradually became modified through time and by local traditions. In the case of complex forms, such as gods with multiple arms, while the piece was being carved additional stone elements would be left as props to lend strength to limbs, and subsequently removed (although in sculpture of the Early Kingdoms period, such props were retained); however, there are some examples, especially in the Bayon style, of images with separately attached arms. The final stage involved the smoothing and often the polishing of the image, especially the face and body.

Of the tools that were employed to carry this out we know next to nothing, but presumably the direct carving was by bronze chisels struck with wooden mallets. Until the day that excavation reveals actual workshops or *ateliers*, this question and many others will remain unanswered.

The overwhelming majority of Khmer stone carving is bound up with the architecture of which it forms part. This includes important mythological motifs in stone,[55] such as

- *Kala* faces. *Kala* is a jawless monster with the head of a lion seen frontally, and two bulging eyes; grasping and chewing a garland, it acts as a magically protective element in lintels placed over doorways.
- *Makara*, a bizarre hybrid between crocodile, fish, tapir, bird and elephant. It is seen in profile, placed at either end of stone lintels.

pl. x
- *Apsaras*, divine dancing girls, shown in relief at very important monu-ments (most notably on the walls of Angkor Wat).

pl. IV
- *Devatas*, female divinities of Indra's paradise, usually framed in flaming arches. These are even more common than *apsaras*.

79
- *Naga*, a cobra with odd-numbered heads (usually seven or nine). This is a serpent god of the waters, invoking 1) the Khmer origin legend of the *naga* princess, 2) the serpent Vasuki used as a rope in the Hindu myth of the Churning of the Sea of Milk, and the *naga* Ananta on whom Vishnu rested during Creation, and 3) the king of the *nagas* who is said to have saved the Buddha from drowning. The *naga* is the mythological animal most repre-sented in Khmer sculpure, notably in the great serpent balustrades flanking causeways and water basins.
- *Garudas*, the enemies of the *nagas*, depicted as anthropomorphic eagles, and revered as the 'vehicle' of Vishnu.
- *Dvarapalas*, youthful divinities guarding doorways.

The entire purpose of these great temple complexes was to provide a beau-tiful home for the gods, and that was the guiding principle behind the magnificently sculpted lintels and doorjambs giving entrance to these sanc-tuaries. The bulk of the decoration of temples is based upon vegetal motifs, particularly the sacred water lily, with elements from the animal kingdom and from mythology. Especially rich in mythological content are the richly carved pediments and 'frontons' (enlarged pediments), such those as on the near-miniature temples of Banteay Srei.

X Pair of *apsaras*, Angkor Wat. The elaborate headdresses and costumes give an idea of the appearance of dancers and other women in the Classic royal court. The white paint was probably added in Post-Classic times.

XI Detail of the Churning of the Sea of Milk relief in Angkor Wat. Demons hold a segment of the serpent Vasuki, which Vishnu used to turn the churn during the process of creation. Classic period, first half of the twelfth century.

XII (*right*) Gilt bronze figure of the crowned Buddha seated in meditation, sheltered by the *naga* serpent Muchilinda. Classic period, possibly twelfth century. Ht 73 cm (28.7 in).

XIII (*below*) Wood figure of a seated worshipper, ornamented with red lacquer, gold leaf and black paint. This sensitive sculpture, found in the Cruciform Gallery of Angkor Wat, is the finest known example of Theravada Buddhist art in Cambodia. Post-Classic period, sixteenth century. Ht 94 cm (37 in).

XIV (*right*) Deified king (?), gilt bronze with silver inlay. This magnificent bronze of unknown provenance may be a posthumous portrait of a deceased ruler. Classic period, second half of the eleventh century. Ht 105.7 cm (41.6 in).

XV Each of the Bayon's thirty-seven surviving towers is embellished with four enigmatically smiling faces, believed to represent either Jayavarman VII or Avalokiteshvara (the Boddhisattva of Compassion), but both may be intended. Classic period, end of twelfth and beginning of thirteenth centuries.

XVI The Phimeanakas temple, from the east. According to Zhou Daguan, a golden tower on its summit was the nightly trysting place of the king and a serpent-woman. Classic period, tenth century.

XVII Row of giant *garudas* fronting the Elephant Terrace; this huge platform was the reviewing stand of Angkor's Royal Palace.

XVIII (*left*) One of Ta Prohm's temples, in the grip of tree roots. French archaeologists deliberately left these structures in their ruined state. Classic period, end of the twelfth century.

XIX (*right*) Face tower at Ta Prohm, Angkor, a huge Mahayana Buddhist monastic complex dedicated by Jayavarman VII in AD 1186 in honour of his mother.

XX (*below*) Wall of a shrine in Ta Prohm, Angkor. The costume and pose of the goddess (*devata*) standing in a niche recalls the earlier *apsaras* of Angkor Wat. The red colouring is not paint but lichen growth. Classic period, late twelfth century.

XXI Buddhist monks in Angkor Wat. Although initially dedicated to Vishnu, this great complex has been Theravada Buddhist since the end of the Classic period.

XXII 'Dance of the *Apsaras*' in the Hall of Dancers, Preah Khan. Following its brutal suppression by the Khmer Rouge, there has been a great revival of classical dance in Cambodia. This troupe is affiliated with Wat Po, in Siem Reap.

Much of the carving, though, might be termed purely 'decorative', 80
although even this must have magical import. Interior walls and pilasters are
often covered with repetitive, low-relief motifs that at times seem to be
reproducing textile designs – perhaps based upon actual examples of
imported Chinese or Indian wall hangings. These vast, decorative programmes must have been laid out first with chalk or ink; Jean Commaille was
the first to suggest the extensive use of stencils, and this technique has been
confirmed by Vittorio Roveda's analysis of such reliefs at Angkor Wat.[56]

Metalworking
We know little about Classic iron-working technology, even though most of
their tools must have been made of iron. Perhaps much of this was produced
by the tribal, aboriginal neighbours of the lowland Khmer, since during the
nineteenth century these were notably skilled iron-smiths.

The greatest of all cult images must have been of metal, but these have not
survived the vicissitudes of war and invasion, cupidity, and the ravages of
time. Some of the finest ones were apparently removed to Ayutthaya by the
Thai during their fifteenth-century conquest of Angkor; these were subsequently looted by the Burmese when they conquered Ayutthaya in 1569.

Almost all the still-existent Classic metalwork consists of fine bronzes cast 81
by the lost-wax technique. Most common are finials, bands, hammock rings, 82
and other bronze paraphernalia from the litters, fans and parasols of the
Cambodian elite, decorated in a wonderfully baroque decorative style similar
to architectural sculpture. Also well-represented in collections are ritual
objects, and statuettes of the Hindu and Mahayanist deities.[57] The larger of
these were cast in several parts, which were then fitted together either with
iron rivets, or else (in the case of limbs) like sections of a pipe. The most
astonishing of the religious statues is the fragmentary, colossal bronze dis- 48
covered in 1936 in the West Mebon, the island in the middle of the West
Baray; seen and described by Zhou Daguan, it depicts the reclining god
Vishnu at the moment of the world's creation, and would have originally
extended at least 6 m (20 ft) when complete.

There are very few extant examples of the magnificent jewelry to be seen
everywhere on the statuary – vast amounts must have been looted by the Thai
armies when they sacked Angkor in the fifteenth century and more may have
been melted down by the Khmer themselves during periods of state contraction. In a tradition that extends back to Oc Eo, Khmer goldsmiths produced
vast amounts of jewelry as well as vessels of gold and silver for the Royal
Palace. If Zhou is to be believed, even women of ordinary rank wore gold arm
bands and rings.

Gold beaters must have been continuously occupied in Angkor and other
Classic centres. Many of the stone statues and probably all the bronze ones
would have been covered in gold leaf. Zhou Daguan relates that the top centre
heads on the Bayon's multifaced towers, as well as the central tower itself, were
golden, and from other sources it seems that all five towers of Angkor Wat were
treated likewise. Even the tower atop the Phimeanakas, where the king was
supposed to have slept nightly with the *naga* goddess, was covered with gold.[58]

78 Figure of a dwarf, from the north end of the Elephant Terrace, Angkor Thom. Classic period, twelfth century.

79 Massive *garuda* figure surmounting a *naga*, from the Preah Khan complex, Angkor. Classic period, late twelfth century. This formed a kind of finial to one of the giant-and-*naga* balustrades of a causeway.

80 Decorative floral relief from Angkor Wat. Such overall, repetitive patterns were probably produced from stencils.

81 Bronze dancing celestial figure (*apasara*), Classic period, late eleventh to twelfth centuries. This beautiful bronze bears a close resemblance to the *apsaras* carved in relief on the Bayon's columns. Ht 39.3 cm (15.5 in).

82 Bronze kneeling woman, late eleventh–early twelfth century, Cambodia. The posture and strongly flexed fingers indicate that this young lady is a dancer. Ht 47.6 cm (18 in).

Pottery and pottery-making

The study of Khmer ceramics is in its infancy. The first archaeologist to take a serious interest in this aspect of material culture was B.-P. Groslier, but his field notes and the collections from his excavations at Angkor were largely lost during the Indo-China War.[59]

Prior to the founding of the Khmer Empire in 802, all clay vessels and pottery roof tiles were unglazed earthenware; after that time, the technique of glazing was introduced, almost certainly from China. It was not much later that the Khmer elite of Angkor and other urban centres began to import high-quality Chinese ceramics. Compared to these exotic and finely made wares, and to the highly sophisticated Khmer art style seen in their metallurgy and stone sculpture, native pottery seems almost like a folk tradition. Khmer ceramics have been characterized as 'heavy, rather brooding, sombre, and serious looking', with simple and almost naïve decoration.[60]

83 Glazed Khmer ceramics of the Classic period. *c* is a lime container in the form of an elephant; *d* is probably a storage jar for wine. Ht. of *d* is 23.3 cm (9.2 in), rest to scale.

83   Almost all Classic Khmer glazed pottery is a kind of stoneware, fired at low to medium temperatures, with two basic glaze colours: a pale, translucent yellowish green, and a dark brown-to-black. The vessel walls have generally been built up by the coiling method, and the piece then finished on a wheel. Some of the earliest Classic wares were produced in a series of kilns on the Kulen Plateau, about 2 km (1.25 miles) southwest of the village of Anlong Thom; these are coated with a clear to yellowish to green glaze derived from wood ash. By the latter part of the tenth century appears what B.-P. Groslier christened as *lie de vin* ('wine lees') ware: thick, flat-bottomed, unglazed stoneware basins and jars, with a thin, violet to red slip; Roxanna Brown suggests that these may have been used as containers for silk preparation and dyeing.[61]

More substantial kilns are known for the Khorat Plateau, in Buriram Province. Probably dating from the eleventh century on, these are constructed of slabs placed on lower walls of laterite, with a single chimney. From them came brown-glazed and green-glazed vessels for the Angkor market – footed jars, bottles, urns with covers and bowls; small elephant effigy jars were probably containers for the lime used with the betel chew. Another set of pottery kilns was discovered in 1995 by a Japanese team from Sophia University, and subsequently excavated by them.[62] These are located near the hamlet of Tani, about 20 km (12 miles) northeast of Angkor Thom. The Tani kilns specialized in the production of ash-glazed and plain bottles and lidded jars.

Serious importation of Chinese glazed pottery began in the tenth century. There were over 5,000 Chinese potsherds in EFEO archaeologist Jacques

Gaucher's excavations in Angkor Thom; in fact, within the Royal Palace excavations of the 1990s, Chinese ceramics greatly outnumbered native Khmer wares.[63] Dawn Rooney suggests that within the royal establishment, Chinese porcelains and celadons were preferred for ornamentation and for serving and eating food, Khmer glazed vessels as containers for religious rituals, and unglazed earthenware for preparing food. Especially common are lidded boxes from Zhejiang Province; white porcelain from Guangdong; and mould-decorated porcelain from Fujian (as late as the thirteenth and fourteenth centuries); and thirteenth-century celadons from Zhejiang.

Daily life in ancient Angkor

Life cycle

Almost everything we know about the daily life of the city's inhabitants comes from the pen of Zhou Daguan, and probably from the occasionally salacious observations of his Chinese colleagues in the capital. His information on the life cycle begins with birth:

> Once a Cambodian woman's child is born, she immediately makes a poultice of hot rice and salt and applies it to her private parts. This is taken off in twenty-four hours, thus preventing any untoward after-effects and causing an astringency which seems to renew the young woman's virginity.[64]

Zhou was clearly fascinated with the deflowering ceremony held for young girls in Angkor, which took place in April. The age at which this rite was performed depended upon the wealth of the family: daughters of rich parents went through it at seven to nine years, poor ones at eleven. The families chose in advance either a Buddhist monk or Shivaite priest for the initiation, and he was showered with gifts such as wine, rice, cloth, silk, areca (betel) nuts and silver.

> The night of the ceremony a great feast, with music, is prepared. In front of the girl's home a platform is erected on which are placed figurines of animals and persons, sometimes ten or more in number, often less. Nothing of this sort is expected of the poor. Following an ancient tradition these figurines remained in place for a week. Next, a procession with palanquins, parasols, and music sets out to fetch the priest. Two pavilions hung with brilliantly coloured silks have been set up; in one of them is seated the priest, the maiden in the other. Words are exchanged between the two, but they can scarcely be heard, so deafening is the music, for on such occasions it is lawful to shatter the peace of the night. I have been told that at a given moment the priest enters the maiden's pavilion and deflowers her with his hand, dropping the first fruits into a vessel of wine. It is said that the father and mother, the relations and neighbours, stain their foreheads with this wine, or even taste it. Some also say that the priest has intercourse with the girl; others deny this. As Chinese are not allowed to witness these proceedings, the exact truth is hard to learn.[65]

The parents were then obligated to 'buy' back the girl from the priest with gifts, otherwise she might never marry.

Couples often had sexual intercourse before they were married. According to Zhou's somewhat chauvinistic opinion, Cambodian women were highly sexed:

> One or two days after giving birth to a child they are ready for inter-course: if a husband is not responsive he will be discarded. When a husband is called away on matters of business, they endure his absence for a while; but if he is gone as much as ten days, the wife is apt to say, 'I am no ghost; how can I be expected to sleep alone?' Though their sexual impulses are very strong, it is said some of them remain faithful.[66]

Sexual behaviour in Classic Angkor must have been fairly relaxed, even between members of the same sex. Our Chinese observer professes shock that groups of ten or more homosexuals can be found in the market every day, soliciting his countrymen.[67]

There is remarkably little archaeological information on disposal of the dead in Classic Angkor. Until the 1960s, no cemetery had ever been found, and B.-P. Groslier was able to say in 1956 'Angkor [is] a city without a necrop-olis'. This changed in 1963, when he discovered and excavated a more-or-less rectangular burial ground on the west side of the Srah Srang[68]; it had been founded in the mid-eleventh century, and continued in use until the fif-teenth. In accordance with Hindu and Buddhist practice, the dead had all been cremated, and the remains placed in large vases. Surrounding them were many offerings, including small porcelain dishes and boxes of Chinese manufacture; various Khmer pottery jars, lids and elephant effigy jars (prob-ably for lime); iron weapons and tools; lead ingots; terracotta *prah patima* moulds (for casting Buddhist votive plaques); and bronze statues of the Bud-dha. That these had been high-status individuals is indicated by bronze mirrors as well as by a pair of bronze litter hooks and two ornamental rings from litter shafts.

Zhou's information on the subject seems to cover the ordinary citizens of the capital, and is reminiscent of Tantric (especially Tibetan) custom rather than Mahayana or Theravada Buddhist. According to him, the dead were simply laid out on straw matting and covered with cloth. Then the corpse was borne in a procession accompanied by flags, banners and music, the mourners scattering fried rice along the way until they arrived at 'some lonely place' out-side the city. There they abandoned the cadaver and went home,

> after seeing that the vultures, dogs, and other beasts are coming to devour it. If all is over quickly, they say that their father or their mother had acquired merit and was receiving the due reward; if the corpse is not eaten, or only partially eaten, this is ascribed to some misdeed committed by the departed one.[69]

He does say, however, that an increasing number of people were resorting to cremation (mostly descendents of Chinese), and that rulers were buried –

meaning by this their ashes – in the *stupas* or *chetdis* (a Theravada practice, as shall be seen in Chapter 8).

Costume and personal appearance

No costumes, dress or textiles of any kind have survived from Classic times, but one can get an excellent idea of these – and of coiffures – from the stone monuments as well as from Zhou's testimony. He describes the strict sumptuary laws that ruled in late thirteenth-century Angkor: high officers and princes could wear fabrics patterned with recurring groups of flowers, ordinary mandarins and female commoners could wear material with two groups of flowers, but only the ruler was permitted fabrics woven in an all-over pattern.[70]

    84

    With the exception of warrior kings and soldiers, who are often depicted with jackets or short bodices ending above the waist, no one had upper body coverings made of textiles – this is indeed a hot climate. A recent study by art historian Gill Green[71] has shown that the prevalent lower body garment is the 'hipwrapper', which all humans or deities wear in one form or another. There are three kinds in Classic Angkor:

84 Pair of *apsaras* from Angkor Wat. They give a good idea of the costume of court ladies in the palace of Suryavarman II.

1) The *chawng kbun* (known today by the modern Khmer term *sampot*), worn by males. A length of cloth is wrapped around the waist and knotted either in front or back; then, the remaining cloth is passed between the legs, and slipped under a waist band or belt at the back or the front. For lower ranked persons like foot soldiers, this was little more than a loincloth, but it became increasingly elaborate as one moves up the social scale.

2) 'Hipcloths', worn by some Khmer soldiers, as well as by women. A length of fabric is wrapped around the hips, brought to the front, and knotted, the free ends being left to hang down in front.

85   3) 'Skirt cloths', an elaborate female garment that hung unhindered from the waist. A length of fabric was wrapped around the body, and cinched with a belt or knotted at the waist. On longer skirt cloths, the end panel was pleated into a bundle that was tucked in at the waist, and allowed to fall forward.

As Green has noted, like so much else in Angkorian culture, these forms are ultimately derived from Indian prototypes – the *chawng kbun* from the well-known *dhoti*, 'skirt cloths' from the sari (and the knotted ones from the Indian *lunghi*).

It is unlikely that the more elaborate hipcloths, as on the *apsaras* or *devata* of Angkor Wat, could have been made of a single piece of cloth. Further, the fabrics of really complex hipwrappers, as well as temple and palace hangings, would have been too wide to have been made on the native backstrap looms described by Zhou. Such textiles must have been imported from China, Champa, Siam (Thailand), and especially India – whose weavings, says Zhou, were noted for their skill and delicacy. The Khmer knew nothing of the culture and weaving of silk, leaving it to Siamese women living in the capital to undertake these tasks.

85   Statue of woman or goddess from the Bakong (Hariharalaya), last quarter of ninth century. She wears a wrap-around skirt cloth, partly pleated, with a folded-over upper extension.

Zhou claims that all Cambodian men and women knotted the hair in a bun,[72] and while this certainly seems to be true for females, men, including the ruler, often appear with very short hair, and some also have buns (as in the famous portrait sculptures of Jayavarman VII). For royal princesses, *devatas*, dancers (both real and mythological), and female musicians, there were splendid, tricorn headdresses, probably made from thin sheets or leaves of gold and silver. Such may be seen, along with even more exotic ones, on the myriad relief *apsaras* and *devatas* of Angkor Wat. The majority of males on the reliefs appear with elongated, slit ears, but it may be that ear pendants were not worn by commoners on the field of battle or in the presence of gods and royalty. All non-slave women were adorned with gold armlets and rings, and both sexes perfumed themselves with sandalwood, musk and the like.

84

Foot coverings of any sort, whether shoes, sandals or slippers, were unknown in Classic-period Cambodia, but women dyed the palms of their hands and the soles of their feet with henna.

Furniture and sleeping arrangements

There were generally no beds in ordinary houses, or in the palace. People slept on bamboo mats laid on wooden floors, although low beds made by the Chinese were gradually coming into use among the well-to-do. Because of the nightly swarms of mosquitoes, cloth mosquito nets were necessary; those in the Royal Palace were silk, woven with gold-spotted threads. There was little furniture of any kind; however, the ruler and other personages of exalted rank sat on low daises.[73]

Relief scenes on the Bayon and elsewhere depict curtains of flower-patterned fabrics, swagged when not in use. Windows in shrines, palaces and in the more upscale houses might be protected from animals (such as monkeys) as well as shaded by lathe-turned, wooden balusters, and were provided with slat blinds that could be rolled up. Umbrellas and other paraphernalia were horizontally suspended from house beams.

Food preparation and cuisine

We have no cookery books from the period of Cambodia's greatness, so it is virtually impossible to reconstruct, for instance, the food served in the Royal Palace. This must have been very different from the daily fare of the ordinary Khmer peasant, which would have largely consisted of cooked rice, fish from the Great Lake and the many waterways, fish paste (*prahok*), and fish sauce (*tik trei*).[74] Our information on food preparation and eating habits is entirely based upon reliefs in the South Gallery of the Bayon and on Zhou Daguan. Zhou tells us that three stones formed a hearth,[75] but the ancient, portable pottery brazier with three-pointed rim is depicted in Bayon kitchen scenes. Rice was hulled with mortar and pestle, cooked in earthenware pots, and served in Chinese pottery dishes or in copperware.

64

Since tables and chairs were largely absent, diners sat on Chinese or rattan mats, or upon animal hides. High-ranking or wealthy families ate from silver or even golden plates, the food being protected from flies by cloths. In the Royal Palace, eating utensils were generally of gold. Southeast Asian practice

86 Food preparation in a field kitchen, on a Bayon relief. Left, a cook pours rice into a pot placed on a clay brazier. Centre, a young pig is about to be lowered into a pot, while a servant blows on the flames. Right, roasting small fish.

dictated that the food was eaten with the right hand; water-filled bowls were kept nearby to rinse the fingers. In the absence of metal spoons, sauces and liquids were scooped up with a special kind of leaf.

There are two sets of Bayon scenes with culinary subjects. One depicts a

86   kind of field kitchen set up in a forest, with rice being cooked, a pig about to be singed or boiled, and small fish (and perhaps frogs, a Cambodian favourite) gripped between bamboo splats being grilled over open flames. The other set involves an elaborately roofed residence, apparently the home of a rich Chinese merchant, with Chinese and Khmer servants; in the kitchen a small deer is bled and the blood is caught in a vessel, while a cook stirs soup with a long, hooked handle.

The residents of Angkor enjoyed alcoholic beverages. There were four kinds of 'wine': 1) mead, prepared from equal parts of honey and water, 2) 'wine' from the leaves of an unidentified tree, 3) rice wine, made from uncooked rice, or left-over cooked rice (today, the preferred variety for this is 'black' rice), and 4) palm sugar 'wine'.[76] In the 'House of the Chinese Man' Bayon relief, a person sips his wine from a small jar through a bamboo tube.

Health and sanitation[77]

Nine out of ten cases of dysentery, according to Zhou, ended fatally. This disease must have been quite prevalent in Angkor and elsewhere in the Empire, given the sanitary practices that he describes. Defecation took place in a trench shared by two or three families; when this was filled, it was covered and sown in grass, and a new one dug. Most of these pits must have drained into the ponds, canals and waterways from which they drew their drinking and cooking water. The only other disease that Zhou describes is leprosy, which seems to have been common, and that he ascribed to the habit of taking a bath immediately after sexual intercourse. He also mentions the long-lasting tradition that there had been a Leper King in Angkor (see Chapter 8). In Zhou's list of Cambodian exports is chaulmoogra, an extract from the seeds of the *Hydnocarpus anthelmintica* tree; this oil is a traditional cure for leprosy in Southeast Asia. There must have been a rich pharmacopoeia available to the capital's citizens; Jayavarman VII had established hospitals throughout his domain to dispense these herbal drugs, which were also available in the markets.

Entertainment and the performing arts

The Indic polities of mainland and insular Southeast Asia were 'theatre states' in anthropologist Clifford Geertz' famous definition of the term (based on his study of nineteenth-century Balinese kingdoms): the spectacular cremations, processions, temple dedications and the like, mobilizing hundreds and even thousands of people,

> were not means to political ends: they were the ends themselves, they were what the state was for. Court ceremonialism was the driving force of court politics; and mass ritual was not a device to shore up the state, but rather the state…was a device for the enactment of mass ritual. Power served pomp, not pomp power.[78]

Nowhere is this more apparent than in the great state processions of South and Southeast Asia, such as the impressive Perahera still celebrated annually in the old Sinhalese capital of Kandy in Sri Lanka (and attended by more than a million citizens). This is what the celebrated reliefs of Angkor Wat's South Gallery are all about: the political, religious and military structure of Suryavarman's empire were laid out for all to see in a grand and thrilling public display that must have been staged in the parade ground immediately in front of the 300-m (984-ft) long Elephant Terrace. Here is the unforgettable testimony of Zhou Daguan, who actually witnessed such an event:

> When the King [Jayavarman VIII] leaves his palace, the procession is headed by the soldiery; then come the flags, the banners, the music. Girls of the palace, three or five hundred in number, gaily dressed, with flowers in their hair and tapers in their hands, are massed together in a separate column. The tapers are lighted even in broad daylight. Then come other girls carrying gold and silver vessels from the palace and a whole galaxy of ornaments, of very special design, the uses of which were strange to me. Then came still more girls, the bodyguard of the palace, holding shields and lances. These, too, were separately aligned. Following them came chariots drawn by goats and horses, all adorned with gold; ministers and princes, mounted on elephants, were preceded by bearers

of scarlet parasols, without number. Close behind came the royal wives and concubines, in palanquins and chariots, or mounted on horses or elephants, to whom were assigned at least a hundred parasols mottled with gold. Finally the Sovereign appeared, standing erect on an elephant and holding in his hand the Sacred Sword. This elephant, his tusks sheathed in gold, was accompanied by bearers of twenty white parasols with golden shafts. All around was a bodyguard of elephants, drawn close together, and still more soldiers for complete protection, marching in close order.[79]

As for the music, in processions shown on the reliefs, the Classic marching band was mainly composed of percussion instruments and long trumpets. A passage from a stela in the Ta Prohm complex has an exhortation:

> Let the procession that surrounds them be full of banners, parasols; let the struck musical instruments make great sounds that charm the spirit; let the male and female dancers dance all around here.[80]

There are many references to music and dance in the inscriptions,[81] since apparently every temple of any importance had its own dance troupe and orchestra, often donated by the king. The SKT inscription records a royal donation of '100 lutes, flutes with a delicious sound, 50 orchestras, copper cymbals, drums, etc.'. These performing artists were privileged *khñum* who could not be employed in inferior labour; in one inscription, a singer and a dancer offer donations of villages, rice fields, revenues, and even other *khñum* to a temple.

Stringed instruments appear as accompaniments to dancers and indoor entertainments, and included angular harps (*pinn*, now virtually extinct in Cambodia), theorbos, violins and *vinas* (lutes). Violins consisted of chords strung on a long tube, while lutes added resonance chambers of one or two gourds. Wind instruments comprise long trumpets, horns and conches. This being Southeast Asia, there was a varied complex of percussion instruments: gongs, bells, handbells, small cymbals, tamtams, barrel drums and tambourines. In a relief in Angkor Wat is a gong circle (*korn vung* in modern Khmer), consisting of nine bossed gongs, being played to accompany dancers. There are no depictions of xylophones, either of wood or metal, a curious absence since these go well back into Khmer prehistory and today form an important part of the *pinn peat* orchestra of contemporary Cambodia.

68

87

Dance and music were inseparable in Classic Khmer culture, and were integral not only to lay entertainments, but also to Brahmanic and Buddhist temple rituals. The *apsaras* – the lovely celestial dancers to be seen throughout the Bayon and other temple complexes – were created from sea foam during the Churning of the Sea of Milk. Their role was to dance for the delectation of the gods on Mount Meru, and their earthly counterpart would have been the large *corps de ballet* of the Khmer king, for, as B.-P. Groslier tells us, 'the royal ballerinas were (and have remained so into our own time) the essential distraction of the palace'.[82] It must not be assumed from the attitudes of the participants seen in sculptures like the famous lintel in Preah Khan's Court of the Dancers that this was some sort of ecstatic performance, for traditional Cambodian ballet is almost a kind of slow-motion dance, with much concentration of the movements of the hands, as in the rest of the Indic world.

On the testimony of the reliefs, there were many diversions for both royalty and commoners in Classic society: cockfights and boar fights, wrestling matches, and circus-like performances of juggling and acrobatics, among others. On the Elephant Terrace are depicted polo matches, gladiatorial con-

88

87 A pair of *apsaras* (celestial nymphs) dancing on lotus flowers, from a column of the Bayon. The gracefully bent-back fingers are still a typical feature of Cambodian dance.

88 Khmer peasants participating in a cockfight, detail from a Bayon relief.

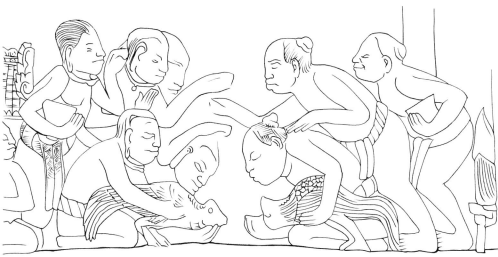

tests and chariot racing. Within the royal palace, princesses could amuse themselves by dancing and playing chess or checkers, and there were even royal boating parties out on the Great Lake (perhaps during the Festival of Waters, see below). One scene carved in an interior gallery of the Bayon depicts a menagerie with zoo-keepers, watched by seated spectators.

Not the least of the pleasures of Angkor's denizens were the frequent baths that they took in the Siem Reap River and in the myriad artificial ponds and basins that dotted the cityscape, as a relief from the heat. Zhou Daguan appreciated one aspect of this pleasant custom:

> Every few days the women of the town, in groups of three or five, stroll down to the river to bathe. Here, at the water's edge, they drop the strip of cotton that clothes them, joining thousands of other women in the river. Even the women of noble birth mingle in these baths and think nothing of it, although they show themselves from head to foot to any bystanders who may appear. Not a day passes without this happening. On days of leisure the Chinese often treat themselves to the spectacle. In fact, I have heard it said that many of them enter the water to take advantage of whatever opportunity offers.[83]

The annual round of religious and profane festivals provided wonderful entertainment for the capital's residents.[84] The Cambodian New Year began in October–November, and was marked by a great public spectacle in front of the Royal Palace. From an immense viewing platform (capable of holding a thousand persons) and decorated with flowers and lanterns, the king and the empire's notables could view the proceedings. Opposite it, for every night of the spectacle, three to six scaffolds were put up to hold a fireworks display. Zhou tells us that the rockets could be seen at a distance of 13 km (8 miles), and that firecrackers as large as swivel-guns shook the entire city with their explosions. The expense for all this was borne not by the king, but by the mandarins and great provincial families.

There was a festival in every month; Zhou observed these:

- Fourth month. This was the time for ball games (about which we know nothing from the reliefs).
- Fifth month. Marked by the festival of 'bringing water to the Buddhas', when Buddha images were bathed by all, including the king.
- Sixth month. 'The festival of floats'. This is still celebrated today during the month Asuj (September–October) – after the people have asked pardon of the Earth and the Water for having polluted them during the course of the year, elaborate little pagodas or pyramids, illuminated by candles and lanterns that have been placed on banana-trunk rafts, are floated out on the waterways. Zhou says that the king viewed this from a belvedere.
- Seventh month. 'The burning of the rice': the newly harvested rice was brought to Angkor Thom's South Gate and burned as a sacrifice to the Buddha. This was watched by throngs of women who had arrived in carts or on elephants.

- Eighth month. 'The month of dancing', a ten-day event in the Royal Palace, to which foreign ambassadors were invited by the king. It was marked by daily performances by actors and musicians, as well as by boar and elephant fights.
- Ninth month. Zhou states that during this was the month of the census, 'when the entire population is summoned to the capital and passed in review before the Royal Palace'.

Curiously, Zhou makes no mention of the Festival of the Waters, celebrated today not only in Cambodia but in the other Buddhist lands of mainland Southeast Asia. This marks the end of the rainy season, and takes place at the time of the full moon in the month Kattik (October–November); during it, boat races are held, in which compete enormous numbers of elaborately decorated pirogues manned by thousands of rowers. That this also took place in Classic Angkor (that is, on the Great Lake) is attested by reliefs in the Southwest Corner Pavilion at Angkor Wat – even court ladies seem to have been out on the water at this time, and a few of them are seen playing a shipboard game of checkers.

Classic Khmer ritual life

With their many thousands of Hindu devotional structures, from the state temples of Angkor down to the smallest village shrines, and with its huge Mahayana Buddhist complexes and attendant monks, Cambodia's cities and countryside must have been bustling with religious activity. It is true that Theravada Buddhism had become strong by the time of Zhou's visit, but the other two religious traditions continued to play important roles.

Brahmanic Hinduism had been all-pervasive during most of the Classic period, until temporarily (and only partially) eclipsed by Jayavarman VII's Mahayanism. Hinduism is not a congregational religion such as Buddhism or Christianity, but is centred on individual devotion and worship of a god or goddess in a ritual that was always under the care of a Brahmin priest. The temple or shrine was there to provide a house in which the deity could take up temporary residence; there he (or she) would have a place to eat, to be bathed, and even to sleep. If everything was well conducted, the god would then come to life in his/her own stone, wood or metal image.

Devotion was a two-way, supernatural contract.[85] To the god the devotee gave offerings of flowers, incense, fruit, clarified butter, coconut juice and the like; in return, the devotee received back from the deity the now-blessed offering (*prasad*), along with the spiritual well-being (*darshan*) that resulted from eye contact with the now-live image. In this sense, each of the thousands of Classic Cambodian sculptures of the gods to be seen in museums, in collections, and in the Angkor conservation facility had once resided in a darkened shrine or sanctum at the centre of a temple establishment, and had been worshipped according to established Brahmanic practice.

The Khmer worshipper, alone or in a group, would have come to the temple with the appropriate offerings, and moved in a set way from the decorated

89 A ritual scene from the Bayon. A king, perhaps Jayavarman VII, prostrates himself before a shrine containing an image of the god Vishnu, while *apsaras* descend from the heavens.

outer structures of the complex towards the central shrine where the god lived, proceeding around the sacred space in an ever-decreasing, clockwise direction (this is *pradakshina*, the auspicious direction). As he neared the sanctum, he passed through structures outside of it in which were halls where the god was taken for his washing, sleeping or entertainment by dancers and musicians.

The sanctum itself was dark and undecorated, and entrance was only allowed to the Brahmin officiant, who acted as an intermediary between the devotee and the deity. The priest took the offering, and in turn offered it to the god, anointing it with the liquid oblations, and decorating the image with garlands. After the image was censed, the priest passed a lamp before it, which was then brought to the worshippers so that they could pass their hands quickly through the flames. Finally, with hands raised and folded palm to palm, the devotee established eye contact with the god, and was granted *darshan*.

89   We may be sure that for the wealthy, and for the ruler and members of the royal family, temple rituals were splendid affairs, with orchestral music, large troupes of temple dancers and temple elephants in procession. But even the king had to prostrate himself humbly before the gods, as Bayon relief scenes of Jayavarman VII worshipping at shrines of the gods Vishnu and Shiva prove. One can now understand why Cambodian artists and architects placed sandstone lintels elaborately carved with garlands and vegetation over temple doors – portals that were guarded by divine youths (*dvarapalas*) and

lovely maidens (*devatas*): it was to make a beautiful home in which a deity might be happy to reside.

On entering a temple, Buddhists, be they Mahayanist or Theravada (as many were by the end of the thirteenth century), paid devotion to the 'Three Jewels' or 'Three Refuges': 1) the Buddha, represented by an image, a *stupa* (burial monument), or a *bodhi* tree, the tree under which the Founder reached Enlightenment; 2) the Dhamma or Dharma, Buddha's teaching, represented by a sermon or informal teaching by the monks; and 3) the Sangha, the community of monks.[86] The devotee showed reverence before the sacred objects by bowing three times while standing or kneeling with the palms joined.

As with Hindu devotion, offerings, accompanied by chanted verses, were made to the images, and usually consisted of flowers, incense, and sometimes a ritual scarf. In Mahayanist practice, the offerings were quite elaborate, with seven different oblations, each in its own bowl. Mahayana Buddhists, who included Jayavarman VII, paid special homage to images of Avalokiteshvara, the Bodhisattva of infinite compassion and mercy; in this branch of Buddhism, images were imbued with the spirit and power of the being they represented, but for the more austere Theravadists, they were merely reminders of Buddha's life and message. Regardless, all images had to be consecrated before they could fulfil their function, whether in a temple like the Bayon or in a pagoda.

Buddhism in Southeast Asia has, and probably had in Classic times, its own annual cycle of festivals, set by full moons; how this was integrated into the festival season described by Zhou is unknown.

Warfare and the military

There seems never to have been a time in Cambodia's history when Khmers were not fighting each other, or waging war on foreign enemies. For the Classic Khmer period, while Zhou Daguan and the inscribed monuments have little to say on the subject, there is abundant pictorial information on armaments, order of battle and actual warfare in the reliefs of Angkor Wat, the Bayon and Banteay Chhmar.[87] Even the Buddha's message of peace and his prohibition on the taking of life did not deter Jayavarman VII from glorifying what seems to have been his great and bloody defeat of the Cham invaders in gruesome detail.

The ordinary Khmer soldiers as well as officers might carry a lance; or a bow, with the arrows being held in a quiver; or sabres of different length; or various sizes of knives and daggers; or a kind of halberd known as a *phka'k*. The latter was basically an iron axe mounted on a long handle curved at one end. At Angkor Wat, the *phka'k* is held in the hands of high-ranking warriors mounted on elephants or horses; it was still in use in the twentieth century for hunting and work in the forest. Crossbows were known, but are extremely rare in the reliefs.

For personal defence, there were two kinds of shields: round ones ornamented with vegetal or flower motifs, and long ones ornamented on the top border. The latter could be grouped together to form a kind of rampart. Both

90 Infantry battle between Cham invaders (left) and Khmer defenders (right), from the Bayon. The Cham can be distinguished by their strange headgear in the form of inverted flowers.

were probably of wood and hide, with metal plaques. Although most warriors wore only a kind of short-sleeved jacket (sometimes resembling the quilted cotton 'armour' in use in Mesoamerica), many were protected by a cylindrical cuirass, often with one or two knives lashed over it for close combat.

90   Far more sophisticated armament is to be seen on the Bayon and at Banteay Chhmar, especially among the infantry. This includes a ballista, mounted either on elephant back or on a wheeled vehicle that could be rolled onto the field of battle; it consisted of two opposed bows, worked by two men, and shot arrows with tremendous force. Michel Jacq-Hergoualc'h, the leading authority on Khmer warfare, believes it may be of Chinese origin. Shield 'ramparts' mounted on wheels are another innovation of Jayavarman VII's reign.

A combat unit consisted of foot soldiers, three to four mounted cavalrymen, and one war elephant. Elephants were reserved for the king and for his highest officers; these stood on roofless, decorated howdahs, with a mahout placed in front to direct the elephant, and wielded various kinds of weapons – the lance-and-shield, the *phka'k*, or the bow-and-arrow. Cavalry horses were ridden without saddle or stirrups, and during combat the mounted knights often stood on their steeds' backs. In the great procession depicted at Angkor Wat, the riders (and some infantrymen) were distinguished by headgear in the shape of eagle or deer heads. War chariots were very similar to *naga*-decorated carts, but were roofless, and drawn by pairs of horses.

Some sections of the Khmer army consisted of foreign mercenaries, such as the colourful Siamese (Thai) unit depicted in the South Gallery relief of Angkor Wat, with their beaded, wig-like headgear and beaded jackets and skirts; these were led by a Thai general mounted on an elephant. Even traditional enemies like the Cham (recognizable from their flower-like headdress) or the Vietnamese could be recruited into the military service of the Angkor state.

The Khmer army on the march must have been an impressive sight – and sound. It was accompanied by military music produced by a huge gong struck by a dwarfish person, long trumpets, bronze castanets, and blasts from conch shells. The ark of Sacred Fire, under the care of Brahmin priests, was carried along into battle, and there were parasols, banners and battle standards. The latter consisted of a staff mounted with the small bronze figure of one of the monkey generals from the *Ramayana*, or of Vishnu mounted on Garuda, or of Garuda by himself. Supplies and food for the army were brought in covered wagons drawn by bullocks, and even on pack elephants, while pigs were driven along the route of march. There were many camp-followers, perhaps the wives and children of the soldiers. Women of far higher rank travelled with the army in palanquins, rickshaws and sedan chairs.

Great naval battles with the Cham appear on the Bayon and at Banteay Chhmar, both sides employing essentially identical ships embellished with *garudas* on the prow and *nagas* on the stern. Each vessel had 20 to 42 rowers plus a steersman, and must have been enormous. These bloody engagements on the waters of the Great Lake included the use of grappling hooks.

Zhou Daguan was unimpressed by Khmer military know-how, denigrating it with the brief statement, 'Generally speaking, these people have neither discipline nor strategy.'[88]

91 A fighting unit of the Khmer army, on a Bayon relief. The great officer in charge rides a war elephant, while his lieutenant is mounted on a horse. The foot soldiers march to the sound of a trumpet, gong and drums.

Thought and culture in Classic Angkor

The Brahmins who brought Indic culture and learning to the royal courts of mainland Southeast Asia during the early centuries of our era continued to play that role throughout the Classic period, and in the royal palaces of Cambodia and Thailand, right into modern times. These intellectuals acted as priests of the temples, teachers, royal chaplains, librarians, astrologers, and in all likelihood architects and calligraphers. It was they who cast the horoscopes for all important events, who interpreted the Vedas and the Hindu laws to the empire's power brokers, who designed temples in which the great gods could reside, who conducted all ritual, who tended and carried the Sacred Fire, and who kept the calendars.

92   All this learning depended upon writing. There are over 1,200 inscriptions known for the ancient Khmer world, almost all from the Early Kingdoms and Classic periods. These were incised into polished stone, and most appear on the doorjambs of temples and on free-standing, four-sided stelae. They are read in horizontal lines from left to right, and from top to bottom, in a complex alphabet derived from the Nagari script of India. There are two kinds of inscriptions. The most prestigious were in Sanskrit, and almost always in the form of poems; as Claude Jacques comments:

> These inscriptions were placed under the gaze of a particular god and seemingly were intended to attract that deity's attention to the person who had had the sanctuary built in his honour or, more often, who was offering him gifts.[89]

Most of these donors were kings, the poems being composed upon their death. They were accompanied by a short eulogy (*prashasti*). Prose texts in

92 Detail of an inscription on the door jamb of a brick tower in the Lolei complex, consecrated in AD 893. Partly in Sanskrit and partly in Khmer, it dedicates the tower to Yashovarman I's parents and maternal grandparents.

Old Khmer comprised the other kind of inscription, frequently appearing on the same stone with the Sanskrit one; these had a very different, more prosaic, and far more informative subject matter. According to Jacques,[90] the overwhelming majority are inventories listing the temple's possessions – land, livestock, servants and furnishings. Some end with an imprecation formula, for example putting a curse upon any violator of the terms of the grant 'as long as the moon and the sun shall last'.

These texts are generally fixed in time by the intricate calendar system of ancient Cambodia, itself partly dependent upon astronomical and astrological considerations.[91] The solar year is given in terms of the Great Era (saka) that began on the Vernal Equinox of AD 79; thus, one is to add 78 to the saka date to reach a year in our system. The digits making up the saka numbers may be spelled out alphabetically, or they may be given by chronograms: for example, saka 1044 (AD 1122) might be given symbolically by 'oceans [4], 'oceans' (again)[4], 'sky' [0], 'moon' [1]. There were 12 lunar months, each divided into a 15-day waxing period and a 15-day waning one. The astrologers were deeply interested in the current position of the moon against the band of stars that runs along the ecliptic in a kind of lunar zodiac; since the sidereal month is about 27 days, there were 27 of these 'lunar mansions' or nakshatras, each with an animal name (the moon generally traversing one mansion a day). Because the lunar calendar was always running ahead of the solar one, extra lunar months were occasionally intercalated in a complex system of Indian origin.

By Zhou Daguan's day, solar years were also expressed in terms of a 12-year cycle, each year named for a specific animal, a system that they had borrowed from the Chinese – perhaps a reflection of Cambodia's rapidly increasing trade with the Middle Kingdom.

Like their counterparts in peninsular India, the Cambodian astrologers were close observers and calculators of the positions of the five visible planets (Mercury, Venus, Mars, Jupiter and Saturn) as these moved across the solar zodiac, which was essentially the same one that is still in use in the Western world. One more calendrical statement appearing in the inscriptions is the day of the seven-day week, each day being linked to one of the planets or to the sun or to the moon, as it is with us. According to Zhou, the ordinary Khmer had no family or personal names, but were known by the day of the week on which they were born.

The Yugas – the huge cosmic cycle of successive creations and destructions – did not enter into their calendrical computations, but they certainly played a role in Cambodian cosmology, as Eleanor Morón Mannikka has shown in her study of the proportions and measurements of Angkor Wat.[92]

Zhou Daguan makes no mention of inscriptions, but he does talk about writing on perishable materials: these are the manuscripts, which probably existed in quantity in the libraries, state archives and temples of Classic Angkor.[93] Not one, however, has survived the vicissitudes of time, history and tropical climate, a tragedy for Khmer scholarship. The religious texts, whether Brahmanic or Buddhist, were contained in palm-leaf books or sas-tra; these consisted of fronds about 50 to 60 cm (20 to 24 in) long, bound

93

together into a stack by loose cords. Each leaf was incised with a stylus, and the scratched lines filled with lampblack. In the Angkor Wat reliefs, Brahmin *pandita* or gurus accompanying the Sacred Fire carry such books in their hands or on their shoulders, while at Banteay Chhmar, a *pandita* reads one accompanied by a Khmer theorbo.

It is likely that all secular books were paper screenfolds. Such accordion-like manuscripts were being produced in Cambodia until the middle of the twentieth century. The paper was manufactured from the inner bark of a member of the mulberry family; it was softened by soaking, then wrung out and finely shredded to separate the white from the brown fibres (these latter being used to produce black paper, the kind mentioned by Zhou). After this had been boiled with white lime and then washed and pounded, the resulting paste was spread onto cloth or screens and left to dry in sheets. White paper was treated with rice powder mixed with water and chalk, and black paper with soot or charcoal. The final stage was to polish the surfaces, and fold the paper into books. Manufactured paper was imported from China; while there is no mention of its use to make books, Zhou reports that the natives derived great amusement at seeing the Chinese use it as toilet paper.

Zhou describes the chalk pencils that were used to write black pages, and says that such pages could be easily erased; accordingly, official documents, such as revenue, corvée manpower and census tallies must have been kept in the white-paged screenfolds, which were written in black ink, probably with bamboo and/or metal pens.

Assuredly some of these paper books contained astronomical tables, for Zhou assures us that their astronomers could calculate solar and lunar eclipses – an impossibility without the accurate accumulation of observational data over a very long period of time.

93 Seated Brahmin gurus reading palm-leaf books, from one of the inner galleries of the Bayon. To the left, a standing Brahmin holds a rosary.

How literate were the Classic Khmer? Surely all the Brahmins of the empire could read and write, and so could the kings and princes, all of whom had been instructed by Brahmin teachers (in contrast to contemporary European rulers such as Charlemagne, who were often illiterate). The vast civil bureaucracy would have found it in their interest as revenue gatherers and beneficiaries to be literate, too. Both Mahayanist and Theravada Buddhist monks would by Sangha rules have to be able to read and recite the sacred texts of their faith. Add to this list the masters of works, the architects, and the master craftsmen who worked in stone and metal, and one can conclude that a substantial minority during Classic times was lettered. Nonetheless, the great majority of Khmer – the free peasants and the slaves – would have been unable to 'read' anything but the imagery of the reliefs and sculptures.

Angkor: city and state

With the exception of B.-P. Groslier, with his vision of an immense 'hydraulic city' containing almost two million souls, until recently few scholars had devoted much thought to what kind of city Angkor really was. As Roland Fletcher has said, 'Angkor still needs to be reappraised as a place where people actually lived.'

There were many cities during pre-modern times in both mainland and insular Southeast Asia. Following a dichotomy first recognized for medieval France, John Miksic of the University of Singapore has proposed that they fell into two groups.[94] *Heterogenetic* cities were found along coastlines and at the borders of ecological zones rather than at their centres; they had few public monuments, and were characterized by entrepreneurship and intensive trade, as well as by high population densities (pre-colonial Malacca would have been an excellent example of such a city).

Orthogenetic cities were located well inland, and were correlated with the production of a surplus staple crop – that is, rice – which could be commandeered by the authorities. Stability and ritual were the prevailing order, and there were impressive monuments of a religious nature. There was no money and little evidence for large markets and significant trade. 'The permanent population of the orthogenetic city was composed of nobles, civil, religious and military bureaucrats, and their staff.' In contrast with heterogenetic cities, overall population density was very low. From everything that we know about Angkor, it would appear to have been orthogenetic. Moving away from our area, so would have been the monumental Classic Maya cities such as Tikal, Copan and Palenque in Mesoamerica, with their royal courts and extremely dispersed patterns of settlement.

A clue as to what at least part of Angkor might have looked like comes from the old Siamese capital of Ayutthaya in Thailand, founded in 1351 and destroyed by the Burmese in 1767. It was a conscious clone of the Khmer capital, Angkor Thom, and covered about the same area; instead of being bounded by a huge moat, it was surrounded on all sides by rivers or by connecting canals, and by a wall. An account of Ayutthaya by a seventeenth-century Dutch traveller states:

> The Streets of the walled Town are many of them large, straight
> and regular, with channels running through them, although the
> most part of small narrow Lanes, Ditches, and Creeks most con-
> fusedly placed; the Citizens have an incredible number of small
> boats…which come to their very doors, especially at floods and
> high water.[95]

Plans and watercolour drawings by Europeans show that it was crisscrossed by canals and streets, with the royal palace in the northwest sector (as
in Angkor Thom); the only densely settled sector lay in the southeast. Comments by an early eighteenth-century observer are relevant here:

> Considering the bigness of the City, it is not very populous…scarce
> the sixth part is inhabited, and that to the South-East only. The rest
> lies desart [sic] where the Temples only stand…there are abun-
> dance of empty space and large gardens behind the streets, wherein
> they let nature work, so that they are full of Grass, Herbs, Shrubs
> and Trees, that grow wild…[96]

The houses of ordinary inhabitants were thatched, single-storey structures of bamboo and wood, built on piles, while foreign traders lived along
the main north-south avenue in more substantial tile-roofed houses. Ayutthaya, whatever its Angkor-inspired beginnings, was slowly evolving from an
orthogenetic to a partly heterogenetic city, due to the easy access that Chinese, European and Arab traders had from its waterways.

Let us first consider Angkor Thom; in recent years its four quadrants have
been surveyed in detail by Jacques Gaucher of the EFEO, using aerial photographs and ground 'truthing'. The main axes of Angkor's capital district
were lined with canals, and, again like Ayutthaya, the Royal Palace was in the
northwest quadrant; elsewhere, apart from the monumental constructions,
there were numerous small water tanks, channels and house mounds. Based
on the results of this survey, Roland Fletcher suggests that while Angkor
Thom could have held as many as 90,000 people (assuming a density of 100
persons per hectare), the population may have been only a quarter of that,
given the amount of open space (as in Ayutthaya); the palace; the major temples; and the single-storey dwellings.[97]

Turning now to the city of Angkor as a whole, a survey carried out there
from 1992 to 1998 by Christophe Pottier has shown that this landscape was
dotted with low mounds that had once supported hamlets of about five to ten
traditional, single-storey houses. These mounds were associated with hundreds of small, local shrines and medium-sized, rectangular water tanks,
recalling Zhou Daguan's statement that 'every family has a pond – or, at
times, several families own one in common'. Based on ground survey and
upon radar imagery and aerial photography, Fletcher now estimates that the
total area of Angkor's urban complex is about 1,000 square km (386 square
miles), within which the people were mainly living along linear features –
canals and roads that extend out from central Angkor for about 20 to 30 km
(12 to 18 miles) in all directions, probably less and less densely occupied as

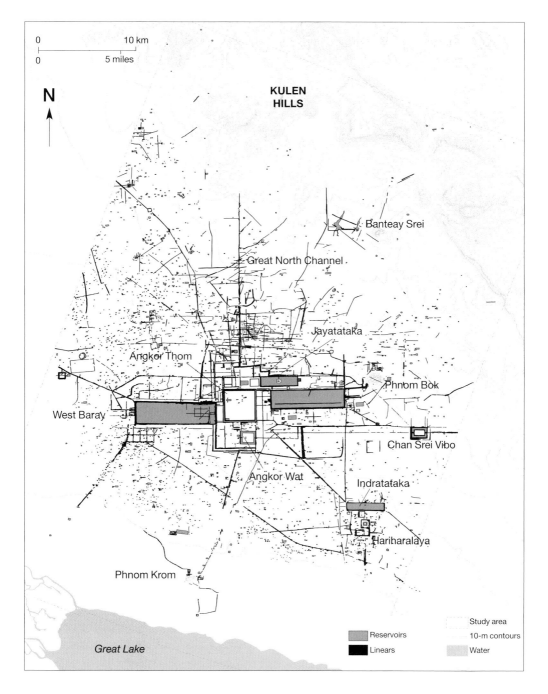

94 The megacity of Angkor, based on AIRSAR remote sensing and ground survey. The linear features are canals, dikes and roads; along with the great *barays*, they generally conform to a grid pattern orientated to the cardinal directions. The myriad small reservoirs are probably ponds belonging to local shrines, hamlets and extended families, and are randomly distributed between the Kulen hills and the Great Lake's high water mark.

one moves towards the peripheries. Angkor Thom, then, was like a kind of spider sitting in the centre of a virtual web of settlement, with large open spaces, including even rice fields, between the 'threads'. This web extended well north of Preah Khan into the foothills of Phnom Kulen; the lovely Banteay Srei was probably at its northern edge.

In Fletcher's words, 'Angkor was therefore a low density, dispersed urban complex with housing along linear features and scattered across the landscape in patches and on isolated mounds.' Groslier's estimate of 1.9 million persons is thus an impossibility. The true figure for Angkor at its apogee, during the reign of Jayavarman VII, was probably a fraction of this, but only a great deal of future research can give us an idea of the total population.

The system of government that made Classic Khmer civilization and the city of Angkor possible was a highly effective and powerful 'top down' one, supported by a command economy and by a massive and all-encompassing, revenue-generating bureaucracy operating on every level from palace to village. Historian David Chandler has summarized this kind of government in both Cambodia of the 1860s, and Cambodia under the rule of Angkor:

> In both cases…government meant a network of status relationships whereby peasants paid in rice, forest products, or labour to support their officials. The officials, in turn, paid the king, using some of the rice, forest products, and peasant labour with which they had been paid. The number of peasants one could exploit in this way depended on the position one was granted by the throne; positions themselves were for sale, and this tended to limit the officeholders to members of the elite with enough money [absent, of course, in Classic times] or goods on hand to purchase their positions.[98]

In an influential 1982 essay, Cornell University historian O. W. Wolters proposed that many of the early polities of Southeast Asia, including the Angkorian one, were *mandalas*; this is a technical Sanskrit term meaning 'a particular and often unstable situation in a vaguely defined geographical area without fixed boundaries and where smaller centres tended to look in all directions for security.'[99] A *mandala* was a 'circle of kings and brahmins', in which one king would lord it over lesser ones, and those kings in vassal or tributary status would continuously try to repudiate this and build up their own network of vassals. This would certainly apply to what we know was going on among rival kings in mainland Southeast Asia *prior* to AD 802. But for most of the time during the next five centuries, in spite of sporadic revolts and foreign invasions that could have occurred in any empire, the Angkor state – that is, the king – had complete control over all Khmer territory. This was enforced out to Cambodia's frontiers not only by his army and his judicial system, but by his roving inspectors (the *tamrvach*) and by periodic census-taking. 'Supreme and extensive political dominion' is how the *Oxford English Dictionary* defines 'empire'. The city of Angkor may not have looked like imperial Rome, but the Classic Khmer Empire over which it ruled lasted as long as the Roman one.

8 · The Post-Classic Period: Decline and Transformation

The very last Sanskrit inscription in ancient Cambodia dates to AD 1327, and describes the accession of a king named Jayavarmadiparameshvara.[1] With this event, the Classic period of Khmer civilization effectively comes to a close. What is here called the 'Post-Classic', and by others the post-Angkorian or Middle Period of Cambodian history and culture, extends from that date until the establishment of the French Protectorate in 1863. Largely because of scholarly neglect, it is by far the least-known epoch, since for almost a century research institutions like the EFEO had with good reason concentrated all their efforts on Classic Angkor and its predecessors. They gave back to the Khmer a large and important part of their history. But ironically, what happened – or what is *said* to have happened – in the Post-Classic somehow seems far more real and relevant to the modern Khmer themselves than all of the royal personages and doings discovered by scholars in the Classic inscriptions, including even the mighty monarchs Suryavarman II and Jayavarman VII.[2]

Yet it is now appreciated that while diminished in grandeur, Khmer culture had a distinctive and vigorous life during these centuries, in spite of the buffeting and territorial shrinkage that Cambodia sustained from the aggressions of the Thai on one side, and the Vietnamese (Annamese) on the other.[3] Here are the most salient traits of the Post-Classic:

- The monarch no longer a *chakravartin*, but merely the king of Cambodia.
- The capital in various locations between the Great Lake and the Delta.
- Theravada Buddhism as the state religion, with Pali rather than Sanskrit as its language.
- Stone temple architecture and *prasats* replaced by wood-built *viharas* ('pagodas') and other monastic buildings.
- State and ancestral temples in disuse; or converted to Buddhist worship and made the object of long-distance pilgrimages.
- Predominance of the Sangha (Buddhist order of monks) in all aspects of life.
- Middle Khmer replaces Old Khmer as the language of the people and of the court.
- Written royal chronicles, but few contemporary stone inscriptions.
- Absence or abandonment of large-scale public works, such as the *barays* and the major canals in Angkor and elsewhere.
- Strong development of maritime trade with China, Japan, and parts of Southeast Asia.
- Marked Thai (Siamese) influence in art, architecture, theatre and court life.

The collapse of Classic Angkor

There are as many theories to account for the downfall of the Classic Khmer civilization of Angkor as there are for the collapse of Classic Maya civilization in Mesoamerica some five centuries earlier, and many of them are remarkably similar.[4] The fact is that at some time early in the fifteenth century, the Khmer Empire had largely ceased to exist, and the capital of Cambodia had been transferred from Angkor to the Quatre Bras region, near the Siem Reap River. This is traditionally dated to 1431, when the Thai are supposed to have invaded and sacked the ancient city (although we shall see that there is some reason to doubt the exactitude of this date).

One persistently advanced theory is that Jayavarman VII had overextended himself by his massive building programmes in Angkor and elsewhere. In Angkor alone, this ruler was responsible for the great monastic complexes of Ta Prohm, Preah Khan and Banteay Kdei, not to mention Angkor Thom, the Bayon and Neak Pean. Outside the capital city, he created (among others) Banteay Chhmar and Beng Mealea, most of the highway and rest-house system of the empire, and his more than 100 hospitals. According to many scholars, this 'building frenzy', as Lawrence Briggs called it, simply exhausted the labour and taxation resources of the Khmer state.[5] It is true that there was never again construction on this scale, or anything near it.

A second possibility is that of outside invasion, in this case by the Thai (the origins of whom will be taken up later on). The historical chronicles, both Cambodian and Thai, suggest that devastating attacks from Siamese armies took place several times in the fourteenth and fifteenth centuries, and that it was these that 1) disrupted the enormous system of *barays* and canals that had underlain Angkorian rice production and 2) introduced Theravada Buddhism, to the detriment of the Hindu and Mahayanist ideologies that had sustained the imperial state and its rulers. As we shall see, these chronologies are internally inconsistent, so that any conclusions based upon them must be taken with a large pinch of salt.

Let us examine the religious hypothesis first. Lawrence P. Briggs – a believer in the reliability of the chronicles – was convinced that the adoption of Singhalese (that is, Theravada) Buddhism was the decisive factor in Angkor's demise:

> The change of religion had more to do with the end of the great period of architecture and art than the ravages of the Siamese and their sack of the capital. The transformation was internal. The soldiers of Ayuthia [Ayutthaya] not so much conquered them with warlike blows as seduced them with the hope of a milder religion. No amount of blows from without could account for the unfinished condition of temples and sculptures begun decades and even centuries before the fall of Angkor or for the systematic mutilation of the images of the hated gods seen everywhere at Angkor. In short, to use a crude expression, the wonderful period of ancient Khmer civilization ended, not so much because the Khmers 'got licked' as because they 'got religion'.[6]

Yet others have pointed out that the same supposedly 'milder' version of Buddhism did not seem to have stopped the rapidly expanding Thai in their military aggressions against Cambodia (which continued until the mid-nineteenth century), nor did it stop the latter from making vigorous counter-attacks, nor did it deter the Burmese from invading Siam and sacking Ayutthaya in 1569. What it *did* do was to make monumental stone temples irrelevant both to the royal cult and to the Khmer people themselves.

Bernard-Philippe Groslier was the most eloquent advocate of the hypothesis that Angkor fell mainly because the massive water-management system on which he claimed the city had depended (his *cité hydraulique*) gradually declined and was abandoned as it silted up through neglect. Recent archaeological survey and excavation by Christophe Pottier and Roland Fletcher have shown that Groslier was at least partially right.[7] Radar images reveal that ancient, bunded rice fields had extended from the relatively flat lands of central Angkor north to the foothills of Phnom Kulen, probably as a result of increasing population pressure as the Classic period progressed. By clearing the lower slopes of forest cover and bringing them into cultivation, Angkor's later rulers had exposed the complex system of *barays* and canals not only to extensive siltation, but also to uncontrollable flooding and erosion. The effects may have been irreversible. If, as seems likely, the *barays* and canals allowed two annual rice harvests (or, more likely, improved yields provided by irrigation) in addition to the one-crop-a-year, flood-retreat farming carried out along the margins of the Great Lake, their loss would have been an ecological disaster.

One final factor should be mentioned. By at least the fifteenth century, the Asia in which Classic Angkor had once flourished had entered into what historian Anthony Reid has called 'The Age of Commerce'.[8] Real prosperity in Southeast Asia now depended upon intensive trade linkages between maritime cities, not upon isolated, inland royal centres, no matter how splendid. Often in the hands of Chinese traders (and Japanese ones, until the Shoguns closed the island kingdom to the outside world), vast amounts of goods travelled down rivers, along coasts, and between countries. By 1431 – the traditional but probably mythic date for the moving of the capital from Angkor – Cambodia's rulers must have realized that it was far more practical to conduct this commerce from the Quatre Bras region, easily reached by junks coming up from the Delta.

But, as we know from the far-better studied demise of the Classic Maya, civilizations – like biological species — usually fall from multiple causes, not single ones. Alterations in the religious paradigm, military incursions, overpopulation and ecological collapse, and the shifting of trade routes and patterns, finished off the Classic, monsoon-forest cultures of both Cambodia and the Maya area.

The sources

Given the fact that archaeological investigations of the Cambodian Post-Classic are virtually nonexistent, the historical and quasi-historical sources on the period loom large in any cultural reconstruction.

As Angkor became gradually abandoned, accurate memories about it disappeared from the collective Khmer memory, or metamorphosed into myth and legend. Yet its most famous building continued in use, under a double name: in Khmer, 'Angkor Wat' means 'the *wat* (Buddhist pagoda) of the city' – an accurate description – while its other Post-Classic name, 'Vishnuloka', evokes both the name of the Hindu god to which it was dedicated, and the posthumous name of its builder, Suryavarman II. A commonly held legend maintains that the capital was once ruled by a 'leper king', and the early French scholars were told that an enigmatically smiling, seated figure (on what is now known as the Terrace of the Leper King) was that personage; however, a Middle Khmer inscription on the statue identifies it as Yama, the Lord of the Dead. According to Cambodian linguist Au Chhieng,[9] Yama's title in Old Khmer was *stach kanlon*, 'King of the Law [i.e. Dharma]', but this was later mistakenly transmuted to *sdach ganlan*, 'Leper King', giving rise to the legend. Phnom Kulen has also attracted myth-makers: Aymonier was shown there what purported to be the stone-cut bath and cremation place of the Leper King, and even today it is commonly believed by local people that many of its features were fashioned by Chinese survivors of a junk that had been shipwrecked on its heights.[10]

The most famous Post-Classic legend, still well-known to the modern Khmer, is the story of the founding of Angkor, in which Indra – the king of the Hindu gods and the faithful servant of the Buddha – plays the key role. Here is Mme Saveros Pou's summary of the tale:

95 Statue of the so-called 'Leper King', as it was *in situ* in 1954. The mottled appearance was caused by lichen growths, and may have given rise to the notion that this was a ruler with leprosy. In actuality, it represents Yama, the Lord of the Dead.

…Indra … had adopted a human son, Ketumala, whom he brought to his celestial realm to enjoy a blissful life. But this happiness could not last very long because the gods all around could not bear [the] human presence and smell any longer. Consequently they got together to ask, even demand, the departure of Ketumala. Indra was shattered, but could not ignore the feelings and concern of his peers. He agreed to send Ketumala back to the earth. The prince was utterly struck by sorrow, for he was attached not only to Indra but also to the joys of celestial life. Indra then ordered the divine architect Bishnukar, alias Vishvakarma, to accompany the prince to the earth and build for him a 'great city as in the kingdom of Indra' – *mahanagar indraprasth*. It was specified in the legend that Bishnukar helped the prince come to terms with his terrestrial new life in building a magnificent palace [Angkor Wat], a true replica of Indra's one… Thereafter, a sacred bull was assigned to the keeping of the city, for whom he built to the southeast a temple bearing the bull's name, *Brah Go* [Preah Ko, in Hariharalaya].[11]

Apart from these legendary accounts, there are the surviving Royal Chronicles, both Cambodian and Thai (the latter from Siam's then capital, Ayutthaya). There are four Cambodian chronicles, all of them dating to the close of the eighteenth and beginning of the nineteenth centuries, and about as many Ayutthayan ones, but compiled at a slightly earlier date. Using two chronologies – one based upon the *chula* era beginning in AD 638, and the other upon the Chinese-derived, twelve-animal cycle – they describe royal events such as births, coronations, abdications, usurpations and deaths; invasions, mainly by the Thai; internecine warfare; and restorations. A meticulous analysis of these by historian Michael Vickery leads him to conclude that the first 150 years of Cambodia's Post-Classic history is 'entirely artificial', that is, pure fiction, a projection backwards in cyclical time of events and personages known to have existed at later dates.[12] It is not until the arrival of European adventurers and missionaries in the sixteenth century that one can begin to anchor Cambodian events to 'real' time.

Why did the Cambodian literati of the time manipulate history in this way? Firstly, they had no records of their own past before the sixteenth century, and popular traditions about this period are dateless. Secondly, during the period in question and even long afterwards, the Cambodian and Thai courts were inextricably linked. Khmer intellectuals were steeped in Thai language and literature, and had come to think that the Ayutthayan chronicles were something to imitate; thus, they forced the Cambodian chronicles into a Thai model.

Even though Sanskrit was no longer used, there is, in fact, a small body of votive inscriptions in the Middle Khmer language from the Post-Classic, though these are relatively rare and in any case, no longer exclusively royal.[13] All are dated by the *saka* era and by the twelve-animal cycle. Many of these can be found in Angkor Wat, and relate to pilgrimages and pious works carried out in this now-Buddhist temple (see below).

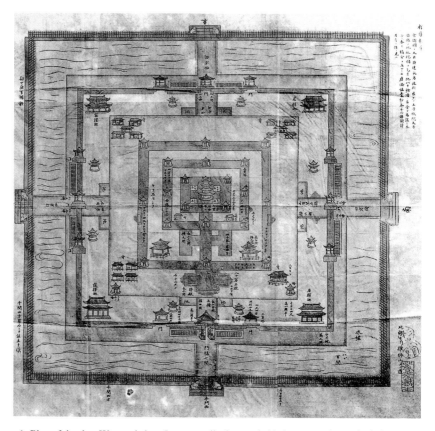

96 Plan of Angkor Wat made by a Japanese pilgrim, probably between 1623 and 1636.

Other information for the Post-Classic comes from graffiti left by Chinese and Japanese merchant-pilgrims to Phnom Kulen and to Angkor's major monuments – in particular to Angkor Wat. Most of these date to the early seventeenth century. The most interesting are painted with brush pens and India ink on the square columns of Angkor Wat's Cruciform Gallery and are deeply Buddhist in nature. It was one of these Japanese pilgrims who must have made the remarkably accurate plan of Angkor Wat now preserved in the library of the Shohohan Museum in Mito, Japan; probably dating to *c.* 1623 to 1636, it contains a clear reference to the famous relief of the Churning of the Sea of Milk.[14]

Another body of documents on Post-Classic Cambodia during the 'Age of Commerce' consists of official Japanese debriefings of Chinese captains and crews of merchant junks that plied between mainland Southeast Asia (including Cambodia) and Japan; following the closing of Japan to the rest of the world in the 1630s by the Tokugawa Shogunate, this shipping had to enter at Nagasaki.[15] The reports are brief, but often contain important economic and even political and social intelligence on seventeenth- and eighteenth-century Cambodia, including this besieged country's relations with its ever-aggressive neighbours.

Finally, there are the accounts of the European missionaries, explorers, diplomats, merchants and adventurers whose arrival and intrigues so often played havoc with indigenous politics and traditional life in the kingdoms of Southeast Asia.[16] The first known *barangs* (Europeans) to arrive in Cambodia were Portuguese missionaries, although traders of that nationality may have preceded them. The pioneer was a Dominican named Gaspar da Cruz, who arrived in 1555 at the court of King Ang Chan – one of Post-Classic Cambodia's greatest rulers — in the then capital, Lovek. Some of these missionaries left valuable, even if slightly garbled, accounts of what they had seen and the kings and courts with which they dealt. The most significant of these is recorded by the official chronicler of the Portuguese Indies, Diogo do Couto, relying on the account of a visit to Angkor by a Capuchin father in 1585 or 1586 (see Chapter 1). As in the New World, on the heels of the missionaries came the adventurers, of whom the Spaniards were the most ambitious, with never-consummated plans to conquer the kingdom. Unfortunately the available documents from these *barang* intrusions are poor in ethnographic details, but they do provide anchor points for some of the chronology in the Royal Chronicles, from the sixteenth century onwards.

Theravada Buddhism and its meaning for Cambodia

'Theravada', 'The Doctrine of the Ancients', was founded on the Pali Canon and fixed by the Third Buddhist Council convened under the reign of India's Emperor Ashoka. Its sacred, literary language is Pali, a tongue of north Indian origin. Theravada doctrines are contained in the Tipitaka, 'three baskets'; these are:

1. The 'basket of discipline', the rules and customs of the Sangha.
2. The 'basket of discourses', the collected sermons and utterances of the Buddha.
3. The 'basket of higher knowledge', commentaries on the Dhamma (Sanskrit: Dharma).

In some respects Theravada is to Mahayana Buddhism as Protestantism is to Catholicism – a conscious return to the life of the Founder and his teachings.

Since the beginning of our era, Sri Lanka has been the fountainhead of Theravada teaching and missionary activities. The sect was introduced into Cambodia during the thirteenth and fourteenth centuries, and perhaps even earlier, but the exact form of propagation is unknown. Art historian Madeleine Giteau believes that the Thai kingdoms and the Burmese court played a part.[17] By the beginning of the fourteenth century, the Thai of the Sukkothaya kingdom had adopted Sinhalese Buddhism; and a Burmese text says that the son of a Cambodian king (perhaps Jayavarman VII) went to Sri Lanka to be ordained, returning to Southeast Asia in 1190. And in Cambodia, Shrindrajayavarman (1308–27), the successor of Jayavarman VIII, left an inscription in Pali; by that time, Theravada Buddhism had become the official religion of the Khmer state – there was never to be a return to Mahayanism.

Theravadism completely penetrated the land of the Khmer, without destroying either the Brahmanical cult of the kings or the folk animism of the masses. Sometimes the monks of the Sangha established themselves near an ancient temple that they then transformed into a Theravada sanctuary (as happened most famously with Angkor Wat, with its two, still functioning monastic complexes). More usually, they sought out a new site, erecting a monastery or *wat* near each village, the *wat* becoming its religious and cultural centre.

97 During the Post-Classic and in modern times, the Cambodian *wat* consists of a somewhat variable set of buildings, mainly built of wood and often surrounded by a moat that is expanded on the east to a lotus-filled pool. The principal *wat* buildings are:

98 • The *vihara*, a rectangular structure in the southeast quadrant of the complex, whose function is to house the Buddhist images. This is orientated east–west, and contains three naves, the central nave resting on two ranks of columns, with a side-aisle or *robieng* bordering it on four sides. The highest part of the nave, called *krih*, is elevated above the *robieng* and covered with a two-sloped roof. Roofed gables jut out from either end at a lower level, giving the 'telescopic' effect so typical of Theravada temples in Southeast Asia. From the gables *naga*-like finials curve upwards. At the west end of the central nave is the main altar, with the gilt image of the Buddha (generally seated in the 'Calling the Earth to Witness' position); numerous other Buddha images are placed below.

97 Theravada Buddhist monastery at the foot of Phnom Krom, on the edge of the Great Lake. The tall structure just right of centre is a cremation pavilion.

98 Wat Traleng Keng, a nineteenth-century Buddhist *vihara* with cruciform ground plan in the old royal capital of Lovek (Quatre Bras region).

- The *uposatha* or Ordination Hall, which serves as the locus for some of the more important rites in the lives of the monks, and as a meeting place for their community. The ground on which it sits and the area immediately adjacent is a highly sacred space, delimited by eight leaf-shaped stones called *sima* placed at the cardinal and inter-cardinal directions. Archaeologically, these stones and the laterite terraces on which the *uposatha* and *vihara* rest are usually the only indication of long-gone monastic complexes of the Post-Classic period.
- The *kuti* (*kot* or *kdei* in Khmer), the living quarters of the monks. These are thatched, pile dwellings not very different from the houses of the Cambodian peasant; the head of the monastery, though, may have more elaborate quarters with a tiled roof.
- The *sala*, an open-sided meeting hall for the faithful, roofed like the *vihara*.
- *Chetdi* or *chetiya*. These are bell-shaped masonry structures with spires, 99 sometimes containing Buddhist relics but more often the cremation ashes of important personages such as royalty or the abbots of monasteries. Often these are the only structures remaining from destroyed monastic complexes, such as the huge royal *chetdis* of the old capital of Udong.

99 Buddhist *chetdi* (stupa) outside the South Gallery of Angkor Wat. Post-Classic period. Such a monument would have housed the ashes of a Theravada monk, or even a precious relic, and indicates the conversion of a Vishnuite temple to a Buddhist one.

97 • The *prah men* or *brah meru*, the cremation pavilion for the funerals of persons of sufficiently high rank for their remains to be housed in a *chetdi* (sovereigns, princes, heads of monasteries).

• A shelter for the *neak ta*, protective spirits of the locality; these are sometimes fragmentary stone statues of Classic date.

Given the fact that the monks of the Sangha do not produce any food, and that they were, and still are, completely dependent upon the alms and offerings of the village faithful among whom they live, it can be seen that there was a degree of intimacy between the clergy and the laity in Post-Classic Cambodia that never could have existed in Classic times.

Angkor as a Theravada Buddhist complex

The city of Angkor may have ceased to be Cambodia's capital in the fifteenth century, but it has never ceased to house Theravada Buddhist communities. Modern visitors are often surprised by the number of devotees that crowd some parts of Angkor Wat and the Bayon, and by the active Buddhist shrines within them. Usually not appearing on tourist maps are several major, still-functioning *wats* within the walls of Angkor Thom; according to Ang Chouléan, these are foci of extensive parishes that include many villages of the Siem Reap region.[18] Laterite platforms that once supported other *wats* can be found elsewhere within the city's confines.

Massive Post-Classic alterations were carried out to some of Angkor's most famous Classic monuments, to convert these to Theravada worship. Most astonishingly, the Shivaite shrine atop Phnom Bakheng, at the very centre of Classic Yashodharapura, was once engulfed by a gigantic masonry statue of the Buddha seated on a lotus – no longer visible because the remains of this image were removed by the Bakheng's EFEO restorers. On a similar scale, the entire west side of the Baphuon was 'remanaged' in the fifteenth century into a colossal relief of the 'reclining Buddha' (actually, the Buddha entering *nibbana* or *nirvana*), using stones that had fallen from the collapsed Classic temple. A similar 'reclining Buddha' was carved into the living rock on Phnom Kulen, where it is still the object of veneration by pilgrims.

Such massive public works could only have been carried out by order of the king. But royal piety was not limited to Buddhism, for one inscription tells us that at some time prior to 1577, a ruler named Tribhuvanadityavarman ordered 'the restoration of Brah Bisnulok ['Holy Vishnuloka', that is, Angkor Wat] to its real former state...he restored the great temple of Brah Bisnulok, the enclosure wall stone by stone; he reconstructed the nine towers of the temple and embellished them by sheathing them in gold.'[19] And we shall see below an earlier intervention at Angkor Wat. Clearly, the Post-Classic kings of Cambodia continued to view this as a royal, Brahmanic temple as well as a Buddhist one. This monument has never faded from the mind of the Khmers.

The approximately forty Middle Khmer texts incised on the pillars and walls of Angkor Wat's first- and third-floor galleries are the work of pious pilgrims, as is the very long inscription on the east face of the Gallery of Bas-Reliefs; they date to the fourteenth through to the eighteenth centuries. In content, they are 'oaths of truth', giving an account of good deeds accomplished by different classes of the faithful, in hopes of a better existence for themselves and others in this life and the next.[20] These, as well as the seventeenth-century Chinese and Japanese Buddhist graffiti painted on columns of the Cruciform Gallery, give valuable information on the social, political and even commercial culture of the epoch.

Geopolitics

As Angkor's power declined, its territorial integrity and even culture came under threat from neighbouring peoples who had played little or no role during the period of Classic greatness. Battered on one side by the Thai (Siamese), and on the other by the Vietnamese (Annamese), Cambodia was 'caught between a rock and a hard place', a perilous situation that continued until the advent of the French Protectorate and even to the end of the twentieth century. Who were these peoples?

The Tai once lived in the area south of the Yangtze River, in the mountainous plateau of Yunnan, as a collection of farming tribes.[21] By the first century BC, various Tai states had been consolidated into the Kingdom of Nanchao; this was an aggressive polity, and by the ninth century AD it had penetrated southward into Burma and eastward to northern Vietnam. However, Nan-chao was overrun in AD 1253 by Kublai Khan and his formidable Mongol army, starting a southward-moving 'ripple effect' that increased the migration of the Tai speakers into mainland Southeast Asia, where some groups had already established a toehold as mercenaries (witness the military unit depicted on the Angkor Wat reliefs). As they infiltrated these lands (see Chapter 3), the Tai took on the culture of the local majority, while keeping their own language. One Tai branch, the Lao, moved into what had been Khmer territory in Laos, establishing a principality at Luang Prabang. Another, the Thai proper, overthrew Khmer rule at the imperial provincial capital of Sukhothaya in the northern Mae Nam Valley; this supposedly took place in 1238 – but all these early dates from the Royal Chronicles must be taken with a degree of scepticism. Towards the end of that century, they also founded the Lanna kingdom at Chiang Mai, in northern Thailand.

Sukhothaya had originally been an Angkorian outpost on Thailand's Chao Phraya Plain.[22] But after its overthrow by the Thai in the 1240s, that was where Thai civilization took shape, and where these 'southern barbarians' (as

100   Thai mercenaries in the Khmer army, detail of a relief in the Third Gallery of Angkor Wat. First half of the twelfth century.

the Chinese called them) absorbed much of the Khmer culture of the Classic period, including urban planning, art and architecture, royal institutions, the Hindu-Brahmanic religious tradition, Khmer music and dance, and the Khmer script. It was also here that the Thai first made their acquaintance with Theravada Buddhism.

Further south, on an island in Thailand's Chao Phraya River, the Thai founded the city of Ayutthaya in the mid-fourteenth century.[23] Here again, the monarchy and administration were modelled on the Angkor state; and it was here that Theravada Buddhism became the state religion of Siam (modern Thailand). Ayutthaya soon became the greatest power in Southeast Asia and, if the Royal Chronicles are to believed, launched many assaults on Angkor, eventually reducing it from an empire to a small state. Early in the Post-Classic, Angkor lost all of its territory in what was to become Thailand, including the Khorat Plateau. The easy access of the Chao Phraya to the Gulf of Thailand attracted many foreign merchants to Ayutthaya; the Chinese were there from the beginning, but during the seventeenth and eighteenth centuries there were sizeable colonies of Portuguese, French, Dutch, English and Malay traders.

At first, the only enemies of the Ayutthaya polity were the greatly weakened Khmer. But in 1569, the more powerful Burmese successfully attacked the city, sacking its treasures, including those treasures that the Thai had taken from Angkor in the previous century. These eventually ended up in Mandalay, where they still are. Ayutthaya rebounded, but was once more conquered by the Burmese in 1767, an event that finished it off as a capital. The centre of government was moved downriver, at first to Thon Buri, and finally to Bangkok, where Rama I, the founder of the present dynasty, was crowned in 1782.

Far more formidable enemies of the Thai appeared to the east of the Khorat Plateau: the Vietnamese (Annamese).[24] In prehistoric times the dominant ethnic group of southeasternmost China and the rich Red River delta of northern Vietnam, these people had been conquered and thoroughly sinicized under the Han Dynasty (206 BC–AD 221). China, in fact, ruled northern Vietnam for the next thousand years, during which their subjects adopted Taoist and Confucian teachings, the mandarin-scholar system of bureaucracy, Chinese rites, writing system and many other customs of their northern neighbours. This does not mean that the Vietnamese ever docilely accepted Chinese domination, and rebellions often broke out, ending with the country's independence in AD 939.

Various local dynasties then ruled Vietnam, with intermittent but ultimately unsuccessful Chinese attempts to retake their former domain. But improved techniques for growing wet rice introduced by the Chinese had led to burgeoning populations in the Red River homeland, and the Vietnamese began pushing south in the search for *lebensraum*. The first to feel the brunt were the Cham of central Vietnam, the old Indianized kingdom that had been converted to Islam; in 1471 Champa was conquered by the Vietnamese, and its people forced out by resettled Vietnamese soldiers, many Cham fleeing to Cambodia. This was not the end, though: the triumphant northerners later invaded the Delta, which could not be defended by the feeble Khmer state, and the important Khmer port of Prei Nokor came under Vietnamese control shortly before 1700; it was eventually renamed 'Saigon'. The final alienation of the Delta from Cambodia came in the course of the next six decades.

Thus, a geopolitical pattern was laid down that has hardly changed over the past five centuries. It was always the policy of Ayutthaya, Sukhothaya and Bangkok to secure the eastern frontier of Thai territory by thwarting Vietnamese designs on Cambodia; it was Vietnam's to simultaneously resist Chinese attempts at domination, and relieve overpopulation by expanding into the lands of weak neighbours like Cambodia and Laos. The rivalry and at times outright conflict between Thailand and Vietnam have continued to reverberate down through the ages. In this struggle, and even in spite of occasional Thai military aggression and territorial takeover, there has been a fundamental sympathy and communality of interest between the Khmer and the Thai, based upon a shared religion, upon many cultural similarities, and upon long-standing linkages between the Thai and Cambodian courts. With the Vietnamese, there has been undying hostility and suspicion on the part of the Khmer, rooted in a very bitter history.

The course of Post-Classic history[25]

Given our conflicting sources, and the extremely shaky chronology that they present, the early centuries of the Post-Classic can be grasped only dimly; even the widely accepted date for the abandonment of Angkor – 1431 – is in doubt. What cannot be doubted, though, is that the Angkor kingdom was repeatedly attacked by the Ayutthaya-based Thai, although the Khmer did occasionally strike back successfully. The transfer of the capital away from Angkor and to the southeastern part of the country seems to have been a piecemeal process. This is the region known to the French as the Quatre Bras, where the Mekong and the Tonle Sap Rivers meet before dividing and going their respective ways through the Delta. Historian David Chandler suggests that the provincial chiefs of this strategically located area had already established direct trade with China, so that it was logical for the Khmer king and his bureaucracy to move here from the far more isolated Angkor.

The initial move seems to have been to Srei Santhor, about 30 km (19 miles) northeast of Phnom Penh, at some time in the fourteenth century; then, briefly, to Phnom Penh itself. By about 1528, the Cambodian court under its first great post-Angkorian king, Ang Chan I, had moved once and for all to the Quatre Bras region, establishing a new capital at Lovek (Longvek), on the right bank of the Tonle Sap River, 50 km (30 miles) north of Phnom Penh.[26] Lovek, like Udong and Phnom Penh – the towns that succeeded it as the capital – was thoroughly international, with foreign quarters for Malay, Japanese and Chinese traders (there were as many as 3,000 of the last in the 1540s). European visitors and the Royal Chronicles describe it and its king in superlative terms. There Ang Chan (who really *did* exist) built a

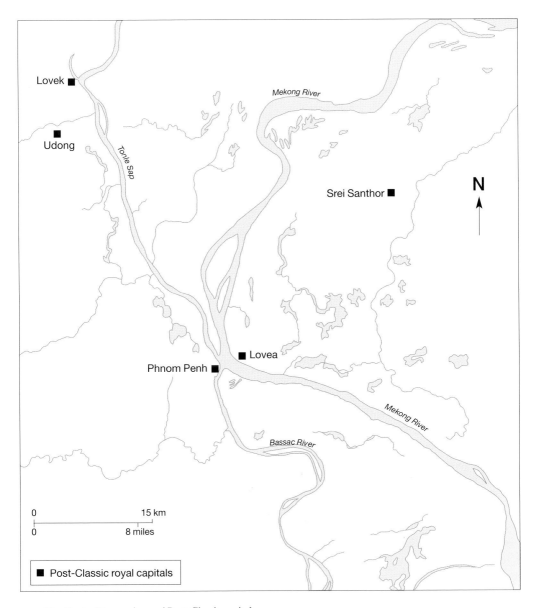

101 The Quatre Bras region and Post-Classic capitals.

golden palace and at least four major *wats*, erecting a huge, four-faced Buddha of wood, the stone foundations of which survive in one of the town's *viharas*. The capital was fortified by earthen ramparts topped with palisades; these ramparts, which form a huge rectangle, are still visible. As we have seen in Chapter 1, the Portuguese chronicler Diogo do Couto, writing in 1599, claimed that forty years before (that is, in Ang Chan's reign) the king had rediscovered the deserted Angkor Thom, and later relocated his capital there, but most scholars think this assertion dubious.

It was during Ang Chan's kingship that the first Portuguese missionary, Gaspar da Cruz, arrived, but he was unsuccessful in gaining converts, blaming his failure on the inability of the Khmer to do anything without the king's assent.[27] A turbulent three decades followed Ang Chan's death in 1566, during which one of his successors flirted dangerously with European powers, i.e. allowing Catholic missionaries to preach, and asking the Spaniards in Manila to help him fight his Thai enemies (luckily, this did not happen). Interestingly, this ruler claimed that for the joint operation, he could field 80,000 troops, 10,000 horses and 12,000 elephants. These figures may have been exaggerated,[28] but even so, it appears that Cambodia was still a power in Southeast Asia.

Even worse for Cambodia, in 1594 Lovek fell to the Thai army after the king and his son had fled to Laos. The Thai capture of Lovek is commemorated in two Khmer legends.[29] One claims that since the Cambodian capital was surrounded by a fence of bamboo hedges, the invaders fired a cannon containing silver coins at the fortifications. The Khmer cut the bamboos to the ground to get the money, and when the Thai returned the next year, the defences of Lovek had vanished. The other has resonated throughout the Post-Classic and even modern history of the country. It states that the reason the Thai king wanted to take Lovek was because two hollow statues were kept in the capital, respectively named *preah ko* ('sacred cow') and *preah kaev* ('sacred precious stone'); within them were golden books containing all the world's knowledge. The victorious Thai carried these off, and thus it is they who have become superior in wisdom, while the Khmer remain in ignorance.

Lovek was reoccupied by the court, but from 1595 to 1599 Cambodia became a target of Spanish imperialism, directed from the Philippines. Two Spanish adventurers, Blas Ruiz and Diego de Veloso, arrived on the scene, and (as Chandler says) seduced the sovereign by their blandishments.[30] More to the point, they initiated a revolution in Southeast Asian warfare with the wholesale introduction of firearms, especially naval cannon. In 1604 the Dominican missionary Gabriel Quiroga de San Antonio tried to draw the Spanish king into invading Cambodia; but the Spanish authorities decided against it, realizing that this action would overstrain their military and financial resources.[31] Catholic proselytizing ended with a major Thai intervention in 1603–04, not to be resumed until three centuries later.

By the seventeenth century, Cambodia had become a maritime kingdom, with an elite that was dependant more upon foreign trade than on revenues from the land. This commerce was almost entirely in the hands of foreigners: Chinese (above all), Japanese, Arabs, Spaniards, Portuguese, Malays from Indonesia, Dutch and English. With the accession of King Chei Chettha II in 1619, the capital was moved to Udong, 9 km (5.6 miles) south of Lovek; this had long been a sacred site. It was during this reign, which lasted until 1627, that the king authorized the Vietnamese king of Hué to open a trading post and receive customs fees in the Delta port of Prei Nokor (Saigon, see above), a disastrous move that by the end of the eighteenth century led to the permanent loss of the whole area and the closing off of the lower Mekong as an outlet for Cambodian trade.

An astonishing event took place in the 1640s that could have changed the whole course of Southeast Asian history: one year after his accession in 1643, the then king, Chau Ponhea Chan (Ramadhipati I), took a Muslim girl as his 'wife of the left', and converted to Islam. Because of his misdeeds, this ruler – a kind of Richard III – was highly unpopular, but he had been assured that Allah would forgive his sins. Simultaneously, his principal wife converted to Catholicism! The results of his rash act, which must have outraged the Sangha, were a revolt of the princes; an invasion and pillage of Cambodia by Vietnamese forces; and the king's assassination.[32]

Cambodia, as Chandler tells us, was now caught in a vice between Thailand and Vietnam. By 1738, the latter had annexed most of the Delta, isolating Cambodia from the overseas world for well over 125 years. The last half of the eighteenth century saw much of the country under only nominal rule from Udong, while the Thai and the Vietnamese armies struggled against each other to establish hegemony over what remained of Cambodia. The declared intention of the Thai was to protect the Theravada Buddhism of the Khmer from the heretical Vietnamese; the intention of the Vietnamese, whether declared or not, was to use Cambodia as a dumping ground for their landless peasantry, retired soldiers, adventurers, and even criminals. Over and over again, the Khmer court was split by divided loyalties, sometimes to the Thai, sometimes to Vietnam; those Cambodian kings who tried to balance the two failed miserably.

That was a bad century for Cambodia, but the first half of the nineteenth century was far worse. In 1794, the Thai had put King Ang Eng on the throne in Udong, at the same time annexing northwestern Cambodia, including Angkor and the rich rice lands of Battambang. His son Ang Chan II (crowned in 1806) leaned in the other direction, and asked for Vietnamese aid during a Thai-Vietnam conflict staged on Cambodian territory. To get even closer to his Vietnamese allies and take advantage of the Delta's trade, in 1812 Ang Chan moved the capital south to Phnom Penh.

A considerable opposition to the king's behaviour had started to build up, exacerbated by the high-handed and cruel way the Vietnamese in the Delta had been treating the native Khmer inhabitants. This came to a head in 1817–20, with the excavation of the huge Vinh Te Canal by forced Khmer labour; a serious anti-Vietnamese uprising took place, headed by monks, ex-monks, and Khmer nobles, but this failed and its leaders were executed.

Then Cambodia entered one of the two darkest periods of its history – the other being the Pol Pot era. In 1832 the Thai attacked the Vietnamese in Cambodia, these being forced to abandon Phnom Penh; when they departed, they took Ang Chan, a true quisling, with them. But then the Vietnamese came back two years later, reinstalling their puppet king and imposing their rule on the rest of the country. From 1834 until 1841, what had once been the greatest empire in Southeast Asia had shrunk to a tiny possession of Vietnam. After annexation, the nobles were forced to wear Vietnamese bureaucratic costumes, and to adopt appropriate mandarin titles. In fact, all Khmer had to take Vietnamese names, and even wear their hair long rather than short. Chinese and low-class Vietnamese poured into the country. The

102 King Norodom, in a photograph taken by John Thomson in 1866. Three years earlier the king had signed the treaty that established the French Protectorate and ended Cambodian independence.

new ruler was now Ang Chan's second daughter Ang Mei, who was crowned in a completely Vietnamese ceremony.

But even this was not enough for the arrogant authorities in Hué. In 1840, the Vietnamese emperor Minh Mang arrested the queen, and took her off to Saigon, along with her regalia (presumably including the Sacred Sword), as well as six of the highest-ranking Khmer officials (*okña*, see below). This sparked a massive and ultimately successful rebellion, ending with the withdrawal of the Vietnamese. Ang Mei's brother Ang Duong, who had been under Thai protection, was put on the throne in 1848, after the Vietnamese had returned the regalia, and once again there was a king ruling from Udong.

Ang Duong is considered by the Khmer to have been one of their greatest rulers, up there with Suryavarman II and Jayavarman VII. He was certainly an enlightened one, and his twelve-year reign was one of peace, if not exactly of prosperity. He initiated public works as well as linguistic reforms (this was when Cambodian intellectuals coined many new and necessary words using Pali models). But Ang Duong could not ignore the geopolitical facts. More or less under the protection of the Thai, he nevertheless worried about the Vietnamese, and made contact with Napoleon III, who had already invaded

Vietnam in 1857 with the intention of adding it to his empire. This did not please Bangkok.

In 1859, the explorer Henri Mouhot visited the aged king at Komput (Cambodia's sole remaining port, on the Gulf of Thailand), as well as Udong, where the 'second king' (Norodom, the *uparaj* or heir apparent) was in residence, in hopes of getting letters for his future visit to Angkor and other parts of the country.[33] Mouhot described Udong as a town of about 12,000 souls, surrounded by a large moat and a parapet, enclosed by a 3-m (10-ft) high palisade. Access was by two gates, one of which opened to a dirty (to him) market-place occupied mainly by Chinese. Udong's settlement pattern as described by Mouhot recalls the linear arrangement at Classic Angkor:

> The longest street, or rather the only one, is a mile in length; and in the environs reside the agriculturalists, as well as the mandarins and other Government officers.

The houses of the inhabitants were of bamboo or planks.

Ang Duong died in 1860, and was succeeded by the same Norodom, the great-grandfather of the present king, Norodom Sihanouk. In 1863 a delegation of French naval officers concluded a treaty with Norodom, 'offering him protection at the hands of a French resident in exchange for timber concessions and mineral exploration rights'. This lopsided agreement was ratified in Paris in 1864 under the joint sponsorship of France and Thailand; in its favour one must say that it prevented Cambodia being entirely gobbled up by its two voracious neighbours.

With the 1863 treaty, Cambodia entered the modern age, as a Protectorate within France's colonial empire. The palace, court and king were transferred to Phnom Penh in 1867, but the ashes of the last Post-Classic rulers of the independent Cambodian kingdom continued to rest under the great *chetdis* of Udong. Self-rule was not to come again to the Khmer until Norodom Sihanouk achieved freedom for his people in the mid-twentieth century.

Post-Classic society and administration[34]

Between the decline of Angkor and the imposition of French rule, there were seven classes of society which were, in descending order of prestige:

- the royal family;
- the clergy (Brahmin priests and Buddhist monks);
- distant relatives of the royal family;
- the mandarin bureaucrats (*okña*, a title equivalent to the *khloñ* of the Classic period);
- the free population;
- debt slaves (or those temporarily committed for debt); and
- hereditary slaves and serfs.

Post-Classic Cambodia was an absolute monarchy, headed by the king (*raj* in Sanskrit and Pali, *sdach* in Khmer), whose power in theory had no limit, only the monks being exempt from his authority. On this individual were

102

bestowed numerous titles, such as 'Raised above Heads', 'Supreme Refuge', 'the Master of the Lower Surface', and so on. The king was the supreme landowner, and all the holdings of those who died went to him by escheat; but the real wealth of his royal domain lay along the alluvial margins of the main rivers and their islands, where rice fields are annually fertilized by rich deposits of mud (the same kind of situation on which the economic power of the pharaohs of Egypt and the Olmec rulers of Mexico had depended). Once crowned, the *sdach* was a sacred being, filled with what anthropologists term *mana*. Étienne Aymonier tells us:

> Inviolable, he is henceforth the object of a cult pushed to adoration. No one is permitted to address a word to him or lay a hand on his sacred person; only his principal wives, by softly caressing his feet, dare to awaken him on urgent matters. His personal name which is never again pronounced is replaced by an equivalent which had been, according to custom, borrowed from the ordinary tongue. He eats alone, surrounded outside by young pages, the sons of mandarins, and inside, by some favourites who serve him and who are in attendance at his meal, while keeping a respectful distance. At his audiences, which he gives seated cross-legged, princes, mandarins, and subjects remain crouching on their knees and elbows, their hands joined at the height of the forehead, which they knock on the ground three times at the beginning and end of the session.[35]

It was strictly forbidden to enter the palace in sloppy or fancy clothes, or clad in black or a shimmering material, or to wear a feather or flower passed through the ear.

In the private apartments to the rear (western part) of the palace were the king's women, 200–300 strong: the harem, concubines, dancers, musicians and singers, all on salary. At the top was the queen, *ag mahisi*, plus other wives; all of these had to be relatives of royal blood, and the king could even marry his own half-sister – only full sisters could not be taken as spouses. As for the harem, the king inherited his predecessor's women, but he continually augmented these with younger females, and let the older (or plainer) ones leave to be married.

Naturally, since the king and his predecessors had huge numbers of children, there were a large number of princes in the royal family. To keep this from getting out of hand, there was an ancient rule that every descendant of royal blood beyond the fifth degree who was not 'reimmersed' by closer alliances or by royal decree ceased to belong to the royal family. Depending on the degree of their relationship, the valid princes were considered to be in line to inherit the kingship (always a complex subject in early Cambodia). Exempt from tithing and taxes, they were often charged with important missions, but otherwise played little role in the country's administration.

As for the clergy, the Brahmins (*baku*), descendants of the Hindu priests of Classic Angkor, formed a patrilineal caste of several hundred families, distinguished from ordinary Cambodians by their long hair, which they wore in a chignon. They were responsible for all the rites and sacraments of the royal

103 The Preah Khan, the Sacred Sword of the Cambodian state, and the palladium of the Khmer people. Probably early Post-Classic, fourteenth century. Formerly in the Royal Palace, Phnom Penh, but disappeared during the Khmer Rouge period. The blade is chased steel; the hilt is enamelled and bejewelled; and the scabbard is gold and silver. To the right are detailed views of the scabbard's segments, chased with scenes from the *Ramayana* (*Reamker*). Total length of sword with scabbard 109 cm (43 in).

palace, including coronations, as well as the guarding of the royal regalia – especially the Sacred Sword, then as always the palladium of the kingdom. 103 Otherwise, they looked and worked just like the rest of the people. Over the *bakus* the king appointed a chief to maintain priestly discipline, as well as chaplains (*parohit*, from the Classic *purohita*) to conduct the rites in the name of the Hindu divinities. When the king went to war, the chaplains went with him, carrying bronze statuettes of the gods; within the palace compound, they prepared lustral water for the sovereign; lit and watched over the Sacred Fire of 12 candles; and set fire to the royal cremation pyre, among their other ritual functions. There was no conflict between worship of the gods and the Buddhist religion, for all these gods were subject to the great laws expounded by the Buddha.

Those above-mentioned relatives of the royal house (that is, those related beyond the fifth degree) were the *Brah Van*, described by Aymonier as a very numerous, patrilineal caste with members scattered across the Cambodian countryside. They had their own chiefs, among whom was the head of the hierarchy of mandarins (see below), who had the responsibility of ensuring that all the old customs were maintained and observed. Beyond the privilege of adding the title *Brah* ('holy') to their names, and of being largely exempt from taxes and corvées, most of them looked and worked just like any other Khmer farmer.

The Buddhist Sangha was very large – one early European source estimated that more than half of all free men in the kingdom were Buddhist monks, which is probably a considerable exaggeration. The king was honoured by being considered the natural protector of Buddhism, a function that he had sworn to fulfil when he was crowned. Although they played no real role in the administration of the country, the Buddhist clergy entered into the lives of every Khmer, not least because all elementary education in Post-Classic Cambodia was in their hands (a situation that is just starting to change at the beginning of the twenty-first century), as were the majority of the festivals that were celebrated across the country throughout the year.

The actual administration was conducted by the mandarin class, in an ingenious and highly effective bureaucratic system that might have originated in the Early Kingdoms period, and was certainly in existence in Classic Angkor. There were about a thousand mandarins in pre-French Cambodia; Aymonier makes the point that they constituted neither a nobility nor a caste, since they filled their offices at the pleasure of the king, and the privileges and honours that they enjoyed could not be transmitted from father to son. Nonetheless, since their sons were often taken on as pages in the court, these would have been in a favourable position for future preferment. All mandarins were ranked according to the honours they received, which went by multiples of one thousand. At the top of the hierarchy were the highest-ranking *okña* – the great mandarins and all the provincial governors, with ten to seven thousand honours (in descending order of prestige); the lesser *okña* below them might have six, five, or four thousand honours. Twice a year, all of these bureaucrats, along with princes, princesses and palace ladies, had to swear an oath of loyalty virtually identical to that instituted by Suryavarman I in AD 1011 (see Chapter 6).

Following ancient custom, just below the sacred personage of the king (*raj* or *sdach*) were the four great Houses, to each of which was allocated a certain number of the 57 provinces into which Cambodia was then divided. The First House was the king's, with 47 provinces; to the abdicated king (*upayu-vraj*) went the Second House, with seven provinces and the dignity of a six-level parasol; the Third House was that of the heir-presumptive (*uparaj*) with five provinces and a five-level parasol; and, finally there was the Fourth House, belonging to the Queen Mother (*brah varrajjini*) or the first princess of the blood, with only three provinces and a four-level parasol. Within each house were a specified number of *okña* mandarins, headed by high officials: the Second House had 50 *okña*, the Third House 40, the Fourth House 20.

Some European visitors, such as Mouhot, mistakenly believed that the *uparaj* was a kind of 'second king'; in reality, royal authority was completely concentrated in the person of the *raj*, who ruled through the five grand-officers of the Council of Senapati (see diagram). The *samtach chauva* was of royal descent, and acted as prime minister and viceroy (the present prime minister,

Hun Sen, has taken the *samtach* title). Under him are the other four, known collectively as 'the four feet of the container' or 'the four columns'; in modern terms, they might be considered the minister of justice, the minister of the interior (and of finance), the minister of the navy, and the minister of war.

An important organizing principle in the palace and in the administration was that of right and left, so that for many offices, the *okña* were paired according to this opposition. This principle applies to the court functionaries, *okña* who formed a body that was apparently separate from the Senapati, although some of their functions must have overlapped. The two in charge of protocol were responsible for introducing mandarins and foreigners at royal audiences, and for overseeing the taking of the biannual oath of allegiance.

Another structural principle is that of the number five, perhaps a reflection of the five peaks of the legendary Mount Meru. This applied not only to the Council of Senapati, but also to the theoretical division of Cambodia into 'five lands', each headed by a very high-ranking *okña* with ten thousand honours, golden seals, and red parasols with golden fringes. On entering his duties, each of these exalted personages – provincial representatives of the five great ministers – sacrificed a buffalo; writing of Cambodia on the eve of the Protectorate, Aymonier commented that this 'relatively noble animal' replaced the condemned man who formed a human sacrifice 'not so long ago'.[36] All the other governors were also *okña*, but of lesser honours, and their sacrifices – a kind of 'entrance fee' for the office – were of less prestigious animals such as oxen or pigs.

104 Table of organization of the Cambodian royal administration on the eve of the French Protectorate, based upon information supplied by Étienne Aymonier. A similar organization probably was in effect throughout the Post-Classic period, and perhaps even in Classic times.

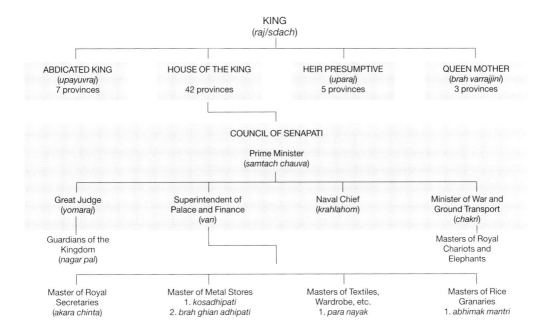

The duties of the governors were to administer justice, to supervise the collection of taxes and rents, and to watch over the levying of corvée labour and the military call-up. Paid no salary, they took a determined amount of the taxes and enjoyed the production of their private lands, not to mention the gifts that subordinates were expected to give their superiors. Supporting them was an army of civil servants, with whom they had to share the revenue. It seems that the Classic institution of the roving inspectors (*tamrvach*) continued to exist in the Post-Classic; nominated by the king, they were the equals and even the rivals of the governors. The title, altered through Thai influence into *tamruot*, is used in modern Cambodia for 'policeman'.

Below all of this ponderous bureaucracy were the free people of the land, free in the sense that they enjoyed basic civil rights, and could settle wherever they wished. Nonetheless, the obligations of this largely rice-farming class were heavy: the entire able-bodied population between the ages of 20 and 50 owed up to 90 days of corvée labour annually. Those outside these age limits were called up for only light labour. Exempt from corvée were the monks, Brahmins, the *Brah Van*, the mandarins and their servants, and all employees of the king.

There was no escaping this corvée, since all males were inscribed by name on census registers that were revised every three years under the supervision of roving commissions. At this point, every person would also choose a particular mandarin or even high official in the capital as his patron. With this personage, who was not necessarily connected with the client's territory, there were mutual obligations: the client owed the patron deference and respect, services, occasional labour, and the usual small gifts, while the latter gave aid and protection (even legal) to the freeman and accommodation when he had to travel to the capital. It was this system through which corvées were mustered, and foot soldiers called up for Cambodia's many wars.

The ultimate support of the entire kingdom was the tax revenue from these small farmers. Taxes were not on land, but on products, especially rice – this was tithing, so one tenth of all the rice and other crops filtered up through the different bureaucratic layers, each official in turn taking his apportioned 'cut', to the king.

Slavery flourished in Post-Classic Cambodia, until abolished by the French. Most slaves (*khñum*) seem to have fallen into this condition through debt, along with their families, and many sold themselves to avoid poverty. Hereditary slaves seem to have been somewhat fewer, although even the Buddhist pagodas could possess such unfortunates, donated to the monasteries by pious laymen. The reverse could also take place: some of the Middle Khmer inscriptions in Angkor Wat describe the manumission of *khñum* as 'meritorious acts', with individuals or even entire families being freed in this way; this might be conditional, though, for instance committing the former slaves to enter the service of a monastery.

Little seems to be known about serfs of the crown. These apparently were descendants of rebels or of great criminals whose death sentences had been commuted, and they lived in their own communities, being obliged like free men to perform corvée labour.

Trade and commerce

Almost all commercial activity during the period was in the hands of foreigners, above all the Chinese. The commercial hub was the Quatre Bras region. As historian Anthony Reid says,

> The great navigable Y-shape formed by the Tonle Sap River and 560 kilometres of the Mekong below the Khone [Khong] Falls formed the natural arteries of Cambodia, whose capital during the age of commerce was always at or near Pnompenh, the major junction of the rivers where ocean-going ships were received.[37]

For example, in 1641 the river market-town of Sambok (near modern Kratie) had a population less Cambodian than Chinese. The latter controlled most of the trade in the surrounding country: for deerskins, gold, rhinoceros horns and ivory the Chinese exchanged salt, chinaware, iron and small bronze gongs.[38]

Japan also wanted deerskins, but there was a brisk market at home for sappanwood, employed for cabinetwork and as the source of a red dye used to colour matting and cakes. During the early seventeenth century, Japanese merchants (most of them from Kyushu, and some even of the Samurai class) would come to Cambodia as 'guests' on the trading ships.[39] While they were waiting for the next ship to return them to Japan, they would go as pious tourists to Angkor Wat; one of the dated graffiti in the Cruciform Gallery states 'I came across the vast seas to offer images of the Buddha on behalf of my parents.'[40]

The Chinese merchant-tourists – one of them a native of Canton – who left votive graffiti in the same place and at the same time were also of fairly high status, for these are in the form of standard, rhymed poems (seven words to a line), completely Buddhist in content.[41]

Post-Classic warfare

Military campaigns were probably conducted in the Post-Classic as they had been in the Classic era, but on a lesser scale: it is doubtful if any king of Lovek or Udong could muster the armies that were fielded by rulers like Suryavarman II. There was no standing army – in times of war, the patron was expected to muster a force of his clients, and place himself or an officer designated by the king at their head. The arms that they bore were substantially like those wielded by Classic warriors, with the addition of firearms and cannon (after 1600). Again, the principle of five ruled, as there were five corps: the vanguard, the rear guard, the right flank, the left flank and the central corps or main body of the army, where the king kept himself with his war elephants.[42] These animals were strengthened magically from time to time by being sprayed with water mixed with human bile (or so say our sources); magical ideas also led the warriors to cover themselves with protective amulets. The king would be surrounded by Brahmins who conducted ritual ablutions, and by soothsayers who were consulted on the placement of military camps and for auspicious days for military operations.

The art of the Post-Classic[43]

There is hardly any surviving Post-Classic architecture dating to before the nineteenth century: if there had been, the Khmer Rouge would have destroyed it in their horrifying campaign to rid the country of all traces of Buddhism. On the other hand, there is a great deal of sculpture, almost all of it in wood, in line with Theravada Buddhism's philosophy of the impermanence of all things. The most significant stone carving consists of the reliefs in the northeast quadrant of Angkor Wat's Gallery of the Bas-Reliefs; according to inscriptions, these were begun in 1546 and completed in 1564. Most observers hold them to be markedly inferior to the Classic reliefs in the rest of the gallery, but they nevertheless are of some iconographic and historical interest. They depict the victory of Vishnu, in his guise as Krishna, over the *asura* demons. As Madeleine Giteau notes, while some of the figures crowded into these scenes show a Classic heritage, others exhibit Thai influence (particularly from Ayutthaya) in costume details, hairdos, textiles, and other items. Even further, clouds carved into the background derive from Chinese conventions.

Nineteenth and early twentieth century visitors to Angkor Wat were impressed by the so-called 'Gallery of a Thousand Buddhas', part of the Cruciform Gallery on the second floor. Here the Khmer monks had gathered many hundreds of Post-Classic wooden images of different ages and provenances, most of which were subsequently removed by the EFEO authorities to the *Conservation d'Angkor*, to Phnom Penh, and to Paris. Certainly the most admired work of art from this great collection of Theravada Buddhist sculptures is the lovely figure kneeling in prayer from Angkor Wat, now in the

pl. XIII

105 The *vihara* in Wat Po, an important nineteenth-century Theravada Buddhist monastery in Siem Reap. The building is surrounded by *chtedis* (stupas) containing the ashes of important religious figures.

106 Detail of a mural in the *vihara* of Wat Po in Siem Reap. The scene is an episode in the *Reamker* (*Ramayana*). Post-Classic period, probably first half of the nineteenth century.

collection of the Museum of Fine Arts in the Cambodian capital; this dates to the sixteenth century. Other statues of the period have been found in various *wats* around the country. As one might expect, the oldest, particularly those from the early Post-Classic capital of Srei Santhor (located to the northeast of Phnom Penh), closely resemble Classic stone sculpture of the Bayon style; as one moves into later centuries, the influence of Ayutthayan Thailand in both style and iconography becomes increasingly stronger.

Originally, the fronts of many of the Post-Classic *wats* probably had elaborate wooden reliefs depicting Hindu protective deities or scenes drawn from the *Ramayana*, as so many of them do in Thailand, but there are very few extant examples.

The art of painting is known only from murals on the inner walls of monastic buildings, but works of art on this scale must have embellished the long-vanished palaces of Lovek and Udong. The subject matter here and in the *wats* would have been drawn from the *Reamker* (the Khmer version of the *Ramayana*) or from the Jatakas – stories of the Buddha's previous existences. Sadly, none of the examples surviving in the country's monasteries predates the first half of the nineteenth century (the remarkable European-influenced murals of Phnom Penh's Silver Pagoda were painted at the beginning of the twentieth century). The most splendid of these can be seen in Wat Po, an important monastic complex in Siem Reap, which has scenes from the *Reamker* carried out in a style heavily influenced by Thai conventions (which themselves were derived from the art of the Khmer!).

105

106

Mental life in Post-Classic Cambodia

Traditional Cambodian thought is enshrined in their literature, both written and oral. It must be admitted that very few proven actual Post-Classic texts have come down to us out of the many thousands that must have once existed: time, wars, and wanton destruction have wrought havoc on manuscripts. Almost all of this literature is imbued with Theravada Buddhist teachings and values.

Curiously enough, scholars refer to the Post-Classic inscriptions of Angkor Wat as 'modern', though these are not modern at all, but are texts in Middle Khmer dating to the fourteenth to eighteenth centuries.[44] A few are quite lengthy, and all of them are 'oaths of truth', giving accounts of 'good deeds' accomplished by different classes of the Buddhist faithful, and expressing wishes for themselves and others in this life and the next. One of the longer ones speaks of the sixteenth-century king who had restored Angkor Wat's ramparts and roof; it goes on to report that the queen had given birth to a son, seemingly an heir apparent, and that the king had come to this great shrine to offer the infant to the service of the 'Triple Jewel'. Accompanying the ruler in this task were members of his harem, Brahmanic specialists, the four great *okña* of the Council of Senapati and court poets. We wish we knew more of the latter. In fact, the longest 'modern' inscription at the site *is* actually a poem, asking for pious favours for the donors, an *okña* and his wife.

The Royal Chronicles have already been mentioned, and these are rich sources for information on Khmer politics, society, history (if treated with caution), and even philosophy.

But the greatest single work of Post-Classic literature is the Khmer version of the *Ramayana*, known to the people of Cambodia as the *Reamker* or *Reamkerti*, 'The Glory of Ram', composed in Middle Khmer between the fifteenth and seventeenth centuries. As early as the seventh century, in the Early Kingdoms period, an inscription mentions a gift to a sanctuary of a manuscript containing the two great Hindu epics – the *Mahabharata* and the *Ramayana* – as well as the Puranas (collections of cosmology and mythology)[45]; and the sculptors of Classic temples like Banteay Srei had an intimate knowledge of every detail in the Indian version of the *Ramayana* story.

Yet, as Mme Saveros Pou has stressed, the *Reamker* is not just an echo of the Indian epic, but a total reworking of it, reflecting Khmer, not Indian, culture, and with a fervently Theravada Buddhist content.[46] Ram (Rama) is not only an avatar of Vishnu, but also a Bodhisattva and simultaneously a Buddha, an upholder of the Dharma. In the story of Sita's abduction by Rab (Ravana) and ultimate rescue by Ram and the monkey army, Ram intends ultimately to conduct his beloved wife to the Supreme Nirvana. In the text, Shiva, Brahma and Indra play subordinate roles, and the latter god acts as the Buddha's faithful servant. Finally, the actions and language of all personages in the *Reamker* – the gods, humans, demons, and animals of the original epic – reflect the teachings of the Buddha.

There are several extant versions of the *Reamker*, in both manuscript and oral form. Until the Khmer Rouge period, an oral version was sung by professional Khmer bards to pilgrims as they made the circumambulation of the

Ramayana scenes in Angkor Wat's galleries (I witnessed this in 1954), and professional storytellers could recite large sections of the Khmer epic to appreciative audiences.[47] And, of course, various episodes of this great story are danced by the Royal Ballet before honoured guests, or presented by shadow-puppet groups to the Cambodian people in general.   107

Lastly, there are the stories, proverbs and aphorisms that have been passed down by word of mouth to the Khmer by their elders since at least the beginning of the Post-Classic, when Theravada values first came into Cambodia. One large body of these is known as 'Wisdom of the Ancients' or 'The Tradition of Olden Times Transmitted from the Distant Past', a collection of sayings and aphorisms for good conduct that may have once been inscribed on palm-leaf books.[48] Here are a few that give something of the down-to-   93 earth flavour of this body of folk literature:

> 'One can control ferocious animals. But as for wicked persons, one must flee far, far away from them.'

> 'As flies gather on filth, so vile persons seek out trouble.'

> 'To cultivate a rice paddy, do it when the soil is warm. To take a wife, do it when your heart is warm.'

> 'Don't argue with women, don't do business with the Chinese, don't get involved in a lawsuit with an official.'

For countless centuries, the traditional Khmer salutation of a person to a superior has always been to raise the hands together while lying prostrate. To justify this age-old custom, one aphorism invokes the image of rice, the Khmer staff of life:

> 'Standing erect it is empty; prostrate, it bears its seed.'

107 Some members of the Royal Ballet, costumed for an episode in the *Reamker* (*Ramayama*), from a photograph taken in Phnom Penh *c.* 1900.

Epilogue

One can say in favour of French rule in Cambodia, which lasted from 1863 until the achievement of independence, that it prevented the country's dismemberment at the hands of Thailand and Vietnam. On the surface, the French conceived of their colonial role in 'Indo-China' as a *mission civilatrice* ('civilizing mission'), but in reality this meant the economic exploitation of its lands and peoples. Compared to Vietnam, where the new rulers imposed their own bureaucracy in place of the local mandarins, the native Cambodian power structure – meaning the king and the royal house – was pretty much left in place. But Norodom, who had signed the 1863 treaty, proved to be far from a French puppet. In 1884, and following a Khmer uprising against their rule, the French adopted a less conciliatory line, and governed the country as a true colony.

Although the French had transformed Vietnam, particularly the Delta, through education, agricultural development and modern infrastructure (to their own advantage as well, of course), they did little of this for the Khmer, who were considered lazy and childlike. To stimulate commerce, for example, they brought in large numbers of Chinese and Vietnamese, a situation deeply resented by the Khmer. In Norodom's successor Sisowath (who reigned from 1904 to 1927) they had a model puppet ruler, who acquiesced to the establishment of rubber plantations and other 'improvements'. On the other side of the balance sheet, though, one must give the French full credit for the establishment of the École Française d'Extrême-Orient and the resurrection and salvation of the country's greatest national treasure: Angkor.

The Japanese occupation from 1941 to 1945 laid the groundwork for the end of French colonialism, which saw reality in 1953 under Ang Duong's great-grandson Norodom Sihanouk, who proved to be not as pliant as the French had hoped. The subsequent history of Cambodia is one of turmoil and tragedy, as the country became embroiled in the general war in Southeast Asia.[49] It was subjected to native, Communist-led insurgencies, Vietnamese intervention, American bombing and political coups, but the ultimate horror was yet to come: the triumph of the Khmer Rouge regime in 1975. By the time of their overthrow by the Vietnamese army in 1978, these fanatical Marxist-Leninists had managed to cause the deaths of an estimated 15 per cent of Cambodia's people, and the self-imposed exile of hundreds of thousands of Khmer to foreign lands.

In the rebuilding of their ravaged country, the Khmer constantly have before them the model of their glorious history – Classic Angkor and its empire. Three of the five towers of Angkor Wat grace its flag; a descendent of its ancient rulers still serves as head of state; and Buddhism is again the state religion. There have been and will continue to be many changes in Khmer life, but the past lives on in the minds of the people.

Rulers of the Khmer

The known rulers of the Early Kingdoms period
Rudravarman (Early sixth century?)
Bhavavarman I (End of sixth century)
Chitrasena-Mahendravarman (End of sixth century)
Ishanavarman I (616?–635?)
Bhavavarman II (637?–mid 650s)
Jayavarman I (657?–681?)
Jayadevi (713 date recorded)

Rulers of the Classic period
Jayavarman II (802–835)
Jayavarman III (*c.* 835–877?)
Indravarman I (877–*c.* 889)
Yashovarman I (889–*c.* 900)
Harshavarman I (*c.* 900–*c.* 923)
Ishanavarman II (*c.* 923–*c.* 928)
Jayavarman IV (*c.* 928–941)
Harshavarman II (941–944)
Rajendravarman II (944–968)
Jayavarman V (968–*c.* 1000)
Udayadityavarman I (1001–1002)
Suryavarman I (1002–1049)
Udayadityavarman II (1050–1066)
Harshavarman III (*c.* 1066–1080)
Jayavarman VI (1080–1107)
Dharanindravarman (1107–1113)
Suryavarman II (1113–*c.* 1150)
Yashovarman II (1150–*c.* 1165)
Jayavarman VII (1181–*c.* 1215)
Indravarman II (*c.* 1215–1243)
Jayavarman VIII (1243–1295)
Indravarman III (*c.* 1296–1308)
Shrindrajayavarman (1308–1327)
Jayavarmadiparameshvara (1327–?)

Visting Angkor

Probably the best time to come to Cambodia is during the first half of the dry season, which begins in late November and continues until the coming of the rains in late May. Late March, April and May can be extremely hot, and much of the land is unpleasantly dry and dusty. Siem Reap, the provincial capital where visitors to Angkor stay, is easily reached by daily flights from either Bangkok or Phnom Penh; there are many modern hotels in the town, from modest to luxurious in quality and price. While Angkor's ruins can be accessed on one's own (perhaps by renting a motorbike), unless one is with a tour it is advisable to engage a guide and a driver, as the site is very large indeed.

Although much of Angkor can be seen in three days, it is far better to spend at least a week, since some of the complexes (particularly Angkor Wat and the Bayon) are worth several visits. One should not overlook Banteay Srei, the exquisite temple to the northeast of the main group.

The serious visitor should not be without a guidebook in hand, either Dawn Rooney's *Angkor*, or Jean Laur's more complete (but heavier) *Angkor: An Illustrated Guide*. Also to be highly recommended is the 1:40,000 map of Angkor published in 1999 by River Books, Bangkok.

Regarding health, the usual precautions in tropical climates should be observed: do not drink unpurified water (or allow ice from it to be put in your drink), and do not eat raw vegetables or unpeeled fruit. Be sure to wear a hat and to apply plenty of sunscreen. The health authorities generally consider Angkor and the Siem Reap zone to be malaria free, but this is not true of the Kulen hills, or elsewhere in the country.

Notes to the Text

Chapter 1

1 Mouhot 1989:279–80.
2 See Heine-Geldern 1966:284–91.
3 The author's early attempts at such a comparative study are Coe 1957 and 1961; see also Bronson 1978.
4 The definitive work on these early discoveries is B.-P. Groslier 1958.
5 Groslier ibid:72.
6 Dagens 1995:26. This small book can be highly recommended for its coverage of the exploration history of Angkor, from the fifteenth century until the modern era.
7 Dagens 1995:28–29 gives a colour reproduction of this extraordinary plan.
8 For an account of Mouhot's life and travels, see the Introduction by Michael Smithers in Mouhot 1989:v–xix.
9 Bouillevaux 1863.
10 Thomson 1867.
11 Detailed information on the Mekong Exploration Commission can be found in Osborne 2000:73–117.
12 Garnier 1996 is an English translation of this work. See also Delaporte 1914–24.
13 Fournereau 1890.
14 Aymonier 1901; 1904; 1999.
15 Lunet de Lajonquiére 1902–11.
16 Coedès 1968 is this great scholar's magnum opus.
17 Briggs 1951.
18 See B.-P. Groslier 1997 for a collection of his major articles on ancient Cambodia. For an account of Groslier's work at Angkor, and his difficulties before and during the Khmer Rouge period, see Prodromides 1997:240–83.
19 The Indian restoration project of 1986 to 1993 is described in Bhandari 1995:112–43.
20 For a full description of APSARA's charter and duties, see Ang Choulean et al 1998.
21 World Monuments Fund 1996. The Preah Khan Project is being coordinated with the Centre for Khmer Studies, in Phnom Penh, and is under the direction of John Sanday.
22 Stark 1998.
23 Moore 1997.
24 The standard work on Thai archaeology is Higham and Thosarat 1998.
25 Bayard 1984.
26 Higham 1989.

Chapter 2

1 Osborne 2000:16–19.
2 The definitive source for all information on the physical and human geography of this area is the great United Nations atlas of the Lower Mekong (United Nations 1968). See also Ng 1979; Delvert 1993; and relevant sections of Stuttard 1943.
3 Ng, Ronald C.Y. 1978; Rigg 1993; Dixon 1978.
4 Information from Mr Supot Hongthong, a native of Surin and my guide in Khorat.
5 Delvert 1993:5–13.
6 Boulbet 1979 is a pioneering geographical and cultural study of Phnom Kulen, with excellent maps.
7 Delvert 1999:18–21. The Great Lake (Tonle Sap) has been declared a national biosphere reserve.
8 Mouhot 1989:21. Lebas 1925 has a detailed description of this remarkable fishery.
9 See relevant sections of Stuttard 1943 for information on the geography and history of the Delta.
10 Zhou 1993:xviii.

11 Stuttard 1943:77–86.
12 Jacob 1978, 1979.
13 Stuttard 1943:87–108 has an extensive coverage of Southeast Asian fauna. For the large mammals of Cambodia (mainly surviving in the Cardamom Mountains) see Desai and Vuthy 1996.
14 Zhou 1993:53.
15 Grist 1986 is a standard general work on rice. See also Hanks 1972 for rice cultivation in Thailand and, by extension, Southeast Asia.
16 Delvert 1961 presents detailed information on rice cultivation in Cambodia, as does Delvert 1998:52–68. An excellent micro-study of one farming village near Angkor is Martell 1975. For rice in the Delta, and the implications of the flood-retreat technique, see Fox and Ledgerwood 1999; for Khorat, see Rigg 1993 and White 1995.
17 van Liere 1980.
18 Zhou 1993:39.

Chapter 3

1 Chandler 1993:13; Coedès 1968:37–38.
2 Porée-Maspero 1950.
3 Coedès 1968:66.
4 Bellwood 1997 is an up-to-date source on the peopling of mainland and insular Southeast Asia, including the Sunda Shelf.
5 The major source for ethnic and linguistic distributions in mainland Southeast Asia is LeBar et al 1964. For current numbers of people speaking the various languages of the area, see the Ethnologue Country Index Web site at: http://www.ethnologue.com/country_index.asp
6 Shorto 1979.
7 Aymonier 1999:224.
8 Kiernan 1988.
9 Bayard:279–80.
10 Shorto 1979:275.
11 Martini 1955:434. The other examples given in this section are taken from the Martini article.
12 Huffman 1970:4–5.
13 Jacques 1999:15–18.
14 Miriam Stark has reminded me that 'large plantations (mostly rubber) were owned and operated by landed gentry Khmer during the post-colonial period and even today, and that generals and politicians commonly own land that they let to tenants (who seem like smallholders)'. Nevertheless, the freeholding of small plots seems the general rule in Cambodia.
15 For Cambodian food and cuisine, see Davidson 1999: 126–27.

Chapter 4

1 Bellwood 1985:39–95.
2 Colani 1926.
3 Mourer and Mourer 1970; Mourer 1977.
4 Chen, Wang, and Zhang 1995.
5 Zhang n.d.
6 Pei n.d.
7 See discussion in Higham and Thosarat 1998:68–76.
8 Higham and Thosarat 1998:91ff.
9 United Nations 1968, map on p. 40.
10 Higham and Thosarat 1998:111–13.
11 Higham and Thosarat 1998:114–17.
12 Mansuy 1902.
13 Information from Miriam Stark.
14 Mourer 1977; Miriam Stark, personal communication.
15 United Nations, ibid.
16 Higham and Thosarat 1998:92–93.
17 Higham and Thosarat 1998:151–56, fig. 29.
18 Solheim and Ayres 1979:66–73.
19 Groslier 1966:159.
20 Malleret 1959.
21 Groslier 1966:195 and pl. 10.
22 Chanthourn 1999; Heang 1999.
23 Moore 1988.

24 Chanthourn 2002; Albrecht et al 2000; Dega 1999; Dega et al 1997.
25 Michael Dega, personal communication.
26 Manh 1999.
27 Kojo n.d.
28 Moore 1997. It should be noted here that the archaeologists working on the 'red soil' sites see no analogue between those sites and the ones in Khorat and the Angkor area (Roland Fletcher, personal communication).
29 See Higham and Thosarat 1998:131–33 for a description of these rock art sites and their possible dating.
30 LeBar et al 1964 is the most accessible source for the culture of the 'mountain tribes' of mainland Southeast Asia.
31 Martell 1975. This excellent study of the circular village of Lovea is one of the very few ethnographies ever undertaken in the Cambodian countryside.

Chapter 5

1 Coedès 1968:27–33; Wheatley 1983:263–73. For early maritime contacts, see also Glover 1996.
2 For example, Coedès 1968 and Briggs 1951.
3 Coedès 1968:42.
4 Yung 2000:13.
5 Yung 2000:14.
6 Briggs 1951:29.
7 See Coedès 1968:276, note 16.
8 Coedès 1968:36.
9 Coedès 1968:65–70, 85–86, 93–94.
10 Briggs 1951:50.
11 Jacques 1979:371.
12 Vickery 1986, 1998.
13 What follows is based upon various sections of Vickery 1998.
14 The routes that these traders might have followed are described in Coedès 1968:27–33.
15 Ray 1998.
16 The religious prohibition on Brahmins 'crossing the black waters' (i.e. ocean) only came into effect in much later times (T.N. Srinivasan, personal communication).
17 Smith 1999.
18 Malleret 1959a, 1960, 1962.
19 Wheatley 1983.
20 Rawson 1967:23.
21 Dao 1998.
22 This and the following two paragraphs are based on Vickery 1998.
23 Jacob 1993.
24 Stark et al 1999.
25 Stark and Sovath 2001.
26 Dowling 2000.
27 Jenner 1980, inscription K 557/600.
28 The *saka* era (also known as the Great Era) begins in March 78 AD. This was in use throughout the Early Kingdoms and Classic periods.
29 Jessup and Zéphir 1997:146–85 illustrates beautiful examples of 'pre-Angkor' (i.e. Early Kingdoms) sculpture, with informative catalogue entries.
30 Lunet de Lajonquière 1902–11.
31 The most complete treatment of Sambor Prei Kuk is Parmentier 1927:44–87. See also Dumarçay and Royère 2001: 39–44. The site is also described in Dumarçay and Smithies 1995:72–79.
32 Briggs 1951:76, 82.
33 Vickery 1998:346.
34 Yung 2000:19.
35 Coedès 1968:65–70.
36 Vickery 1998:80–81.
37 Cummings 1996:247.
38 Freeman 1996:200–05.
39 Santoni 1998. Roland Fletcher (personal communication) believes that the actual occupation area is much larger than the bounded town.
40 Leidy 2000.

Chapter 6

1 Jacques 1992. Much of the material in the present chapter is based upon Briggs 1951:88–261; Jacques 1999; and Jacques and Freeman 1997.
2 Finot 1915 is the definitive study of the SKT stela.
3 Boulbet 1979; Boulbet and Dagens 1973.
4 Finot 1915:88 (translated by MDC).
5 Jacques 1999:44–45. See also Aeusrivongsa 1976.
6 Vickery 1986.
7 Boulbet and Dagens ibid.
8 Finot ibid.
9 Jacques and Freeman 1997:62–69.
10 Briggs 1951:104.
11 Jacques and Freeman 1997:73.
12 These hypothesized sight lines are based upon published maps, and on my own visits to Phnom Bakheng, Phnom Bok, and Phnom Kulen.
13 The architecture and significance of Phnom Bakheng are discussed in Dumarçay and Royère 2001:55–62.
14 o'Naghten 2000:50–53.
15 This important point was first made by Stern 1954.
16 Jacques and Freeman 1997:83–85.
17 Briggs 1951:114.
18 Parmentier 1939:15–52.
19 For descriptions and illustrations of sculptures in the Koh Ker style, see Jessup and Zéphir 1997:188, 210–16.
20 Briggs 1951:124.
21 Dumarçay and Royére 2001:62–70.
22 The classic monograph on Banteay Srei is Parmentier, Goloubew and Finot 1927. This is still the only major Khmer monument to have been fully published in all its detail.
23 Jessup and Zéphir 1997:191.
24 Briggs 1951:151–52.
25 Briggs 1951:110. Preah Vihear is described in considerable detail in Parmentier 1939:270–342; vol. 2 of this work has complete plans.
26 Briggs 1951:168.
27 Dumarçay and Royère 2001:71–79.
28 For the recent history of the Baphuon, see Prodromidès 1997:252ff.
29 Zhou 1993:3. In his account, Zhou mistakenly places the recumbent figure in the Eastern Baray, rather than the Western.
30 For a description and excellent illustrations of Phimai and its sculpture, see Siribhadra and Moore 1992:228–63.
31 Murai et al n.d.
32 For an account of Suryavarman II's life and works, see Jacques and Freeman 1997:147–97, as well as Briggs 1951:187–204.
33 Siribhadra and Moore 1992:267–305.
34 The bibliography for Angkor Wat is enormous. Up-to-date descriptions can be found in Jacques 1999:116–20; Rooney 1997:125–46; and Roveda 2002. The classic, three-volume study of the temple complex is Finot, Goloubew, and Coedès 1929–32.
35 Coedès 1947:68–85.
36 Stencel, Robert, Fred Gifford, and Eleanor Morón 1976; Mannikka 1996.
37 Nafilyan 1969.
38 Marc Franiette, personal communication. Roland Fletcher (personal communication) has his doubts about the reality of this Cham invasion, noting that Angkor Wat, for instance, bears no signs of any such destruction, and that the burning of the wood-built Royal Palace may not have been arson, but accidental.
39 Jayavarman VII's life and accomplishments are given in Briggs 1951:209–36 and Jacques and Freeman 1997:204–76.
40 Zhou 1993:2.
41 For the Bayon, see Stern 1927; Jacques and Freeman 1997:246–67; Dumarçay and Groslier 1967, 1973.

42 Jacques 1999:133.
43 Jacques 1999:138–42.
44 Groslier 1937.
45 Jacques 1999:156.
46 Jacques 1998:203

Chapter 7

1 Zhou 1993 and 2001 are based on the French edition of Pelliot 1951. Corrections to Pelliot's translation can be found in Yang 1994.
2 Aymonier 1900–04; Moura 1883.
3 See Mabbett 1978; Mestier du Bourg 1970.
4 Mabbett 1977; Sarkar 1976.
5 Jacques 1976.
6 Zhou 1993:21.
7 Jacques, ibid.
8 Aymonier 1900:55–56 (trans. MDC).
9 Mabbett 1978:10.
10 Zhou 1993:7.
11 Aymonier 1900:58.
12 Zhou 1993:73.
13 Groslier 1998:98.
14 Roland Fletcher (personal communication) feels that the Phimeanakas surely lay near the front entrance of the palace complex, or was in the middle of its front portion.
15 Zhou 1993:13.
16 Mabbett ibid.
17 Pottier 1997.
18 This section on the state bureaucracy is largely based upon Zhou 1993; Mabbett 1978; and Sahai 1977b.
19 Zhou 1993:63.
20 Zhou 1993:11.
21 Zhou 1993:9.
22 Ricklefs 1967.
23 Zhou 1993:33.
24 Zhou 1993:29.
25 Groslier 1979 is this scholar's most complete statement of the hypothesis.
26 Dumarçay and Royère 2001:xvii–xxix.
27 Roland Fletcher, personal communication.
28 The areas for these *barays* have been measured from the JICA base map of Angkor.
29 Groslier 1979:189–91.
30 Articles highly critical of Groslier's *cité hydraulique* hypothesis are van Liere 1980; Grunewald 1982; Stott 1992; and Acker 1998.
31 Roland Fletcher, personal communication. See also Fletcher 2000–01.
32 Zhou 1993:41.
33 Zhou 1993:43.
34 Zhou 1993:45.
35 The Classic Khmer system of taxation and revenue is covered in Sahai 1977a and b; and Jacques 1986.
36 The unfortunate yet ludicrous *affaire Malraux* is well chronicled in Prodromidès 1997:126–67.
37 Groslier 1921:95–96.
38 Lunet de Lajonquière 1902–11.
39 Information from Mr. Suphot Hongthong, my guide in the Khorat Plateau.
40 Dumarçay and Royère 2001:105.
41 Jacques 1999:156.
42 Zhou 1993:61.
43 Thorel 2001:43.
44 But one inscription stipulates that it was forbidden to bathe elephants in the Srah Srang, the 'royal bathing pool'; see Jacques 1999:74.
45 Quoted in Thaitawat 2000.
46 Dumarçay and Royére 2001:10–12.
47 Dumarçay and Royère 2001:14–17.
48 See Freeman 1996:52–53.
49 Dumarçay and Royère 2001:15.

50 However, according to Roland Fletcher (personal communication), the principal culprit for damage to the temples is the water table, which now fluctuates markedly every year and would not have done so in the Classic period. The distortions of the temples are due to expansion and contraction of clays in the soil.
51 Giteau 1974:48.
52 o'Naghten 2000:100. Trans. By MDC.
53 Groslier 1921:219.
54 In Jessup and Zéphir 1997:132.
55 See Roveda 1997:75–76 for a listing and description of these mythological motifs.
56 Discussed in Groslier 1921:225–27 and in Roveda 2002:224.
57 Readers are referred to the descriptive notes for Classic bronze objects in the National Gallery of Art catalogue (Jessup and Zéphir 1997).
58 Zhou 1993:2.
59 Marc Franiette, personal communication. But see Groslier's pioneering study (Groslier 1981).
60 The most complete description of Khmer ceramics is Brown 2000:41–55. Particularly important for the study of this subject are the essays in the first number of *Udaya* (*Journal of Khmer Studies*), April 2000.
61 Brown 2000:44.
62 Aoyagi et al 1998.
63 Dupoizat 1999.
64 Zhou 1993:15.
65 Zhou 1993:18–19.
66 Zhou 1993:15.
67 Zhou 1993::15.
68 Courbin 1988.
69 Zhou 1993:37.
70 Zhou 1993:7.
71 Green 2000.
72 Zhou 1993:13.
73 Zhou 1993:59.
74 For possible cuisine, see Davidson 1999 and Thaitawat 200.
75 Zhou 1993:59.
76 Zhou 1993:55.
77 Almost all of our information on this subject comes from Zhou 1993:35 and 39.
78 Geertz 1980:13.
79 Zhou 1993:72.
80 Coedès 1906.
81 For ancient Khmer music, see G. Groslier 1921:125–28; B.-P Groslier 1997:89–93; Sam et al 1998.
82 Groslier 1997:89.
83 Zhou 1993:69.
84 Zhou 1993:29.
85 Burton 1993:56–75 has an excellent discussion of Hindu devotional practise.
86 See Harvey 1990:170–95 for Buddhist devotion.
87 The most complete study of Khmer armaments and warfare, profusely illustrated, is Jacq-Hergoualc'h 1979 (on which this section is based).
88 Zhou 1993:71.
89 Jacques 1999:15–16.
90 Jacques, ibid:16–17.
91 Eade 1995.
92 Mannika 1996.
93 For Classic Khmer books and manuscripts, see Zhou 1993:27; Groslier 1921:1–7; Becchetti 1994; and Jacques 1999:17–18.
94 Miksic 2000.
95 Joost Schouten, quoted in Sternstein 1965:94.
96 E. Kaempfer, quoted in Sternstein 1865:98–99.
97 Information in this and the subsequent two paragraphs is personal communication from Roland Fletcher.
98 Chandler 1993:142.
99 Wolters 1982:16–33.

Chapter 8

1 Briggs 1951:252; Jacques 1998:205.
2 Ang 1998.
3 See Thompson 1997 for an overview and appreciation of 'Cambodia after Angkor'.
4 Mabbett 1978:8 lists and discusses various theories about the Classic Khmer 'downfall'; see also Mabbett and Chandler 1996:204–17.
5 Briggs 1951:258–59. Roland Fletcher comments that it was not Jayavarman VII's building program that was expensive, but the later maintenance of these great complexes.
6 Briggs 1951:260
7 Roland Fletcher, personal communication.
8 Reid 1988.
9 Au 1968.
10 Aymonier 1999:228–29. I was told the tale of the Chinese junk by villagers on Phnom Kulen, during my visit in November 1999.
11 Pou 1992:19.
12 Vickery 1979.
13 Lewitz 1972; Mak 1995:18.
14 Dagens 1995:28–29.
15 Ishii 1998.
16 The indispensable study of these European sources on Post-Classic Cambodia is Groslier 1958.
17 This section on Theravada doctrines and history, as well as the Theravada monastery, is based upon Giteau 1975:2–19 and Dalet 1936.
18 Ang 1998:44–45.
19 Jacques and Freeman 1997:296.
20 Lewitz ibid.
21 See Bunge 1981:6–18 for the early history of the Tai (and Thai) people.
22 Taylor 1992:169–70.
23 Taylor 1992:168–73.
24 For the pre-colonial history of Vietnam, see Le 1955.
25 A basic study of the Post-Classic history of Cambodia is Chandler 1993:77–98. See also Groslier 1958 and Mak 1995.
26 Giteau 1975:74ff.
27 Chandler 1993:82.
28 One late sixteenth century source, Christoval de Jaque, states that King Reamea Chung Prei had only 400 war elephants (Groslier 1958:154), a more likely figure.
29 See Chandler 1993:85–86.
30 Chandler 1993:86.
31 Quiroga de San Antonio 1998.
32 Mak 1995:259.
33 Mouhot 1989:196.
34 Most of this section is based upon Étienne Aymonier's unsurpassed account of Cambodia as it was on the eve of the French Protectorate (Aymonier 1900:1–102).
35 Aymonier 1900:58 (translation MDC).
36 Aymonier 1900:71.
37 Reid 1993:54.
38 Reid 1993:312–13.
39 Ishii 1998:2–6, 153–93.
40 Shimizu 1965:238 (translation by Professor Edward Kamens).
41 Information from Dr Su Wei of the Department of East Asian Languages and Literatures (Yale University), who examined my photographs of these graffiti.
42 Aymonier 1900:74–75.
43 The standard source on the art of Post-Classic Cambodia is Madeleine Giteau's great compendium (Giteau 1975).
44 Pou 1975a.
45 Bizot 1989:26.
46 Pou 1975b.
47 For a modern oral version, see Bizot 1989.
48 Bernard-Thiérry 1955.
49 For the tragic history of post-colonial Cambodia, see Chandler 1996. For the Khmer Rouge ('Pol Pot') genocide, see Kiernan 1993.

Further Reading

An absolutely indispensable bibliographic reference for early (pre-Protectorate) Cambodia is Bruguier 1998. The first volume is arranged by author, and the second by topic (including sites and geographic locations).

Abbreviations:
EFEO – École Française d'Extrême-Orient
BEFEO – Bulletin de l'École Française d'Extrême-Orient

AEUSRIVONGSA, NIDHI 1976 The *Devaraja* cult and Khmer kingship at Angkor. In *Explorations in Early Southeast Asian History: the Origins of Southeast Asian Statecraft*, ed. K.R. Hall and J.K. Whitmore, 107–48. Ann Arbor: Center for South and Southeast Asian Studies.

ACKER, ROBERT 1998 New geographical tests of the hydraulic thesis at Angkor. *South East Asia Research* 6(1):5–47.

ALBRECHT, GERD, MIRIAM NOËL HAIDLE, CHHOR SIVLENG, HEANG LEANG HONG, HENG SOPHADY, HENG THAN, MAO SOMEAPHYVATH, SIRIK KADA, SOM SOPHAL, THUY CHANTHOURN AND VIN LAYCHOUR. 2000 Circular Earthwork Krek 52/62: recent research on the prehistory of Cambodia. *Asian Perspectives* 39(1–2):20–46.

ANG, CHOULÉAN 1998 Angkor: la science, la tradition et leur défi pour les khmers. *Third Symposium on the Bayon, 18–19 December 1998, Working Documents*, 40–47. Siem Reap.

ANG, CHOULÉAN, ERIC PRENOWITZ AND ASHLEY THOMPSON 1998 *Angkor. Past, Present and Future.* Phnom Penh: APSARA.

AOYAGI, YOJI, TASUO SASAKI, MASAKO MARUI, AND ETSUKO MIYATA 1998 Investigation of the Tani Kiln Site Group, Angkor. In *Renaissance culturelle du Cambodge*, 257–66. Tokyo: Institute of Asian Studies, Sophia University.

AU CHHIENG 1968 À propos de la statue dite du 'Roi Lepreux'. *Journal Asiatique* 256(2):185–201.

AYMONIER, ÉTIENNE 1900 *Le Cambodge 1. Le royaume actuel.* Paris: Ernest Leroux.

—— 1901 *Le Cambodge 2. Les Provinces Siamoises.* Paris: Ernest Leroux.

—— 1904 *Le Cambodge 3. Le groupe d'Angkor et l'histoire.* Paris: Ernest Leroux.

—— 1999 *Khmer Heritage in the Old Siamese Provinces of Cambodia.* Bangkok: White Lotus.

BAYARD, DONN T. 1979 Comment. In *Early South East Asia*, ed. R.B.Smith and W.Watson, 278–80.

—— 1984 A tentative regional phase chronology for Northeast Thailand. In *Southeast Asian Archaeology at the XV Pacific Science Congress* (ed. D.T. Bayard), 161–68.

BECCHETTI, CATHERINE 1994 Une ancienne tradition de manuscrits au Cambodge. In *Recherches nouvelles sur le Cambodge*, ed. F. Bizot, 47–61. Paris: EFEO.

BELLWOOD, PETER 1997 *Prehistory of the Indo-Malaysian Archipelago* (revised edition). Honolulu: University of Hawaii Press.

BERNARD-THIÉRRY, SOLANGE 1955 Sagesse du Cambodge. *France Asie* 12(114–15):436–39. Saigon.

BHANDARI, C.M. 1995 *Saving Angkor.* Bangkok:White Orchid.

BLURTON, T. RICHARD 1993 *Hindu Art.* Cambridge (Mass.): Harvard University Press.

BOULBET, JEAN 1979 *Le Phnom Kulen et sa région.* Paris: EFEO.

BOULBET, JEAN AND BRUNO DAGENS 1973 Les sites archéologiques de la région du Bhnam Gulen. *Arts Asiatiques*, t. 27. Paris.

BOUILLEVAUX, CHARLES-ÉTIENNE 1863 *Ma visite aux ruines cambodgiennes en 1850.* Saint-Quentin.

BRIGGS, LAWRENCE P. 1951 *The Ancient Khmer Empire.* Philadelphia: The American Philosophical Society.

BRONSON, BENNET 1978 Angkor, Anuradhapura, Prambanan, Tikal: Maya subsistence in an Asian perspective. In *Pre-Hispanic Maya Agriculure*, ed. P.D. Harrison and B.L. Turner, 255–300. Albuquerque: University of New Mexico Press.

BROWN, ROXANNA M. 2000 *The Ceramics of South-East Asia. Their Dating and Significance.* Chicago: Art Media Resources.

BRUGUIER, BRUNO 1998 *Bibliographie du Cambodge ancien.* 2 vols. Paris: EFEO.

BUNGE, FREDERICA M. (ed.) 1981 *Thailand. A Country Study.* Fifth edition. Washington: Department of the Army.

CHANDLER, DAVID 1993 *A History of Cambodia* (second edition). Chiangmai (Thailand): Silkworm Books.

—— 1996 *Facing the Cambodia Past.* Chiang Mai (Thailand): Silkworm Books.

CHANTHOURN, THUY 2002 *Banteay Kou: Memotian Circular Earthworks.* Phnom Penh: Royal University of Fine Arts.

CHEN, BAOZHANG, WANG XIANGKUN AND ZHANG JUZHONG 1995 Finds and morphological study of carbonized rice in the Jiahu Neolithic site in Wuyang County, Henan Province. *Chinese Journal of Rice Science* 9(3):129–34.

COE, MICHAEL D. 1957 The Khmer settlement pattern: a possible analogy with that of the Maya. *American Antiquity* 22(4):409–10.

—— 1961 Social typology and the tropical forest civilizations. *Comparative Studies in Society and History* 4(1):65–85.

COEDÈS, GEORGE 1906 La stèle de Ta Prohm. *BEFEO* 6:44–81.

—— 1947 *Pour mieux comprendre Angkor.* Paris: Maisonneuve.

—— 1968 *The Indianized States of Southeast Asia.* Honolulu: University of Hawaii Press.

COLANI, MADELEINE 1926 Découverte d'industries paléolithiques dans la province de Hòa-Bình, Tonkin. *L'Anthropologie* 36:609–11.

COURBIN, PAUL 1988 La fouille du Sras-Srang à Angkor. In EFEO, *Collection de Textes et Documents sur l'Indochine* 17:21–58. Paris.

CUMMINGS, JOE 1996 *Laos* (2nd edition). Hawthorn (Australia): Lonely Planet.

DAGENS, BRUNO 1995 *Angkor. Heart of an Asian Empire.* New York: Harry N. Abrams.

DALET, ROBERT 1936 Esai sur les pagodes cambodgiennes et leur annexes. *La Géographie* 65:135–53.

DAO LINH CÔN The Oc Eo burial group recently excavated at Go Thap (Dong Thap Province, Viêt Nam). In *Southeast Asian Archaeology 1994: Proceedings of the 5th International Conference of the European Association of Southeast Asian Archaeologists* 1:111–17. Hull, England: Centre for Southeast Asian Studies.

DAVIDSON, ALAN 1999 *The Oxford Companion to Food.* Oxford and New York: Oxford University Press.

DEGA, MICHAEL F. 1999 Circular settlements within Cambodia. *Bulletin of the Indo-Pacific Prehistory Association* 18:181–190.

DEGA, MICHAEL F., VET KOU, CHAMROEUN CHHAN, AND SAMEH KOUM 1997 Circular earthworks in Kampong

Cham: 1996 Archaeological Research. *Bulletin de Liaison des Recherches au Cambodge 3, EFEO* 13–16. Phnom Penh.

DELAPORTE, LOUIS 1914–24 *Les monuments du Cambodge*. Paris: Ernest Leroux.

DELVERT, JEAN 1961 *Le paysan cambodgien*. Paris and The Hague: Mouton.

—— 1993 *Le Cambodge* (2nd edition). Paris: Presses Universitaires de France.

—— 1998 *Le Cambodge* (3rd edition). Paris: Presses Universitaires de France.

DESAI, AJAY, AND LIC VUTHY 1996 *Status and Distribution of Large Mammals in Eastern Cambodia*. Cambridge: Flora and Fauna International.

DIXON, C.J. 1978 Settlement and environment in northeast Thailand. *Journal of Tropical Geography* 46(1):1–10.

DOWLING, NANCY 2000 New light on early Cambodian Buddhism. *Journal of the Siam Society* 88(1,2):122–31.

DUMARÇAY, JACQUES, AND BERNARD-PHILIPPE GROSLIER 1967, 1973 I *Le Bayon, histoire architecturale du temple*, II *Inscriptions du Bayon*. Paris: EFEO.

DUMARÇAY, JACQUES, AND MICHAEL SMITHIES *Cultural Sites of Burma, Thailand, and Cambodia*. Kuala Lumpur and New York: Oxford University Press.

DUMARÇAY, JACQUES, AND PASCAL ROYÈRE 2001 *Cambodian Architecture, Eighth to Thirteenth Centuries*. Leiden: Brill.

DUPOIZAT, MARIE-FRANCE 1999 La céramique importée à Angkor: étude préliminaire. *Arts Asiatiques* 54:103–16.

EADE, JOHN C. 1995 *The Calendrical Systems of Mainland South-East Asia*. Leiden: E.J. Brill.

FINOT, LOUIS 1915 L'inscription de Sdok Kak Thom. *BEFEO* 15:53–106.

FINOT, LOUIS, VICTOR GOLOUBEW, AND GEORGE COEDÈS 1929–1932 *Le Temple d'Angkor Vat*. 3 vols. Paris and Brussels: G. Van Oest.

FLETCHER, ROLAND 2000–2001 Seeing Angkor: new views of an old city. *Journal of the Oriental Society of Australia* 32–33:1–27.

FLOOD, GAVIN 1996 *An Introduction to Hinduism*. Cambridge: Cambridge University Press.

FOURNEREAU, LUCIEN 1890 *Les ruines d'Angkor*. Paris: Ernest Leroux.

FOX, JEFF, AND JUDY LEDGERWOOD 1999 Dry-season flood-recession rice in the Mekong Delta: two thousand years of sustainable agriculture? *Asian Perspectives* 38(1):37–50.

FRÉDÉRIC, LOUIS 1981 *La vie quotidienne dans la peninsula indochinoise à l'époque d'Angkor*. Paris: Hachette.

FREEMAN, MICHAEL 1996 *A Guide to Khmer Temples in Thailand & Laos*. Bangkok: River Books.

FUJIWARA, HIROSHI 1990 *Khmer Ceramics from the Kamratan Collection in the Southeast Asian Ceramics Museum, Kyoto*. Singapore: Oxford University Press.

GARNIER, FRANCIS *Travels in Cambodia and Part of Laos. The Mekong Exploration Commission Report (1866–1868) — Volume 1*. Bangkok:White Lotus.

GEERTZ, CLIFFORD 1980 *Negara. The Theatre State in Nineteenth-Century Bali*. Princeton: Princeton University Press.

GITEAU, MADELEINE 1957 *Histoire du Cambodge*. Paris: Didier.

—— 1974 *Histoire d'Angkor*. Paris: Presses Universitaires de France.

—— 1975 *Iconographie du Cambodge post-angkorien*. Paris: EFEO.

—— 1996 *Histoire d'Angkor*. Paris and Pondicherry (India): Kailash.

GLAIZE, MAURICE 1948 *Les monuments du groupe d'Angkor*. Saigon: Portail.

GLOVER, IAN C. 1996 Recent archaeological evidence for early maritime contacts between India and Southeast Asia. In *Tradition and Archaeology: Early Maritime contacts in the Indian Ocean*, ed. H.P. Ray and J.-F. Salles, 129–58. New Delhi:Manohar.

GREEN, GILL 2000 Textiles at the Khmer court. *Arts of Asia* 30(4):82–92.

GRIST, DONALD H. 1986 *Rice*. London and New York: Longman.

GROSLIER, BERNARD-PHILIPPE 1958 *Angkor et le Cambodge au XVIe siècle d'après les sources portugaises et espagnoles*. Paris: Presses Universitaires de France.

—— 1966 *Indochina*. Geneva: Nagel.

—— 1979 La cité hydraulique angkorienne: exploitation ou surexploitation du sol? *BEFEO* 66:161–202.

—— 1981 Introduction to the ceramic wares of Angkor. In *Khmer Ceramics. 9th–14th Century*, ed. Diana Stock, 9–39. Singapore: Southeast Asian Ceramic Society.

—— 1998 *Mélanges sur l'archéologie du Cambodge*. Paris: EFEO.

GROSLIER, BERNARD-PHILIPPE, AND JACQUES ARTHAUD 1957 *The Arts and Civilization of Angkor*. New York: Praeger.

GROSLIER, GEORGE 1921 *Recherches sur les Cambodgiens*. Paris: Augustin Challamel.

—— 1937 Bantay Chmar, ville ancienne du Cambodge. *L'illustration* 3(4909):352–57.

GRUNEWALD, FRANÇOIS 1982 À propos de l'agriculture dans le Cambodge medieval. *Asie du Sud-Est et Monde Insulindien* 13(1–4):23–38.

GUÉRET, DANIELLE 1998 *Le Cambodge. Une introduction à la connaissance du pays khmer*. Paris and Pondicherry (India): Kailash.

HANKS, LUCIEN M. 1972 *Rice and Man. Agricultural Ecology in Southeast Asia*. Honolulu: University of Hawaii Press.

HEANG, LEANG HONG 1999 Pottery from the Groslier Circular Earthworks Site, stored in the National Museum, Phnom Penh. Paper presented at the Conference on Circular Earthworks in Cambodia, 14–19 November 1999. Phnom Penh.

HEINE-GELDERN, ROBERT 1966 The problem of transpacific influences in Mesoamerica. In *Handbook of Middle American Indians*, Vol. 4, ed. Gordon F. Ekholm and Gordon R. Willey, 277–95. Austin: University of Texas Press.

HERBERT, PATRICIA, AND ANTHONY MILNER 1989 *South-East Asia Languages and Literatures: a Select Guide*. Whiting Bay (Scotland): Kiscadale.

HIGHAM, CHARLES 1989 *The Archaeology of Mainland Southeast Asia*. Cambridge: Cambridge University Press.

—— 2001 *The Civilization of Angkor*. London: Weidenfeld & Nicholson.

—— 2003 *Early Cultures of Mainland Southeast Asia*. Chicago: Art Media Resources.

HIGHAM, CHARLES, AND RACHANIE THOSARAT 1998 *Prehistoric Thailand*. Bangkok: River Books.

HONDA, HIROSHI, AND NORIKI SHIMAZU 1997 *The Beauty of Fired Clay Ceramics from Burma, Cambodia, Laos, and Thailand*. Kuala Lumpur: Oxford University Press.

HUFFMAN, FRANKLIN E. 1970 *Cambodian System of Writing and Beginning Reader*. New Haven: Yale University Press.

ISHII, YONEO (ed.) 1998 *The Junk Trade from Southeast Asia. Translations from the Tōsen Fusetsu-gaki, 1674–1723*. Singapore: Institute of Southeast Asian Studies.

JACOB, JUDITH M. 1978 The ecology of Angkor. Evidence from the Khmer inscriptions. In *Nature and Man in South East Asia*, ed. Philip A. Stott, 109–27. London: School of Oriental and African Studies.

—— 1979 Pre-Angkor Cambodia: evidence from the inscriptions in Khmer concerning the common people and their environment. In *Early South East Asia. Essays in Archaeology, History and Historical Geography*, ed. R.B.Smith and W.Watson, 406–26. New York: Oxford University Press.

—— 1993 Pre-Angkor Cambodia: evidence from the inscriptions in Khmer concerning the common people and their environment. In *Cambodian Linguistics, Literature and History. Collected Articles*. Ed. David A. Smyth. 299–316. London: School of Oriental and African Studies.

JACQ-HERGOUALC'H, MICHEL 1979 *L'armament et l'organisation de l'armée khmère*. Paris: Presses Universitaires de France.

JACQUES, CLAUDE 1976 À propos de l'esclavage dans l'ancien Cambodge. In *Actes du 29e Congrès Internationale des Orientalistes, Asie du Sud-Est Continental* 1:71–76. Paris.

—— 1979 'Funan', 'Zhenla': the reality concealed by these Chinese views of Indochina. In *Early South East Asia*, ed. R.B.Smith and W.Watson, 371–79. Oxford: Oxford University Press.

—— 1992 On Jayavarman II, the founder of the Khmer Empire. In *Southeast Asian Archaeology 1990, Proceedings of the Third Conference of the European Association of Southeast Asian Archaeologists*, ed. Ian Glover, 1–5. Hull (England): Centre for South-East Asian Studies.

—— 1998 À propos de modifications dans quelques temples d'Angkor et loeur signification pour l'histoire khmère. In *Southeast Asian Archaeology 1994*, ed. P.-Y. Manguin, 195–206. Hull (England): Centre for South-East Asian Studies.

—— 1999 *Angkor*. Cologne: Könemann.

JACQUES, CLAUDE, AND MICHAEL FREEMAN 1997 *Angkor. Cities and Temples*. London: Thames and Hudson.

JESSUP, HELEN IBBITSON, AND THIERRY ZÉPHIR, eds. 1997 *Sculpture of Angkor and Ancient Cambodia. Millennium of Glory*. Washington: National Gallery of Art.

KIERNAN, BEN 1988 Orphans of genocide: the Cham Muslims of Kampuchea under Pol Pot. *Bulletin of Concerned Asia Scholars* 20(4):2–9.

KIERNAN, BEN (ed.) 1993 *Genocide and Democracy in Cambodia. Yale University Southeast Asia Studies* 41. New Haven.

KOJO, YASUSHI n.d. Circular earthworks and ethnographic parallels. (unpublished paper dated 16 November 1999).

LAUR, JEAN 2002 *Angkor. An Illustrated Guide to the Monuments*. Paris: Flammarion.

LE THANH KHOI 1955 *Le Viêt-nam, histoire et civilisation*. Paris: Éditions de Minuit.

LEBAR, FRANK M., GERALD C. HICKEY, AND JOHN K. MUSGRAVE 1964 *Ethnic Groups of Mainland Southeast Asia*. New Haven: HRAF Press.

LEBAS, J. 1925 Les pêcheries du Lac Tonlé-Sap (Cambodge). *Annales de Géographie* 34:69–73.

LEIDY, DENISE PATRY 2000 Prakon Chai and the art of Southeast Asia in the 7th to 9th centuries. *Arts of Asia* 30(4):28–41

LEWITZ, SAVEROS 1972 Les inscriptions modernes d'Angkor Vat. *Journal Asiatique* 260:107–29.

LUNET DE LAJONQUIÈRE, ÉTIENNE-EDMOND 1902–1911 *Inventaire déscriptif des monuments du Cambodge*. 3 vols. Paris: EFEO.

MABBETT, IAN W. 1978 Kingship in Angkor. *Journal of the Siam Society* 66(pt 2):1–58.

MABBETT, IAN, AND DAVID CHANDLER 1995 *The Khmers*. Oxford: Blackwells.

MAK PHOEUN 1995 *Histoire du Cambodge de la fin du XVIe siècle au debut du XVIIIe*. Paris: EFEO.

MALLERET, LOUIS 1959a *L'archéologie du delta du Mékong: 1. L'exploration archéologique et les fouilles d'Oc-éo* (2 vols.). Paris: EFEO.

—— 1959b Ouvrages circulaires en terre dans l'Indochine méridionale. *BEFEO* 49(2):409–34.

—— 1960 *L'archéologie du delta du Mékong: 2. La civilisation matérielle d'Oc-éo* (2 vols.). Paris: EFEO.

—— 1962 *L'archéologie du delta du Mékong: 3. La culture du Founan* (2 vols.). Paris: EFEO.

MANH, PHAM DUC 1999 The prehistoric lithophone at Loc Ninh (Binh Phuoc – Vietnam). Paper presented at the Conference on Circular Earthworks in Cambodia, 14–19 November 1999, Phnom Penh.

MANNIKKA, ELEANOR M. 1996 *Angkor Wat: Time, Space and Kingship*. Honolulu: University of Hawaii Press.

MANSUY, HENRI 1902 *Stations préhistoriques de Samrong-Sen et de Longprao (Cambodge)*. Hanoi: Schneider.

MARTELL, GABRIELLE 1975 *Lovea: village des environs d'Angkor*. Paris: EFEO.

MARTINI, FRANÇOIS 1955 La langue cambodgienne. *France-Asie* 12(114–15):428–35. Saigon.

MESTIER DE BOURG, HUBERT DE 1970 La première moitié du XIe siècle au Cambodge: Suryavarman Ier, sa vie et quelques aspects des institutions à son époque. *Journal Asiatique* 258(3–4):282–313.

MIKSIC, JOHN N. 2000 Heterogenetic cities in premodern Southeast Asia. *World Archaeology* 32(1):106–20.

MOORE, ELIZABETH H. 1988 *Moated Sites in Early North East Thailand*. Oxford: BAR International Series 400.

—— 1997 Circular sites at Angkor: a radar scattering model. *Journal of the Siam Society* 85:107–19.

MOUHOT, HENRI 1989 *Travels in Siam, Cambodia and Laos, 1858–1860*. Singapore: Oxford University Press.

MOURA, JEAN 1883 *Le Royaume du Cambodge* (2 vols.). Paris: Ernest Leroux.

MOURER, CÉCILE, AND ROLAND MOURER 1970 The prehistoric industry of Laang Spean, Province Battambang, Cambodia. *Archaeology and Physical Anthropology in Oceania* 5:128–46.

MOURER, ROLAND 1977 Laang Spean and the prehistory of Cambodia. *Modern Quarternary Research in Southeast Asia* 3:29–56.

MURAI, SHUNJI, PANJAI TANTATSANAWONG, AND SURAT LERTLUM n.d. Discovery of ancient water reservoir in historical town of Phimai, Nakornrathchasima, Thailand: application of airSAR for archaeology study. Web site: http://www.gisdevelopment.net/application/archaeology/general/archg0016.htm.

NAFILYAN, GUY 1969 *Angkor Vat. Description graphique du temple*. Paris: EFEO.

NG, RONALD C.Y. 1978 Man and land in northeast Thailand. In *Nature and Man in South East Asia* (ed. P.A.Stott), 34–48.

—— 1979 The geographical habitat of historical settlement in mainland South East Asia. In *Early South East Asia. Essays in Archaeology, History and Historical Geography* (ed. R.B.Smith and W.Watson), 262–72.

O'NAGHTEN, HEDWIGE MULTZER 2000 *Les temples du Cambodge. Architecture et espace sacré*. Paris: Geuthner.

OSBORNE, MILTON 2000 *The Mekong. Turbulent Past, Uncertain Future*. New York: Atlantic Monthly Press.

PARMENTIER, HENRI 1939 *L'art khmèr classique. Monuments du quadrant Nord-Est* (2 vols.). Paris: EFEO.

PARMENTIER, HENRI 1927 *L'art khmèr primitif* (2 vols.). Paris: EFEO.

—— 1939 *L'art khmèr classique* (2 vols.). Paris: EFEO.

PARMENTIER, HENRI, VICTOR GOLOUBEW, AND LOUIS FINOT 1926 *Le Temple d'Içvarapura (Bantay Srei, Cambodia)*. Paris: G. Vanoest.

—— 1939 *L'art khmèr classique* (2 vols.). Paris: EFEO.

PEI, ANPING n.d. Pengtoushan culture crop remains in Chinese prehistoric agriculture (1988) On Website http://www.carleton.ca/~bgordon/Rice/papers/pei88a.htm.

PELLIOT, PAUL 1951 *Mémoires sur les coutumes du Cambodge de Tcheou Ta-Kouan*. Paris: Adrien-Maisonneuve.

PORÉE-MASPERO, ÉVELINE 1950 Nouvelle étude sur la Nāgi Somā. *Journal Asiatique* 238(2):237–67.

POTTIER, CHRISTOPHE 1997 Nouvelles données sur les couvertures en plomb à Angkor. *BEFEO* 84:183–220.

POU, SAVEROS 1975a Inscriptions modernes d'Angkor. *BEFEO* 62:283–353.

—— 1975b Les traits bouddhiques du Ramakerti. *BEFEO* 62:355–68.

—— 1992 *Dictionnaire VieuxKhmer-Français-Anglais. An Old Khmer-French-English Dictionary*. Paris: Centre de Documentation et de Recherche sur la Civilisation Khmère.

—— 1990 From Old Khmer epigraphy to popular tradition: a study in the names of Cambodian monuments. In *South-

east Asian Archaeology 1990, ed. Ian Glover, 7–24. Hull (England): Centre for South-East Asian Studies.

PRODROMIDÈS, MAXIME 1997 *Angkor. Chronique d'une renaissance*. Paris and Pondicherry: Kailash.

QUIROGA DE SAN ANTONIO, GABRIEL *A Brief and Truthful Relation of Events in the Kingdom of Cambodia*. Bangkok: White Lotus.

RAWSON, PHILIP 1967 *The Art of Southeast Asia*. New York: Praeger.

RAY, HIMANSHU PRABHA 1998 *The Winds of Change: Buddhism and the Maritime Links of Early South Asia*. Delhi: Oxford University Press.

REID, ANTHONY 1988 *Southeast Asia in the Age of Commerce 1450–1680*. Vol. 1: *The Lands Below the Winds*. New Haven: Yale University Press.

RICKLEFS, M.C. 1967 Land and the law in the epigraphy of tenth-century Cambodia. *Journal of Asian Studies* 26(3):411–20.

RIGG, JONATHAN 1993 Rice, water and land: strategies of cultivation on the Khorat Plateau, Thailand. *South East Asia Research* 1 (2):197–209.

ROONEY, DAWN 1997 *Angkor. An Introduction to the Ruins*. Hong Kong: Asia Books.

ROVEDA, VITTORIO 1997 *Khmer Mythology*. Bangkok: River Books.

—— 2002 *Sacred Angkor. The Carved Reliefs of Angkor Wat*. Bangkok: River Books.

SAHAI, SACHCHIDENAND 1977a Fiscal administration in ancient Cambodia. *The South East Asian Review* 1(2):123–38.

—— 1977b Territorial administration in ancient Cambodia. *The South East Asian Review* 2(1):35–50.

SAM, SAM-ANG, PANYA ROONGRUANG, AND PHONG T. NGUYÊN 1998 The Khmer people. In *The Garland Encyclopedia of World Music, Vol. 4: Southeast Asia*, 151–217. New York and London: Garland.

SANTONI, MARIELLA 1998 Fouille d'un monument préangkorien dans la ville ancienne associée à Vat Phu (Province de Champassak, Laos). In *Southeast Asian Archaeology 1994* (ed. P.-Y. Manguin), 1–20. Hull (England): Centre for Southeast Asian Studies.

SARKAR, KALYAN KUMAR 1976 Ancient Cambodian society as known from Old Khmer inscriptions. In *Actes du 29e Congrès Internationale des Orientalistes, Asie du Sud-Est continentale* 3:191–96. Paris.

SHIMIZU, JUNZO 1965 The inscriptions by some Japanese, found in Angkor Vat [in Japanese]. In *Indo-Chinese Studies: Synthetic Research of the Culture of Rice-cultivating races in Southeast Asian Countries* 1, ed. Nobuhiro Matsumoto, pp. 223–65.

SHORTO, H.L. 1979 The linguistic protohistory of mainland South East Asia. In *Early South East Asia*, ed. R.B.Smith and W.Watson, 273–78. Oxford: Oxford University Press.

SIRIBHADRA, SMITTHI, AND ELIZABETH MOORE 1992 *Palaces of the Gods. Khmer Art & Architecture in Thailand*. Bangkok: River Books.

SMITH, MONICA L. 1999 'Indianization' from the Indian point of view: trade and cultural contacts with Southeast Asia in the first millennium C.E. *Journal of the Economic and Social History of the Orient* 42(1):1–26.

SOLHEIM, WILHELM G. II AND MARTI AYRES 1979 The late prehistoric and early historic pottery of the Khorat Plateau, with special reference to Phimai. In *Early South East Asia*, ed. R.B.Smith and W. Watson, 63–77. Oxford: Oxford University Press.

STARK, MIRIAM T. 1998 The transition to history in the Mekong Delta: a view from Cambodia. *International Journal of Historic Archaeology* 2(3):175–204.

STARK, MIRIAM T., AND BONG SOVATH 2001 Recent research on emergent complexity in Cambodia's Lower Mekong delta. *Bulletin of the Indo-Pacific Prehistory Association* 21(5):85–98.

STARK, MIRIAM T., P.B. GRIFFIN, P. CHUCH, J. LEDGERWOOD, M. DEGA, C. MORTLAND, N. DOWLING, J. BAYMAN, S. BONG, V. TEA, C. CHHAN, AND K. LATINIS 1999 Results of the 1995–1996 field investigations at Angkor Borei, Cambodia. *Asian Perspectives* 38(1):7–36.

STERN, PHILIPPE 1927 *Le Bayon d'Angkor et l'évolution de l'art khmer*. Paris: Paul Geuthner.

—— 1954 Diversité et rythme des fondations royales khmères. *BEFEO* 44(2):649–87.

STOTT, PHILIP 1992 Angkor: shifting the hydraulic paradigm. In *The Gift of Water. Water Management, Cosmology and the State in South East Asia*, ed. Jonathan Rigg. 47–58. London: School of Oriental and African Studies.

STUTTARD, J.C. (ed) 1943 *Indo-China*. Cambridge: Naval Intelligence Division.

SWEARER, DONALD K. 1995 *The Buddhist World of Southeast Asia*. Albany: State University of New York Press.

THAITAWAT, NUSARA 2000 *The Cuisine of Cambodia*. Bangkok: Nusara & Friends.

THOREL, CLOVIS 2001 *Agriculture and Ethnobotany of the Mekong Basin*. Bangkok: White Lotus.

THOMPSON, ASHLEY 1997 Changing perspectives: Cambodia after Angkor. In *Sculpture of Angkor and Ancient Cambodia. Millennium of Glory*, ed. H. I. Jessup and T. Zéphir, 22–32. Washington: National Gallery of Art.

THOMSON, JOHN 1867 *The Antiquities of Cambodia*. Edinburgh: Edmonston & Douglas.

UNITED NATIONS 1968 *Atlas of Physical, Economic and Social Resources of the Lower Mekong Basin*. New York: United Nations.

VAN LIERE, W.J. 1980 Traditional water management in the lower Mekong basin. *World Archaeology* 11(3):265–80.

VÉANG, THIOUNN 1921–22 Prah Khan (l'épée sacrée du Cambodge). *Arts et archéologie khmers*, t. 1, pp. 59–63. Paris: Éd. géographiques, maritimes et coloniales.

VICKERY, MICHAEL 1979 The composition and transmission of the Ayudhya and Cambodian chronicles. In *Perceptions of the Past in Southeast Asia*, ed. by Anthony Reid and David Marr, 130–54. Singapore: Asian Studies Association of Australia.

—— 1986 Some remarks on early state formation in Cambodia. In *Southeast Asia in the 9th to 14th Centuries*, ed. David G. Marr and A.C.Milner, 95–115. Singapore: Institute of Southeast Asian Studies.

—— 1998 *Society, Economics, and Politics in Pre-Angkor Cambodia*. Tokyo: Centre for East Asian Cultural Studies for Unesco, The Toyo Bundo.

WHEATLEY, PAUL 1983 *Nagara and Commandery: Origins of the Southeast Asian Urban Traditions*. Chicago: University of Chicago Press.

WHITE, JOYCE C. 1995 Modeling the Development of early rice agriculture: ethnoecological perpectives from northeast Thailand. *Asian Perspectives* 34(1):37–58.

WOLTERS, O.W. 1982 *History, Culture, and Region in Southeast Asian Perspectives*. Ithaca: Southeast Asia Program.

WORLD MONUMENTS FUND 1996 *Preservation Priorities: the Angkor Challenge*. New York: World Monuments Fund.

YANG BAOYUN 1994 Nouvelles études sur l'ouvrage de Zhou Daguan. *Recherches nouvelles sur le Cambodge* (ed. François Bizot), 227–34.

YUNG, PETER 2000 *Angkor. The Khmers in Ancient Chinese Annals*. Oxford: Oxford University Press.

ZHANG, JI-WEN n.d. *Origin of Rice Agriculture on the middle and lower Yangtze River*. On Website at http://www.carleton.ca/~bgordon/Rice/papers/zhang6.htm.

ZHOU DAGUAN (CHOU TA-KUAN) 1993 *The Customs of Cambodia*. Translated from the French by J. Gilman d'Arcy Paul. Third edition. Bangkok: The Siam Society.

—— 2001 *The Customs of Cambodia*. Edited and translated from the French by Michael Smithies. Bangkok: The Siam Society.

Sources of Illustrations

Unless otherwise indicated, images are © Michael D. Coe.

Colour plates
I NASA/Jet Propulsion Laboratory
VIII © Georg Gerster
XII © The Asia Society, New York
XIII Photo © Luca Tettoni
XIV The Metropolitan Museum of Art. From the collection
of Walter H. and Leonore Amenberg, 1988. (1988.355).
Photo © 1988 The Metropolitan Museum of Art.
XIX Photo © Michael Freeman

In-text illustrations
1 Delaporte, Louis 1880, *Vogaye au Cambodge*. Paris:
Librairie Charles Delagrange
2 Delaporte, Louis 1880, *Voyage au Cambodge*. Paris:
Librairie Charles Delagrange
4 Photo © Jeff Chouinard
5 ML Design
9 ML Design
10 Aymonier 1900, vol. 1, fig. 26
11 Left: Drawing Blane Smith, from a photo by John
Stubbs, World Monuments Fund.
11 Right: Drawing Blane Smith
13 ML Design
14 From Mourer and Mourer 1970
15 Drawing Blane Smith based on Albrecht et al
2000, fig. 2
16 Drawing Blane Smith based on Albrecht et al
2000, fig. 5
17 From Albrecht et al 2000, various figures
18 From Chanthourn 1999, various figures
20 Photo © Jeff Chouinard
21 ML Design
22 Drawing Blane Smith, based on Malleret 1959a, pl. 12
23 Redrawn by Blane Smith from Wheatley 1983
24 Redrawn by Blane Smith from Malleret 1962
25 Photo © Luca Tettoni
26 © The Cleveland Museum of Art, 2002, John L.
Severance Fund, 1973.106
27 From Parmentier 1927, plates 29–30
28 From Parmentier 1927, fig. 12
29 From Parmentier 1927, fig. 22
30 From Parmentier 1927, fig. 5
32 © The Asia Society, New York
33 Photo © Michael Freeman
34 Redrawn by Blane Smith from Jessup and Zéphir 1997,
pp. 204–05

36 Photo © Luca Tettoni
37 Redrawn by Blane Smith from Jessup and Zéphir 1997,
p. 146
38 Drawing Blane Smith
39 ML Design
42 ML Design
43 Photo École Française d'Extrême-Orient, Paris
44 Photo © Luca Tettoni
45 From Parmentier 1939, pl. 21.
47 Redrawn by Blane Smith from Briggs 1951, fig. 19
48 Photo © Michael Freeman
50 ML Design
54 Drawing Blane Smith
56 Photo © Luca Tettoni
57 Photo © Jeff Chouinard
63 ML Design
65 Photo © Michael Freeman
66 ML Design
67 Drawing Blane Smith from a photo by Michael D. Coe
68 Drawing Blane Smith from a photo by Michael D. Coe
69 Museum of Fine Arts, Boston. Keith McLeod Fund;
1973.146
70 Drawing Blane Smith from a photo by Michael D. Coe
71 Redrawn by Blane Smith from B.-P. Groslier 1957, p. 92
72 ML Design
73 Drawing Blane Smith
75 © The Asia Society, New York
77 Photo © Luca Tettoni
81 Museum of Fine Arts, Boston. Denman Waldo Ross
Collection; 22.686
82 © The Asia Society, New York
83 Redrawn by Blane Smith; *c* from Fujiwara 1990, rest
from Honda and Shimazu 1997
84 Photo © Jeff Chouinard
85 Redrawn by Blane Smith from Jessup and Zéphir 1997,
p. 201
86 Drawing Blane Smith from a photo by Michael D. Coe
87 Drawing Blane Smith from a photo by Michael D. Coe
88 Drawing Blane Smith from a photo by Michael D. Coe
89 Drawing Blane Smith from a photo by Michael D. Coe
94 Map courtesy of Damian Evans and Roland Fletcher
96 Photo École Française d'Extrême-Orient, Paris
98 From Dalet 1936, fig. 2
100 Drawing Blane Smith from a photo by Michael D. Coe
101 ML Design
102 Photo John Thomson
103 Véang 1921–22, plates I and III
107 Redrawn by Blane Smith from Dumarçay 1991, pl. 15

Index